EYES ALL
OVER THE SKY

EYES ALL
OVER THE SKY

Aerial Reconnaissance in the First World War

James Streckfuss

CASEMATE
uk
Oxford & Philadelphia

Published in Great Britain and the United States of America in 2016 by
CASEMATE PUBLISHERS
10 Hythe Bridge Street, Oxford OX1 2EW, UK
and
1950 Lawrence Road, Havertown, PA 19083, USA

© James Streckfuss 2016

Hardcover Edition: ISBN 978-1-61200-367-2
Digital Edition: ISBN 978-1-61200-368-9 (epub)

A CIP record for this book is available from the British Library

Printed in the United Kingdom by TJ International

For a complete list of Casemate titles, please contact:

CASEMATE PUBLISHERS (UK)
Telephone (01865) 241249
Fax (01865) 794449
Email: casemate-uk@casematepublishers.co.uk
www.casematepublishers.co.uk

CASEMATE PUBLISHERS (US)
Telephone (610) 853-9131
Fax (610) 853-9146
Email: casemate@casematepublishing.com
www.casematepublishing.com

*In memory of Sharon Streckfuss, whose contributions
to this project and to my life are beyond evaluation,
and who left us all much too soon*

Contents

List of Maps

Acknowledgements

One of the first lessons learned in writing history is that it is never a solo process. Everyone needs help along the way and I can testify to having had a great deal of valuable assistance from many people during the research and writing of this book. Of course the History Department faculty of the University of Cincinnati stand out for their close involvement in guiding the dissertation that provided the starting point, particularly Dr. Christopher Phillips, Dr. Willard Sunderland, and Dr. Martin Francis. Dr. John H. Morrow, Jr., of the University of Georgia, had been a valued friend and colleague for several years prior to the start of this project, and his work in this field continues to inspire countless researchers and writers. Several other UC historians, though not directly involved in the final product, nevertheless contributed through the examples they provided in demonstrating how this kind of work should be done. Dr. Daniel Beaver, with whom I was privileged to study during his last year at UC, Dr. Thomas Sakmyster, Dr. John K. Alexander, Dr. David Stradling, and Dr. Edward Ross Dickinson, now at the University of California, Davis, all made me a better student of history.

Outside the University of Cincinnati community many friends, most of whom I came to know through the old Cross and Cockade Society, or the current League of World War I Aviation Historians and Cross and Cockade International, loaned research material or provided other help along the way. Funding for my research junket to London to mine the vast holdings of the British National Archives' Public Record Office and the Moore-Brabazon and Laws Collections at the Royal Air Force Museum came from the late Bruce and Ralph Hooper of the Elizabeth S. Hooper Foundation. This family foundation, named in honor of their mother, maintained a long and impressive record of supporting organizations that honor the service of men and women who have worn the uniform of this country and I am myself honored that they chose to support my efforts as well. Staff members of the National Archives Public Records Office perform their jobs in a highly professional manner, juggling the demands of several hundred curious researchers every day. Amidst the chaos they never failed to lend whatever assistance I needed. The same can be said of the staff at the Royal Air Force Museum, especially Peter Elliott, who arranged for a waiver of the rules so that I could bring a digital camera into the facility at a time before cameras were regularly allowed. During my stay in London, Michael and Shibohan Herne were extremely gracious hosts who made me feel more like family than a temporary boarder.

Colonel Terry Finnegan, USAF (Ret.), and Dr. Birger Stichelbaut both served as valuable sounding boards and people with similar views on the role and importance of aerial reconnaissance. Dr. Stichelbaut's efforts in organizing the 2006 Images of Conflict: Military Aerial Photography and Archaeology conference in Ypres, Belgium, where we all had the chance to share ideas, were especially appreciated. The University of Ghent's Department of Ancient History and Archaeology and the In Flanders Fields Museum also deserve thanks for their sponsorship of the conference. Steve Suddaby and Colonel Steve Ruffin, USAF (Ret.), provided many good suggestions and advice. Noel Shirley, who served for more than a decade as assistant managing editor of *Over the Front*, shared much primary source material without which there would have been little said here about naval aviation. The late Peter Grosz and the late Neal O'Connor, both of whom still stand as giants in the field of First World War aviation research, taught the world most of what is known about German aerial operations in the Great War. What little they did not cover, my friend Peter Kilduff has done, and he was also generous with his help. Aaron Weaver, as always, was a great help when it came to photographs. Sydney Barth, a young talent, and soon to be a design student at UC's College of Design, Architecture, Art and Planning, graciously provided the maps.

Several years before beginning graduate school, I had the opportunity to spend a few days rummaging through the records at the US Air Force Historical Research Agency and the library at the Air War College during a visit to Maxwell Air Force Base funded by a grant provided by the USAF HRA. The documents copied during that visit were essential to the chapter on balloon operations. I have not had a formal opportunity to thank agency officials for that generosity until now and would like particularly to mention Dr. Robert Johnson, of the Archives Division. Annie Pinder, of the UK Parliamentary Archives, also proved helpful answering an email query in a timely manner.

The people at Casemate, particularly Clare Litt, who provided valuable editorial advice, and Katie Allen who designed the cover, were instrumental in turning the original manuscript into the finished product.

The largest measure of gratitude goes to my family. My late mother, Ruby Streckfuss, and my sister, Virginia Gutzwiller, both learned long ago the question "what would you like for Christmas" often led to very odd answers. In this case, several holiday seasons spent shopping at the US National Archives collecting a complete set of the Gorrell Report on microfilm, an acquisition that ultimately saved immeasurably in both travel time and expense. Finally, my late wife, Sharon, our son, Erich, and most recently, my fiancé Lucy Ginther, all endured many disruptions in their lives over several years in support of this research. In addition, they all regularly lent their technical expertise when called upon, helping solve more than a few hardware and software problems. Erich also allowed me to conscript him for a couple days service as research assistant photographing records at the National Archives' College Park, Maryland, facility, saving me another road trip. To everyone I express my thanks. Any and all mistakes are mine alone.

Those interested in reading more First World War aviation history should consider membership of two outstanding historical organizations: The League of World War I Aviation Historians, www.overthefront.com, and Cross & Cockade International, www.crossandcockade.com.

Note on Sources and Terms

Two major collections supplied the bulk of the research material used here. Most data on American aviation originated with the National Archives and Record Administration's (NARA) Gorrell's History of the Air Service, while British records came mostly from the massive Air 1 file in the United Kingdom National Archives' Public Record Office (TNA: PRO).

Following the First World War, Air Service Colonel Edgar Gorrell collected the records of each American aviation unit in France. Gorrell's goals included writing an official US Air Service history. Although he did not complete that task, the data he compiled remains available within Record Group (RG) 120 within the NARA's Records of the American Expeditionary Forces (World War I). Informally termed the "Gorrell Report," the material is divided by subject matter and identified by series letter and volume number. The complete report is available as publication M990 of NARA's microfilm series and is now also accessible online. An example of a citation to a Gorrell Report document is "Thomas E. Hibben, 'Topography: Lecture delivered at the Second Aviation Instruction Center,' M990, p. 1, R34, F759, Gorrell's History of the Air Service, Ser. J, vol. 3, RG 120, Records of the American Expeditionary Forces (World War I), NARA." This source form identifies the author, document title, microfilm publication, internal page number within the lecture, microfilm reel and frame number, and the larger publication's series letter and volume number within RG 120.

British Air Ministry records reside in the United Kingdom's National Archives Public Record Office facility at Kew in some twenty-seven hundred boxes coded Air 1. The department code "Air" identifies Air Ministry records, and the "1" is the series number. Occasionally a series code contains a second number, in which case the numbers are separated by a stroke. Series numbers are followed by piece numbers, which identify individual items within the file. Complex piece numbers consist of several numbers divided by strokes. Internal page numbers within the file complete the citation. As an example of a complete citation: "'No. 4 Squadron Reconnaissance Reports, August 1914: Appendices to War Diary,' Air 1/744/204/3/8, TNA: PRO, 42," contains the document title, department code and series number, piece number, location of the file in the National Archives (TNA) Public Record Office facility (PRO), and the internal page number. Where authorship of a document is known the author's name heads the citation.

The Moore-Brabazon Papers (MBP) and Frederick Laws Papers (FLP), both housed at the Royal Air Force Museum (RAFM) at Hendon, England, contain considerable material on British aerial photography. The US Air Force Historical Research Agency (USAF HRA) at Maxwell Air Force Base, Alabama, possesses duplicate copies of much of the information contained in the Gorrell Report as well as many other US Air Service Balloon Section records that proved particularly useful in the writing of Chapter 3. French documents housed at the Service Historique de l'Armée de l'Air (SHAA), Service Historique de l'Armée de l'Marine (SHAM) and Service Historique de l'Armée de l'Terre (SHAT), at Chateau de Vincennes near Paris were consulted for information on French aviation and US Naval Aviation units located in France. Surviving German records, especially the *Nachrichtenblat der Luftstreitkräfte* (*Air Force News*), the official newspaper of Germany's first air force, published between January 1917 and the autumn of 1918, and the *Kommandeur der Flieger* (aviation commander) reports, produced within the several German armies for internal circulation, provided much of the information not gathered from British and American intelligence sources.

Abbreviations

Adm.	Admiral or Admiralty
AEF	American Expeditionary Forces
AFB	Air Force Base (US)
BEF	British Expeditionary Force
CMM	Chief Machinist Mate
Cpte.	*Capitaine* (French captain)
DMA	Director of Military Aeronautics (British and US)
Ens.	Ensign
Fl. Abt	*Flieger Abteilung* (German Flying Section)
Fl. Abt. (A)	*Flieger Abteilung (Artillerie)* (German Artillery Flying Section
GPO	Government Printing Office (US)
GQG	*Grand Quartier General* (French General Headquarters)
Hptm.	*Hauptmann* (German captain)
Jasta	(Abbreviation for a German *Jagdstaffel*, a fighter squadron)
JG	(Abbreviation for a German *Jagdgeschwader*, a fighter group or wing)
Kofl	*Kommandeur der Flieger* (German Army Aviation Commander)
Kogenluft	*Kommandierende General der Luftstrieftkräfte* (German Commanding General of the Air Force)
NARA	National Archives and Records Administration (US)
OHL	*Obersten Heeresleitung* (German Army High Command)

PlM	Prussian *Ordern Pour le Mérite* (Order of Merit)
RAF	Royal Air Force (British)
RAdm.	Rear Admiral
Reihenbildzug	(German serial photographic section)
RFC	Royal Flying Corps (British)
RNAS	Royal Naval Air Service (British)
Stofl	*Stabsoffizier der Flieger* (German Aviation Staff Officer)
VAdm.	Vice Admiral

Introduction

No modern military analyst would challenge the suggestion that the development of air power fundamentally altered the way human beings fight wars. Movement into the third dimension removed restrictions that had limited military and naval operations for centuries. The possibilities inherent in aerial warfare immediately fascinated military authorities and social commentators. As early as 1908 the novelist H. G. Wells took a futuristic look at what the world might experience when the first bombers appeared in *The War in the Air*.[1] The following year, Louis Blériot became the first to fly across the English Channel, forever ending the feeling of safety British men and women took from living on an island. Less than a year and a half later, American Eugene Ely made the first flights from and to naval vessels. Within the next two years, army commanders in the United States and throughout Europe began ordering aircraft and experimenting with them during practice maneuvers. In 1912, when Italy and Turkey went to war, a handful of military airmen received their baptisms of fire. The continent's major powers watched these earliest military aerial operations unfold and by the time the rest of Europe erupted in war in the summer of 1914 all of the belligerent nations had taken the first steps towards organizing an air force to work with their armies and navies. As airmen, airplanes, airships, and balloons took their places with the ground and sea forces that went off to war, no one could yet possibly know how significant a role they would play in the fighting.[2]

Reconnaissance and bombing dominated early military thinking about the potential use of aircraft. During the Napoleonic wars and the American Civil War, armies began using balloons to observe the enemy generally and to provide firing advice to the artillery.[3] Count Ferdinand von Zeppelin visited the United States as a Prussian military observer to the Union Army during the latter conflict and the balloons he inspected started him thinking about the giant airships that would later become synonymous with his name. Once those airships achieved performance and endurance adequate to fly round-trips from bases in Germany to destinations in England, British citizens began fearing that Wells's futuristic predictions might actually come true. That Germany would use its zeppelins to bomb their homes.

During their maneuvers in 1912 and 1913, British commanders attached aviators and airplanes to each of the opposing forces to test the feasibility of aerial reconnaissance. The army that made more effective use of its reconnaissance fliers won on each occasion, an early indicator of what would become aviation's leading wartime role. During the war itself, aerial reconnaissance, observation, and photography contributed to every aspect of operations. Reconnaissance crews bringing back reports of enemy troop and supply movements aided in the planning of successful operations and occasionally, such as at the battles of the Marne and Tannenberg, proved key factors in avoiding disasters. Pilots and airplane and balloon observers became instrumental parts of the artillery regulation process. Aerial photographers provided the primary material from which military cartographers drew the thousands of maps printed daily on both sides of the lines. And in the war's second half, naval aviators supplied escort and sentinel service to the millions of troops and even greater millions of tons of supplies crossing the Atlantic in naval convoys.

Bombing was more problematic. Early aircraft ran on generally unreliable low-horsepower engines, with insignificant lifting power. The situation improved after the war began. Over its course both sides experimented with strategic bombing: Russia with the world's first multi-engine bomber, the *Ilya Muromets*; Germany with zeppelins and giant aircraft; and the British with squadrons stationed in eastern France within range of industrial targets in Germany. In the last months of the conflict, Britain, France, Italy, and the United States fielded an inter-Allied bombing force that might have carried the air war to Berlin had the fighting continued into 1919. By the armistice in 1918, however, aircraft performance had not progressed to such an extent that aerial bombers could claim to have contributed significantly to the Allied victory.

Historians who have written about aviation in the First World War have remarked on a supposed lack of appreciation the war's ground commanders had for their airmen. There is some evidence to support this argument. For example, prior to the war French General Ferdinand Foch, who became supreme Allied commander in 1918, is quoted as having described the military value of airplanes as "worthless."[4] British Expeditionary Force Commander, Sir Douglas Haig, is also sometimes cast as having a low opinion of the usefulness of the air units under his overall command.[5] Actions taken by senior commanders, however, reveal a belief in aviation's value that existed from the war's outbreak and continued to mature over the course of the conflict. In 1914, for example, Russian military leaders, desperate for the resources required to build an air arm that could compete with Germany's, struck a deal with their French ally to trade ground troops for aviators. Under the terms of the agreement, Russia received two aeronautical missions to help them build an aviation program. In exchange, Russia sent an entire brigade of "some 1,610 officers and 65,000 men" to fight with the French on the Western Front.[6] By the opening of the battle of the Somme in July 1916, Haig wrote to the War Office urging enlargement of the Royal Flying Corps to fifty-six squadrons.[7]

Air war chroniclers have also concentrated their efforts largely on bombing and fighter operations, two aspects of aviation that can be vigorously studied independently of the ground or naval wars. This work contends that this narrow focus has minimized the connections between aerial and ground and naval operations to such an extent that the importance of aviation to the broader history of the war has been lost. Aviation has been portrayed as a romantic contrast to the slaughter on the ground, an alternate view of the war that kept civilian morale alive. Military flying has also been categorized as a novel experiment that contributed little to the struggle's outcome and only achieved its true potential in the Second World War.

The historiography of First World War aviation has developed in a number of directions since the war ended in 1918, only a small handful of which have included comprehensive treatments of aerial reconnaissance, observation, and photography or their impact on the way in which the belligerent powers conducted military and naval operations. This book seeks to highlight the significant influence reconnaissance and observation crews and aerial photographers had on the way the First World War developed. A related goal involves explaining why, in the face of overwhelming evidence that aviation's various reconnaissance functions constituted its primary worth to the belligerent powers, the historiography took another path, one that has barely acknowledged the existence of this division of air power. Evidence from the postwar period points to the conclusion that the struggle for independence that air power advocates in the United States and Europe provoked with Army and Navy leaders forced them to concentrate their efforts on building strong bombing and aerial combat arms.[8] The observation crews that had proved so essential during the war fell victim to political considerations after the armistice.

The research presented here traces the development of aviation's various reconnaissance functions from their earliest debut in the eighteenth and nineteenth centuries through the end of the First World War. An examination of the fighter pilot's allure is included to develop an understanding why his exploits overshadowed the more militarily significant work of the reconnaissance crews. Finally, the financial and political struggles that affected air forces in the postwar period are examined to determine why military planners, and ultimately historians, abandoned their focus on aerial reconnaissance in favor of strategic bombing. Ultimately, the goal is to restore aviation to the story of the Great War by demonstrating that by putting eyes all over the sky aviators significantly altered the manner in which operations were conducted in the war's other dimensions.

CHAPTER 1

Desire and Capacity Lock Horns

The basic element of war is uncertainty. The man who developed an organization to make a business of getting the latest information of the inevitable changes, and who then would act, was the man who created and conducted a successful war organization.
—H. A. Toulmin, Jr., *Air Service: American Expeditionary Force, 1918*

At a campaign stop in Wisconsin on August 18, 2004, President George W. Bush had this to say in defense of his plan to redeploy American forces abroad: "When you can replace land troops with more effective aircraft it means people are stationed at home and they can be deployed rapidly and it's less unsettling times for our troops, less rotations, less pressure on the system, plus taxpayer savings."[1] Clearly, the forty-third American commander-in-chief believed that aircraft have made a difference in the conduct and understanding of war. He would no doubt accept, without argument, that a military's three-dimensional operational capability fundamentally changes a government's decisions on *how* to make war.[2]

Most authors and historians who analyze either the First World War in its entirety or specifically the role played by aviation during the 1914–1918 war are not so generous in their assessment of the airplane's significance to the twentieth century's first global conflict. The historical consensus at the outset of the twenty-first century is that aviation played a minor role at best in the conduct and outcome of the First World War. Because air power was in its infancy during the twentieth century's teen years, many who write on the First World War appear to believe it was of little practical use. Air power specialists and military historians alike argue the Second, not the First World War, firmly established the potential of the air weapon through demonstrations of might such as the Luftwaffe's attempt at a blitz of England in the summer of 1940 and the American and British bombing campaigns over France and Germany during the years 1942–1945.

A close study of the first air war reveals another way to think about the significance of aviation, one focused on the importance of reconnaissance, photography, and observation. While this air power model is seemingly less aggressive and far less suited to quantifiable analysis than the bombing model that developed during the Second World War, it is clear that during the First World War events on the ground and on the water could not, and would not, have developed the way they did in the absence of aviation. This reconnaissance-based model took root shortly after the war began in the summer of 1914 and was firmly in place when the United States entered the First World War in April 1917. By the time the United States associated itself with the Allied powers, British, French and Italian military leaders had gained extensive experience with aviation. By comparison, in the years since the first flights at Kitty Hawk and Dayton, Army and Navy commanders in the United States had largely neglected aviation's potential. Europe's lead made Allied influence over the US Air Service inevitable. Under considerable pressure to build an air service from scratch as quickly as humanly possible, American aviation leaders chose to imitate the French and the British and set about constructing an air power model that utilized aviation primarily as the eyes of its army and navy.

American fascination with the potential of destructive air power did not begin during the First World War, but rather developed in response to the rush to downsize the US military following the war. American, British, French, and German experiments with strategic bombing during the First World War failed to develop the airframe, engine, or navigation technology capable of delivering an impressive bomb load. Despite this failure, between the wars, American air power theorists continued to put their faith in the idea that devastation could rain down from the sky. Finances dictated their choice. Shrinking budgets combined with a military culture dominated by tradition and seniority to make the Army and Navy formidable opponents in a war over finances. To prevail the fledgling Air Service had to convince those with power over the purse that they could win any future war faster than either the Army or Navy, and at a lesser cost in both money and blood.

Strategic air power's apparent success in the Second World War confirmed arguments that military leaders, historians, and the American public had made about aerial bombing's war-winning possibilities since the end of the previous world conflict. Several factors proved the power of strategic bombing, including the Luftwaffe's near-win in the Battle of Britain, the havoc that the US Eighth and Fifteenth Air Forces, and Royal Air Force Bomber Command, wreaked in occupied France and in Germany, and the climactic end to the war in the Pacific following the dropping of atomic bombs on Hiroshima and Nagasaki. The destructive power of aviation evident during the Second World War made inevitable a historical reexamination of the First World War's aerial campaign. By contrast, especially after historians had witnessed the campaigns from 1939 to 1945, the Great War's bombing programs seemed miniscule at best, without impact on the war fought in the trenches of Europe and on, or below, the waters of the Atlantic, North Sea, and the Mediterranean.

Twentieth-century aviators were not the first warriors to witness such dramatic changes in military and naval doctrine brought about by the introduction of a new weapon. Nineteenth-century soldiers had endured the beginning of the transition to modern warfare. Modern technology, including mass-production techniques, began to exert its influence on the battlefield in the century prior to the First World War. Forces fighting in the American Civil War had been obliged to entrench to protect themselves from enemy troops using rifled weaponry that extended the effective firing range from a half-mile to as much as two miles for artillery and that included early forms of rapid-fire weapons. They witnessed death and destruction on a scale hitherto unprecedented.[3] Following the American Civil War and into the early years of the twentieth century, the Gatling and other machine guns proved useful to those in need of enhanced firepower. In particular, American mining companies employed private armies that intimidated potential and actual strikers by threatening to turn these weapons upon them if they did not return to work.[4]

Europe's aristocratic officer corps, still commanding the British, French, and German armies, did not always find the new weaponry gentlemanly. These officers' traditional schooling in the art of charging across open battlefields either on horseback with the lance, or on foot with rifle and bayonet in hand, sustained a culture that made them reluctant to embrace automatic weapons. Their attitudes implicitly placed a romantic vision of the past over military efficiency. In 1852, British officers and members of the crew remained aboard the sinking ship HMS *Birkenhead,* sacrificing their lives so that the women and children on board could reach safety in the available lifeboats.[5] That this attitude toward personal bravery and gentlemanly conduct had not disappeared by the eve of the First World War, and in fact had spread beyond the military, is demonstrated in April 1912 accounts of the sinking of the *Titanic.*[6] Within this mindset masculinity became the dialectical "other" to intelligence. Culturally, this attitude allowed technological advances that offered easier ways to kill or defend to frequently take a back seat to demonstrations of bravery. "In the code of the gentlemen intelligence was a little suspect."[7] Consequently the machine gun did not figure significantly in European warfare until the ground stalemate of the First World War largely eliminated mobile warfare.[8] The gentlemanly embrace of a more traditional and romantic form of warfare also make it easier to understand command decisions to send British troops leisurely marching across No-Man's-Land on the opening day of the battle of the Somme and the early reluctance to abandon horse cavalry in favor of aerial reconnaissance.

In his study of English chivalry, historian Mark Girouard restricts his social and military analysis to Great Britain, but makes clear his belief that chivalry's romantic influence was just as strong in continental

Europe and the United States. In support, in addition to the example of heroism on the RMS *Titanic*, he cites Kaiser Wilhelm II's talk "about putting on 'shining armor' and the war posters of Germany and her allies" at the outbreak of the First World War.[9] Furthermore, civilian and military yearnings to preserve a less violent, chivalric form of war romanticized both friendly and enemy forces.[10]

Whatever their romantic notions of combat, well before the development of the airplane inventors saw opportunity in harnessing technology, often as a deterrent to battlefield casualties or to war itself. In June 1877, Richard Gatling wrote that he had been prompted to invent the rapid-fire gun by a desire to save rather than lose lives. His gun would allow armies to achieve maximum results against the enemy with a minimum number of soldiers.[11] The path to perfecting the automatic gun and the airplane intersected in the work of Hiram Maxim, inventor of the weapon that became the basis for "machine" guns used by both sides between 1914 and 1918. Maxim also put his talents to use trying to perfect the airplane. In 1892, while involved in unsuccessful attempts to create an aircraft power plant, Maxim wrote: "give us a motor and we will very soon give you a successful flying machine."[12] The world did not have long to wait. On December 17, 1903, Orville and Wilbur Wright made the first successful powered flights at Kitty Hawk, North Carolina. Five years later, they tried to market their flying machine to the US Army, theorizing that aerial reconnaissance would render the prospect of armed conflict too difficult for any nation to risk going to war.[13]

American progressivism was at its peak at the time the Wright Brothers solved the problem of powered flight. Perhaps no other contemporary invention better symbolized progressives' faith in society's capacity for continual improvement than did the airplane. At the beginning of the century, as powered flight became widespread, anything seemed possible, much as landing men on the moon proved humankind capable of anything in the late twentieth century. But the seemingly ideal relationship between the airplane and the progressives' goal of a better society did not immediately translate into governmental interest in the Wright Flyer.

Appreciation for the Wrights' achievement took some time to develop. The brothers' attempts to interest the US and British governments fell on deaf ears until 1908 when the US government placed its first order for a Wright aircraft.[14] During the same year Wilbur Wright traveled to Europe to demonstrate the brothers' invention to other prospective customers and to disarm skeptics who doubted the Americans' claim to have been first in flight.[15]

As the nineteenth century turned into the twentieth, Europe's budding aviators were as interested as their American counterparts in developing a successful airplane. Understandably, the European aviation community valued its own claim to the title of first aloft.[16] Several European pioneers had managed to take to the air before Wilbur Wright arrived on the continent to showcase his invention and his piloting skills. However, doubts over reports about the Wrights' success vanished when the elder Wright brother flew at Le Mans in 1908. The ability to remain in the air for long distances and periods of time, all the while under perfect control, were all skills the French had yet to master. As British aviation historian, J. M. Bruce observed, "French national pride had been dealt a severe blow: to many French citizens of the time the conquest of the air and the development of mechanical flight was, or should be, a French prerogative."[17]

The Wrights did not long wear the mantle of aviation leaders. Worldwide excitement generated by the earliest flights in the United States and Europe brought with it government and media interest. Competition for government contracts as well as prize money offered by newspapers intent on increasing sales brought out a bumper crop of prospective aviators. The romance of flight ensured an adoring public's support for their feats of derring-do. The competitors included men who were already stars in other fields, men such as auto accessories magnate Louis Blériot, wealthy automobile and yacht racer Thomas Sopwith, international playboy Hubert Latham, and tennis star Roland Garros.[18]

In powered flight's first decade, aviators set and broke records for endurance, altitude, speed, and distance flown on an almost daily basis. The most significant aerial achievement shattered a military in addition to an aviation barrier. On July 25, 1909, Frenchman Louis Blériot flew across the English Channel from Calais to Dover ending the centuries of British national security that came with life on an island. "Britain, the world's greatest naval power, had been forced to recognize that its navy might no longer be able to defend it against all future forms of attack from abroad."[19] The British public had good reasons to be concerned. Suddenly intellectual curiosity and fear seemed to pull the world simultaneously in opposite directions. People once eager for the future to arrive now began to fear that their future might include death at the hands of the airplane.

Attitudes towards aviation's role in future military operations varied among Europe's military commanders from a "characteristically conservative" approach taken by the British to the more confident French, who proclaimed an early test had achieved "spectacular results."[20] George Holt Thomas, British agent for France's Farman Aircraft, "had made it his business to attend the [September 1910] French maneuvers and vigorously reported that their army viewed matters in a very different way from the British, and had proved that aeroplanes were essential for reconnaissance."[21] British commanders responded by assigning Capt. Bertram Dickson, an early aviator, to their own war games later the same month. Dickson initially felt "cold-shouldered by his former colleagues, the regular officers of the Army."[22] The official historian of the Royal Air Force, Sir Walter Raleigh, attributed the lukewarm reaction to the cavalry's natural preference "to carry out the work of reconnaissance in the usual way," adding "men believe in the weapons they are skilled to handle."[23] As with Wilbur Wright at Le Mans, doubts about the airplane's ability to produce results vanished when Dickson returned from a flight on September 21. His report provided a "far more detailed picture of the enemy's movements than they had been able to glean from their own cavalry scouts. As a result, the commanding general of the 'Red' Army altered his plan."[24] Romantic visions of warfare were beginning to take a back seat to military efficiency and modern technology.

In contrast to the British military's early reluctance to include aviation in its war plans, and to the Wrights' somewhat pacifist view that airplanes might make the prospect of armed conflict intolerable, Germany leapt quickly to develop military aviation technology. As early as the 1860s Count Ferdinand von Zeppelin sought to build an aerial weapon capable of winning a war. As an official Prussian military observer during the American Civil War, Zeppelin had been impressed by the use and the even greater potential of balloons by combat forces. By the mid-1870s, Zeppelin had begun work on the line of airships that would bear his name. Within a decade military necessity would begin to influence his research when Germany's neighbor and frequent enemy, France, developed a lighter-than-air ship dubbed *La France*.[25]

After a series of setbacks, and at a time when most airplanes could stay in the air for only a few minutes, Zeppelin achieved mentionable success in September 1907 when his *LZ 3* [*Luftschiff Zeppelin*] remained aloft for eight hours. In response to this flight, the German military took an interest in Zeppelin's work and offered to purchase an airship if he could design one capable of remaining airborne for a 24-hour round trip of 435 miles.[26] Zeppelin set about improving on his aircraft's performance and in November 1909, just four months after Blériot crossed the English Channel in his lightweight and underpowered single-seater, Model XI, Zeppelin showcased the remarkable endurance and weight-carrying capability of his new ships by offering the world's first airline flights.[27]

The military implications of Germany's developing an airship capable of flying long distances while carrying heavy loads were not lost on the British. Just a year earlier, British novelist Herbert G. Wells chronicled a fictional worldwide conflict in which the threat represented by the invention of airships and airplanes triggered a war between the United States and Germany, a preemptive clash initiated by a German government nervous over the prospect the United States might develop a successful air weapon before it could do so itself.[28] Now that Louis Blériot had crossed the English Channel and Ferdinand von Zeppelin was constructing airships capable of even more impressive feats, the threat appeared real. Articles appearing in Great Britain's *Flight* magazine between 1909 (some even prior to the Blériot cross-channel flight) and just after the beginning of the First World War in 1914 document the development of an extensive discussion about the potential of air power. Those same articles also illustrate the British public's fear of attack and how their fear drove the conversation toward consideration of aircraft as an active weapon. Thus began the cultural devaluation of aerial reconnaissance.

Establishing a link between reconnaissance, artillery, and bombing accurately reflected one of several paths aviation would take during the war. Alluding to the airship's reconnaissance potential, Col. F. G. Stone analyzed a translated German article that emphasized observation's value to naval artillery and the vulnerability of British land targets to attack by airship-aided naval vessels.[29] Stone chose to concentrate heavily on speculation surrounding the prospective worth of airships as bombers. Rather than advocate for airships as an effective means of gathering information on enemy movements, the article instead focused on the load-carrying capability of rigid and non-rigid lighter-than-air craft, as well as the range from various bases on the European continent to possible targets in Great Britain, the need to conduct experiments aimed at developing Britain's own capacity to mount an aerial offensive, and the potential means of defending the island against attack from the air. Comments received on the Stone article, published in 1909 in the journal *Flight*, concentrated solely on the bombing discussion, entirely ignoring reconnaissance.[30]

Military analysts were not always blind to aviation's potential as a better means of reconnaissance. In a less one-sided examination early the following year, John E. Capper, a colonel in the Royal Engineers, discussed reconnaissance within an analysis of the potential military capabilities of dirigibles and airplanes. Capper discussed the broad range of aviation possibilities, including the need for aerial superiority, bombing, and transport, and divided reconnaissance into "strategical" and "tactical" subcategories.[31] Capper concluded an army equipped with aircraft would benefit by "the collection of intelligence, the moral result on the enemy, the minor destruction of supplies, etc, [and] assisting the G.O.C-in-C [general officer commanding-in-chief] to control his troops in battle."[32] Interestingly, given the course eventually taken during the war and particularly considering his engineering background, Capper entirely dismissed the possibility of aircraft assisting the artillery in any way.

Capper's rational, though slightly flawed evaluation notwithstanding, the general tone of the prewar discussion of aviation's military potential regularly centered on the more sensational topic of aerial attack. In their March 5, 1910 issue, the editors of *Flight* devoted a full page to a review of R. P. Hearne's *Airships in Peace and War*.[33] *Flight*'s unnamed reviewer borrowed two maps from Hearne, the first of which accurately depicted the area on both sides of the English Channel illustrating the distances between various points in Germany and potential targets in England. Hearne had written in reference to the map: "Now, if we glance at the diagram, it will be noted that a straight run of 380 miles would take the Zeppelin from Lake Constance to Sheerness, one of our important naval centres. If she chose to attack, we have absolutely nothing that could stop her." Building on this sense of helplessness, Hearne continued, "She would travel over Germany, France, the Channel, and England during the night without the least fear of detection, and could strike with literally the suddenness of a bolt from the blue. An airship of the modern type is practically an invisible enemy and this matter of invisible attack is the most terrifying feature of aerial warfare."[34]

The imagined results of an aerial attack grew to such proportions that it proved possible for some writers to predict theoretical consequences in excess of the known outcomes of earlier sea invasions. In a letter appearing in the June 11, 1910 issue of *Flight*, Harold Ingersoll compared the possibility of attack from the air to a sea assault on England, theorizing aerial bombardment would be worse:

> We find that an attacking force from over sea must cross the boundary between sea and land, and we know therefore what parts to defend, and where to expect attack. The air having no boundaries, we cannot locate a possible aerial attack and consequently not only the edge of the country, but its whole area must be defended. Therefore, in aerial warfare we possess no insularity.[35]

Building the kind of insularity from attack Ingersoll desired mandated good intelligence on enemy activities, the kind of information aerial reconnaissance might be expected to produce. In fairness to the editors of *Flight*, they did not yet embrace the idea that aerial attack would constitute the *raison d'être* of military aviation. In fact, a January 13, 1912 editorial in the publication enthusiastically endorsed Capt. Henry R. M. Brooke-Popham's prediction that reconnaissance would be aviation's primary contribution to future warfare.[36] In doing so, however, the editorial segued neatly into a discussion of the likelihood that the need to protect the reconnaissance machines would develop rapidly into a shooting war of the kind that H. G. Wells had predicted in his novel, *War in the Air*.[37] For the first time *Flight*'s editors were able to cite actual wartime experience, noting Italian reports of aerial action in its conflict with Turkey—the first war in which heavier-than-aircraft participated—that made it possible to predict "the only method of preventing the hostile aeroplane from gaining the information it has set out to obtain is by means of a counter attack by friendly air-craft."[38]

The tendency to emphasize an aircraft's ability to attack and defend over its primary mission as an intelligence gatherer soon found a more influential voice. In the May 18, 1912 issue of *Flight*, Brig. Gen. David Henderson speculated on the features necessary to a good reconnaissance airplane.[39] Henderson, the British Army's one-time director of military intelligence, who then served as director of military aeronautics, and who would lead troops in France two years later as the Royal Flying Corps' first general officer commanding, predicted the evolution of two types of military airplanes in wartime, "a fighting machine and a scouting machine."[40] Beginning with the attributes necessary for a good fighter, Henderson speculated, "the fighting aeroplane [would] be required to overcome the air forces of the enemy, if possible to drive them to the ground; at any rate to inflict damage upon them, and, in spite of opposition, to penetrate far enough to gain accurate information of the dispositions of the enemy's forces."[41] Conceding the two types might merge into one, Henderson outlined the qualities necessary to a modern fighter or reconnaissance machine, including speed, silence, invisibility, maneuverability, and a good view of the ground. Four of these features were essential to the aircraft's survival in the presence of hostile forces; only one was crucial to its observation function.[42]

Despite Henderson's focus on the ability of a commander to send out a reconnaissance force capable of handling its own defense and returning with valuable information about the enemy, the editors of *Flight* and their readers were more concerned with the prospect of surviving an aerial assault. As 1912 came to an end and Britons felt the tension of an imminent war on the continent, Winston Churchill, then first lord of the Admiralty, attempted to assure his countrymen "that all necessary precautions would be taken to protect [British] naval establishments against aerial observation or attack."[43] In the absence of that protection, however, Churchill conceded an unidentified airship had been "heard over Sheerness about 7 o'clock on the evening of October 14th." This admission led *Flight* to complain, with less concern over espionage than physical damage that "Neither Sheerness nor any other place on the whole of our coasts would have been in a position to offer any defence against its attack."[44] Completing the shift from concern over potential enemy reconnaissance to that of worry over the danger of aerial attack, *Flight* offered an article on the same page, written by a Berlin-based German army official, Hptm. von Stockhausen, who boasted about the zeppelin's bomb-carrying capability. Emphasizing the point while also highlighting Germany's lead in the development of a large load-carrier, Stockhausen asked: "What nation possesses an airship at all approaching in value to our Zeppelin cruisers? Is there one unrigid [sic] or semi-rigid airship which can attain such speed or has such carrying powers? Can one of them hold an exact course or remain stationary over a definite point?"[45]

The threat posed by zeppelins figured prominently in the debate over British Naval estimates the following year. Churchill, for his part, although recommending that his country "develop long-range airships of the largest type," hoped to minimize the danger represented by Germany's lead in airship technology.[46] As he prophesized in his address to Parliament, "If war breaks out to-morrow, foreign airships no doubt might do a certain amount of mischief and damage but it is foolish to suppose that in their present stage of development they could produce results which would decisively influence the course of events." Opponents countered by raising disturbing questions of Churchill. "Was the Admiralty really satisfied that our dockyards, magazines, and other naval establishments were secure against the possibility of serious overhead attack? Did Mr. Churchill consider that the question of secret rendezvous for a fleet at sea in time of war was not seriously affected by the new problem of airships?" Adding to the debate, Lord Charles Beresford said he believed aircraft would revolutionize war. "It had removed one of [Great Britain's] great natural defences, the fact that [it is] an island."[47] Another member, Walter Hume Long, summed the matter up concluding in a fearful manner, "if half that was said about this new method of warfare was true, the very existence of the country might be threatened."[48]

Worries over national security had a dramatic effect on the 1914 Navy estimates and nearly every aviation category showed sharp increases over the previous year's budget. The total for "aircraft, building and repair by contract," had more than tripled, from £113,300 to £375,000; amounts for the accommodation of airships had risen from £72,000 to £94,000, while that for seaplanes had gone from £22,000 to £51,500; and Air Department salaries had more than doubled from £2,371 to £5,371. In human terms the Navy's Air Department had grown to 125 officers and 500 other ranks and was expected to continue growing throughout the year to a total of 180 officers and 1,400 to 1,500 men.[49]

In the year before the outbreak of war, British and French aviation designers might have liked to develop greater offensive and defensive capabilities, but their capacity dictated an emphasis on reconnaissance.[50] Airframes were too frail and engines too low-powered to allow them to build heavy bombers comparable to Germany's zeppelins and they had yet to develop a single-seat fighter. Churchill justified the emphasis on reconnaissance when he told the House of Commons: "No assistance can be more valuable than the assistance rendered by aeroplanes and seaplanes in bringing information in regard to which time is vital to the bases where the patrol flotillas are held in readiness." But the public's fear of attack dictated an effort to develop more aggressive elements, which Churchill also acknowledged. The future prime minister cautioned, "passive defence against [an aerial] attack is perfectly hopeless and endless. The only real security which sound military principles will rely upon is that you should be master of your own air."[51] To achieve that mastery, the first lord of the Admiralty backed up his bet on observation by adding a nod to bombing. "Of course," he told Parliament, "the heavy seaplanes which we are deploying now will carry heavy explosives which can be dropped on transports and disturb a landing, even before the patrol flotilla can arrive." Churchill went on to say his seaplanes would "carry wireless telegraphy which enables them to signal 120 miles effectively," and concluded that, "in the third place, these [seaplanes] will be of great value for the defence of vulnerable points."[52] In sum, Churchill envisioned aviation as a three-part defense-in-depth, with what would today be called a "search and destroy" capacity ranking first, a reconnaissance component second, and a defender-of-last-resort capability third.

As Europe edged closer towards the most cataclysmic conflict the world had yet to know, rapidly advancing technology crossed paths with tradition, imagination, and fear to set the stage for aviation becoming a vital player in war. Within little more than a decade, powered flight had progressed from its tentative beginnings at Kitty Hawk to the point where aviators were about to add a third dimension to modern warfare. As reconnaissance auxiliaries to the world's armies and navies, airplanes, airships, and balloons would soon shape the way Europe fought its Great War.

CHAPTER 2

The Fighter Pilot Mystique

These men—these names headed by that of 'Captain Ball, V.C., D.S.O., M.C., Légion d'honneur'—they would not soon be forgotten by those who fought. Indeed the final and greatest Decoration to which so many had already attained would ensure that their names lived on for evermore.

—Duncan Grinnell-Milne, *Wind in the Wires*

A real man fights the war. He does not just observe it. Fascination with the fighter pilot dates from early 1915 when the victory scores of the first successful combat aviators moved beyond kill number one, and the world began to take notice of aerial warfare. From those simple beginnings, the fighter pilot has achieved near cultural status in the history of the First World War. Atop this pedestal, fighter pilots have overshadowed the achievements of reconnaissance and observation fliers to a point where the latter are all but forgotten. Understanding the development of this mystique requires an appreciation of how the fighter pilot's image appealed to two distinct audiences: those who sought the masculine satisfaction of risking their own lives fighting in the air, and the broader public who idolized them.

The aerial image most frequently associated with the opening months of the First World War depicts Allied and German aviators waving as they passed harmlessly by one another on their respective reconnaissance and bombing missions. Harmless as the aviators were to one another, the military value of those early reconnaissance missions prompted ground commanders on both sides to embrace aviation and to begin plotting ways to bring to an end the enemy's intelligence-gathering aerial sorties. Blinding the enemy meant bringing down their aircraft before crews could report what they had seen, and so began the habit of carrying aloft pistols, rifles, and for the especially daring, light machine guns. By the war's first anniversary, crews engaged in aerial combat on a regular basis. While in the sky, aviators were in constant danger.

On the ground, whether assigned to pursuit, reconnaissance, or bombing squadrons, fliers enjoyed a comfortable existence. As such, many men opted for war in the air despite its dangers. Unlike their ground-bound counterparts, aviators did not wage war against rats, mud, and lice, enemies in some ways more demoralizing than the opposite side's machine guns and artillery. Infantrymen served regular rotations in the trenches, where a miserable war with nature was a constant companion. By contrast, aviators lived in relative luxury. Boarding with local villagers or lodging in Nissen huts or tents, as most airmen regularly did, appeared palatial to the average trench-dweller.

The aviator's relatively comfortable life began in training. Aviation training generally took place well to the rear of the front lines. Even in France, where the Western Front lay within easy reach by airplane or railroad, training facilities were in areas undamaged by the war. The Lafayette Escadrille's Edwin C. Parsons fondly remembered a French training custom called "*pannes de château*, meaning château breakdowns. A pilot would disappear for anywhere from three days to a week and come back with a smug face and a tale of having made a forced landing, but fortunately, oh so fortunately, near a big château, where he was royally entertained."[1] Diarists among a group of American pilots who trained with Italians at Foggia recorded almost daily trips from the training camps into town to shop and dine at local restaurants and frequent leave to Rome and other Italian cities.[2] Elliott White Springs, writing under the guise of the "unknown aviator," raved about his training in England with the Royal Flying Corps, with whom he began his instruction, at Oxford's Christ Church College. "We have champagne with our meals at $2.10 a bottle! This is indeed the life!"[3]

When the US Air Service set up its own facilities in France in 1917, American training officers copied their British and French counterparts' luxurious approach to instruction. Harvey Conover, who went to France as an ambulance driver before transferring to aviation, commented on the new training base at Tours. "[T]he quarters are very comfortable, the food good, the authorities in charge very lenient and accommodating, and everything seems to point to a most pleasant prospect," he wrote. "To summarize the whole outlook we have just three things to do—Eat, Sleep, and Fly. Who could ask for anything more agreeable?"[4]

Once through their training, fliers continued to enjoy a relatively relaxed life on the ground. A photograph of Manfred von Richthofen's command, *Jagdstaffel* (Fighter Squadron) 11, taken while stationed at Roucourt, France, shows the unit living in a local château.[5] *Bombengeschwader* (Bombing Squadron) 3, a German unit quartered near Ghent, Belgium, reported taking advantage of the opportunities offered by the presence of local women, fishing in lakes, walking through parks, swimming and boating on the Lys, good food and drink in the city's restaurants, and exposure to local art.[6] Some of the Americans who trained at Foggia later served with an Italian bombing *squadriglia* (squadron) whose officers pooled their funds to purchase a squadron box at the local opera house.[7] When not close enough to take advantage of amenities offered by a town or city, airmen relied on their own creativity to enhance their surroundings. British ace Albert Ball built and furnished his own hut near his airfield. "It became something of a club on occasions. He played gramophone records and other pilots dropped in to listen." Outside his hut, Ball planted a garden where he grew vegetables and flowers.[8]

In the class-conscious European societies of the early twentieth century, an officer's commission brought enhanced social prestige. Although learning to fly did not always guarantee promotion to the officer corps, in some armies it helped. The US Air Service accorded its prospective aviators "cadet" status during their training days, something akin to an officer in training. Full commissions, and the social standing that accompanied them, were the exception rather than the rule prior to completion of flight instruction.[9] In the British forces, aviator wings were generally but not exclusively reserved for officers. Indeed, the

Royal Flying Corps' leading ace, James McCudden, began his flying career as a sergeant pilot. Germany, Austria-Hungary, and France were much more frugal in commissioning their aviators. All three nations maintained large numbers of non-commissioned aircrew and reserved commissions for those fliers who distinguished themselves in combat.

Several armies employed mixed crews of non-commissioned pilots and commissioned-officer observers and in those cases the observer commanded the airplane even though he did not control its movements. The pilot's status as little more than aerial chauffeur provided many with a professional incentive, in addition to social reasons, to abandon two-seater work for the freedom of single-seat fighters. German pilot Josef Doerflinger began his career flying two-seaters, but when unjustly blamed for a crash, he took the opportunity to transfer to single-seat fighters where he would no longer have to put up with someone in the back telling him what to do.[10]

A transfer to fighters might solve the non-commissioned pilot's professional situation, but his social problems remained, making the quest for officer rank an important goal for those on the lower end of the military's social ladder. Analyzing a photo of twenty-eight-victory ace, Benno Fiala Ritter von Fernbrugg, and four men under his command, historian Martin O'Connor points to "the hard line drawn in the Dual Monarchy between officers and NCOs."[11] The men flanking Fiala in the photo are two officers and two non-commissioned officers. Fiala has his arms draped around the two officers—a not-so-subtle indication of the social closeness enjoyed by the three—while the two NCOs stand marginalized at the edges of the group. The two NCOs' outstanding military accomplishments make Fiala's distinction appear particularly contrived. Stefan Fejes and Eugen Bönsch, who stand outside their commander's affectionate embrace, both scored sixteen victories in air combat, while Michael Dorcic and Franz Rudorfer, who enjoy pride of place next to Fiala, were far less successful. Rudorfer achieved eleven victories, while Dorcic did not score at all.[12]

American aviation cadets waiting for their lieutenant's bars also yearned for social advancement. Within a year of the their country's declaration of war some 38,000 Americans had volunteered for aviation training.[13] Because the construction of training facilities lagged behind this flood of volunteers, many men sat idle as fields were constructed. Approximately a thousand cadets who had progressed rapidly through American ground schools on the strength of promises of flight training in Europe and early commissions were put to work instead building the Third Aviation Instruction Center at Issoudun, France. Assignment as common laborers insulted many on the verge of status and privilege, causing morale to fall to the point of "near mutiny."[14]

The American situation in Italy differed little from that in France, where the group training at Foggia were also forced to wait for their commissions. One cadet confided to his diary, "I have hope that this tangle about the first and second lieutenancies may be straightened out soon, as all the fellows who finished after I did but before the 15th of December (1917) received firsts."[15] Another cadet celebrated his eventual commission by writing, "I am a Second Lieutenant ASSORC (Air Service Signal Officer Reserve Corps). I am an officer now and treated as such."[16] Being treated as an officer was apparently worth the wait for newly minted 2/Lt. Sherwood Hubbell, who went on to record the privileges that accompanied his new rank. "Seven other fellows and myself have moved from the big room [shared by the non-commissioned cadets] into a very comfortable little room." Given that as a non-commissioned cadet Hubbell and his friends had been subject to early morning roll calls and camp restrictions, Hubbell was elated no longer to be so burdened. "We can sleep as late as we want. [W]e are absolutely free to go in and out of camp whenever we please. Last, but not least, we can now take hot baths. The officer's bathroom contains a splendid tub and has a water-heater. This is a real luxury."[17]

If the promise of luxury came with aviation duty regardless of flying assignment and social status came by way of the officer's commission without regard to the type of duty the aviator fulfilled, one might wonder what drew men to aspire to fight in the air rather than serve as bombers or reconnaissance fliers? Analyzing Royal Air Force pilots serving in the Second World War, historian Martin Francis distinguished between the types of courage required to fly bombing missions versus serving on fighters. The RAF "actively discouraged" bomber crews from the sort of "reckless bravery" required of a fighter pilot because "teamwork and the disciplined and systematic implementation of highly specific objectives were seen as much more desirable."[18] He might as well have been discussing the difference between the First World War's fighter pilots and their reconnaissance colleagues. The distinctions are the same. The fighter pilot could afford a little recklessness. He had only his own life to risk and the more daring his behavior the greater his chances of victory. The reconnaissance crew, on the other hand, required both discipline and teamwork in the pursuit of photographs or enemy intelligence and displays of recklessness might jeopardize rather than further those objectives. But their jobs lacked the glamour, the potential for glory, and the emphasis on masculinity that came with service in fighters. And men aspired to be heroes.

Writing about war in general, William Manchester quoted an old soldier's saying, "a man won't sell you his life, but he'll give it to you for a piece of colored ribbon."[19] With a world war subjecting it to mass slaughter, an emotionally depressed public also craved heroes. Trench warfare appeared to render irrelevant warfare's land-based supermen, the horse-mounted cavalry. With the exception of 1916's battle of Jutland, German battleships rested largely stagnant in their ports, negating the possibility of a modern Trafalgar. With these traditional sources of heroes unavailable, the world turned its eyes skyward. Who then would become aviation's champions? With aerial reconnaissance undiscussed in the press and aerial bombing carrying the stigma of attacking the helpless, the new and adventurous fighter pilots, who battled each other in apparently equal contests, held out the greatest promise of heroism.

In the nineteenth century and before young soldiers looking for honor and glory joined the cavalry. Racing across the battlefield atop a bleached charger, lance in hand, provided a romantic view of war not available to those who fought on foot. Frederick the Great held that "good cavalry" made a commander "master of the land," and that where infantry suffered by war, cavalry acquired "perfection."[20] But the American Civil War had proven "the conventional wisdom from past wars that called for massed cavalry to break enemy lines and formations was much outmoded." Cavalry still remained capable of a wide range of reconnaissance tasks, including the provision of "a screen behind which friendly forces could mass." They could also "watch enemy movements and report them" and protect "friendly forces by stopping enemy patrols" and "gather information about the country and the enemy, and prevent enemy cavalry from doing the same." Cavalry's biggest contribution, however, came prior to the battle, when the information it brought back "might determine the outcome of campaigns and battles before they ever occurred."[21]

Those serving in the cavalry during the First World War's opening battles remained hopeful those same opportunities would remain open to them. In 1918 cavalry would confirm that it could still prove effective during mobile actions such as those fought at Amiens, Megiddo, Vittorio-Veneto, and in Macedonia, but when movement on both the Western and Eastern Fronts came to a standstill in 1914 the outlook for cavalry's future looked bleak.[22] At that early point in the war, young men with a hunger for heroism began looking elsewhere for adventure. Serving in the cockpit of a modern airplane offered the same feel, the same chance for one-on-one contests of bravery, and the same test of manhood that came in the saddle of a cavalry mount. "Aerial combat could be imagined as similar to medieval rituals of combat."[23]

One of those looking for something new out of the war was a young Canadian cavalryman, William Avery Bishop. He would end the war as Canada's top-scoring fighter pilot. Bishop began his wartime account, *Winged Warfare*, with the observation:

> It was the mud, I think, that made me take to flying. Everything was dank, and slimy, and boggy. I had succeeded in getting myself mired to the knees when suddenly, from somewhere out of the storm, appeared a trim little aeroplane. It landed hesitatingly in a near-by field as if scorning to brush its wings against so sordid a landscape; then away again up into the clean grey mists.[24]

A member of a Canadian cavalry unit, the Mississauga Horse, at the war's outset, Bishop entered the conflict with dashing images of cavalry actions, noting he had "fully expected that going into battle would mean for me the saddle of a galloping charger."[25] While the reality of modern ground warfare ran contrary to those mental images, the freedom of action and the potential for individual achievement offered by fighting in the air brought an opportunity to fulfill them. Bishop decided at the moment of his encounter with the airplane: "there was only one place to be on such a day—up above the clouds and in the summer sunshine. I was going into the battle that way. I was going to meet the enemy in the air."[26]

Not just any airplane would fulfill ambitions like Bishop's. The mounted cavalryman could perform both his reconnaissance and battle functions on the same horse. But when airplanes began taking over for the horse, aviation technology divided the horse cavalry's combined functions, creating two distinct types of aircraft, one to fly reconnaissance, observation, and photography missions, and the other to fight in the air. Two-seat reconnaissance types were generally slow, stable, and not as capable of defending themselves as fighters. By contrast, fighters were fast, nimble, and well armed.[27] It would not be long before the men who flew these aircraft were thought of as possessing the same qualities.

Manfred von Richthofen, eventually the war's leading fighter pilot, shared Bishop's desire for the kind of heroic opportunity seemingly no longer available on the ground. Like Bishop, Richthofen had also chosen cavalry service prior to the advent of war in Europe. But just as Bishop's war seemed to have quickly bogged down in the mud, Richthofen's mired down in a sea of never-ending boredom. He first traded his cavalry mount for a job "in the trenches at a spot where nothing happened."[28] Then, after a series of equally unexciting assignments, Richthofen wrote that he had "had enough of it. I sent a letter to my Commanding General and evil tongues reported that I said to him: 'My dear Excellency! I have not gone to war in order to collect cheese and eggs, but for another purpose.'"[29] Whatever its exact wording, the letter worked and Richthofen obtained his desired transfer to aviation.

The United States of America's official neutrality at the outset of the First World War proved equally frustrating to many young Americans in search of romantic adventure. Edmond C. C. Genét, lineal descendant of revolutionary France's notorious first ambassador to the United States, "Citizen Genét," took matters into his own hands. He jumped ship in Veracruz, Mexico, deserting the Navy to join the French Foreign Legion. Enlistment in Europe's war promised more excitement than America's troubles with Mexico. But service in the trenches proved too anonymous for Genét, so after two years the young veteran secured a transfer to military aviation. Explaining his decision to his mother, Genét wrote: "If anything does happen to me you all surely can feel better satisfied with the end than if I was sent to pieces by a shell or put out by a bullet in the infantry. The glory is well worth the loss. I'd far rather die as an aviator over the enemy's lines than find a nameless, shallow grave in the infantry."[30]

The personal goals of would-be aviators like Genét meshed nicely with the national objectives of all the belligerent powers. Shortly after the war began, a group of eager young Americans, prevented by their nation's neutrality from flying under their own colors, initiated a campaign to organize an all-American squadron within French aviation. Grasping the propaganda potential inherent in accounts of American volunteers fighting on behalf of the Allied cause, French commanders approved the scheme and in the process created an aerial legend. By the spring of 1916, enthusiasm for the idea had attracted "more than fifty Americans" to the ranks of French military aviation, an unofficial gaggle the *New York Times* dubbed the "Franco-American Flying Corps."[31] In May their efforts to organize a homogenous group were realized when the French created Escadrille N. 124 ("N" referring to the squadron's Nieuport single-seat pursuit aircraft) as a fighter squadron, staffing the unit exclusively with American pilots. The unit immediately became known as the Escadrille Américaine (American Squadron). Two days following the squadron's formation the *New York Times* reported on the unit's participation in French aerial operations over the lines, noting several pilots by name, and that the French anticipated formation of an additional three American units.[32] Reacting to the news, Germany mounted a diplomatic protest against the Escadrille's existence, arguing that allowing US citizens to fly over the lines in French aircraft violated American neutrality. The remonstration prompted the unit to change its name to L'Escadrille Lafayette, a tribute to the Marquis de Lafayette's service in the American Revolution. To preserve their American identity, the Lafayette Escadrille's members adopted a distinctive insignia, an American Indian with a red face and sporting a red, white, and blue war bonnet.[33] Less politically charged, the new name and insignia nonetheless held romantic imagery and ultimately contributed to the near mythological status the American volunteer squadron came to enjoy.

Within a massive Allied propaganda campaign aimed at pulling the United States into the war, publicity in the United States about the exploits of the Lafayette Escadrille conditioned American readers to accept the idea of their countrymen under arms and, more important, in service to the Allied cause. Victor Chapman's death in combat prompted three separate articles in the *New York Times*, in which *Times* reporters identified him as "a member of the Franco-American flying corps" and the "American escadrille."[34] In one of these tributes Chapman's father, prominent American essayist John Jay Chapman, extolled American youth to follow his son's example, saying "I am proud that he joined the French army, and I think that every American boy ought to do the same." Press attention did not confine itself to the American media. "The German papers," remarked Georges Thénault, the Lafayette's French commanding officer, "occupy themselves with us, and this publicity is perhaps the best propaganda, for it shows which side the youth of America is on. There is no volunteer squadron in Germany!"[35] No less an interested party than the ambassador to France, Myron Herrick, shared Thénault's opinion of the propaganda value of his squadron. "The influence upon sentiment at home was tremendous," Herrick marveled. "Amid the haggling of notes and the noise of German protestations, here were Americans shedding blood for a cause in which the heart of the American people was already enlisted."[36]

In addition to its airplanes, the Lafayette Escadrille possessed ample connections to money, political influence, and to the press, all valuable assets in the quest for glory. Founding members Norman Prince and William Thaw came from huge American wealth. Prince's father, Frederick Prince, had large estates in the eastern United States and in France, while Thaw's father, Benjamin, had accumulated a fortune as a businessman in Pittsburgh.[37] Dr. Edmund Gros, a Paris-based American physician rumored "to have the largest medical practice in Europe," provided French political connections and an introduction to American millionaire William Vanderbilt.[38] Vanderbilt, in turn, donated money to fund monthly allowances for Lafayette pilots over and above their small French military salaries.[39] If all that was not enough to guarantee attention from the press, Lafayette pilot Kiffin Rockwell sent regular reports from the front to his brother Paul, a wounded infantryman working as a war correspondent, and provided him access to his fellow pilots.[40]

James Norman Hall sought to do more than simply report on the *Lafayette Escadrille*. A prewar American newspaper reporter, Hall had enlisted as an infantryman in the British Expeditionary Force on the outbreak of hostilities to get a firsthand look at the fighting. His experiences in the trenches formed the basis of his first book, *Kitchener's Mob*, published in 1916.[41] Honorably discharged after more than a year in British service, Hall re-enlisted with the French in order to try flying. Assigned to the Lafayette Escadrille in June 1917, he served sporadically over the next eight months—interrupted by a wound and a brief posting to another French unit—until the Lafayette transferred en masse to the US Air Service in February 1918. In his second book, *High Adventure*, Hall chronicled his aerial career as a member of the Lafayette, an association that did not end with the squadron's passage out of French service, or even with the end of hostilities.[42] After the war, Hall teamed up with another Lafayette Flying Corps veteran, Charles Bernard Nordhoff, to write the more or less official two-volume history of American volunteer airmen in the French military, *The Lafayette Flying Corps*.[43]

Rockwell's and Hall's reports from the Lafayette Escadrille, as extensive and firsthand as they might have been, did not begin to satisfy the extent of the American public's craving for news of the American pilots flying under the French flag. Books by or about members of the Lafayette Escadrille (and the larger Lafayette Flying Corps made necessary by the enormous response to formation of the original *escadrille*) began to appear as early as 1917. Ten would make it into print before the war ended.[44] Public interest in the history of the American flying unit endured in the decades following the war, and shows no sign of fading. Escadrille veteran Edwin C. Parsons published three editions of his wartime aerial memoirs between 1937 and 1963.[45] Following his death in action the day after the United States declared war on Germany, Edmond Genét's executors published his wartime correspondence as *War Letters of Edmond Genét* and more than six decades later, in 1981, a companion volume followed offering Genét's diary.[46] In total to date, more than thirty Lafayette Escadrille and Lafayette Flying Corps books and two feature films have appeared over the near century since the war.[47]

Romance, glory, and individualism also exerted a strong pull on another would-be fighter pilot, Edward V. Rickenbacker. Rickenbacker already enjoyed considerable fame as a racing driver prior to America's entry into the Great War. But like Genét, Richthofen, and Bishop, the future American ace of aces longed for more:

> The rush of an airplane through the sky awoke within me every instinct of sportsmanship and desire. There was but one element in the game of war aviation that troubled me. Could I play my part in a life-and-death contest such as had been going on in the air over France for the past three or four years?[48]

Rickenbacker thought of the European aviators as knights and wondered whether they might possess "a particular gladiatorial characteristic" he might not find in himself.[49]

Comparisons of fighter pilots to medieval knights among the public were already common before Rickenbacker likened them to gladiators. Fascination with knights and other remnants of medieval culture had enjoyed something of a revival in Europe and the United States during the nineteenth century, with the works of Sir Walter Scott becoming favorites of the elite reading public.[50] In such an environment extension of the term to aviators, many of whom hailed from these nations' upper classes, was natural. Strictly speaking, use of the term "knight" had a factual as well as a metaphorical basis. The entry-level grade of the multi-level French order, the *Légion d'Honneur*, referred to its members as "*Chevalier*" and several of the multiplicity of German orders carried the title "*Ritter*," both the equivalent of an English "knight."[51] Americans soon took up the comparison. Upon hearing of the death of Lafayette Escadrille pilot Victor Chapman, John Jefferies, a Harvard classmate of Chapman's likened his friend to "Prince Rupert or Richard Plantagenet."[52] Another family friend wrote the tragic news reminded him of "the times of the Mediaeval Knight."[53] Chapman's father embraced the comparisons, writing that his son's acceptance as an aviator "was, to him, like being made a Knight."[54] Characterizations of the first military pilots as knights spread quickly throughout published literature.[55] When introducing an early postwar collection of New England aviators' biographies, A. Lawrence Lowell compared the fliers to "paladins of romance."[56]

Despite the popularity of "knight," "ace" quickly became the standard reference term for successful fighter pilots. Prior to the First World War, writers commonly applied the term "ace" to anyone who excelled in a particular field, especially sports. Given the crossover between other sports and aviation, the press understandably applied the sports term to early fliers. In the first decade of powered flight aviators measured progress in their field by records set in speed, altitude, flight duration, maneuvers perfected, and obstacles crossed. Contests, such as the 1909 international aviation meet at Reims, France, and the prize won by Frenchman Louis Blériot for the first successful aerial crossing of the English Channel, provided incentives and venues in which to set or break those records. Those competitions attracted widespread press attention not only due to the novelty of flight but also because several of the competitors, such as Thomas Sopwith and Roland Garros, were either wealthy young men or already well known as sports figures. The term "ace" found its way into common military usage during the early days of the Great War when Roland Garros became the first pilot to score more than one aerial victory.[57] Once established in the military aviation vernacular, the term "ace" quickly spread into the popular culture becoming a regular fixture in book titles and themes. During the last year of the war the word turned up both in a biographical work of the recently deceased French fighter pilot, Georges Guynemer, and in a fictional offering by budding aviation writer, Laurence LaTourette Driggs.[58] In "Aces of the Air," French Cpte. Jacques De Sieyes characterized flying as "a game—an amazing game, a game of adventure, of countless thrills, of soul-stirring excitement, a game in which courage, daring, resource, determination, skill, and intelligence achieve honor in life or, if the fates so decree, glory in death."[59]

The actions of all the wartime powers bear out De Sieyes's observations. The war's successful fighter pilots were the objects of a seemingly endless supply of both honor and glory. German combat pilots, for example, began receiving rewards immediately on the occasion of their first aerial conquest, an achievement officially marked with the gift of the *Ehrenbecker* (Honor Goblet), an elaborately engraved silver goblet issued to *"Dem Sieger in Luftkampf"* ("The Victor in Air Combat"). Successful German naval pilots were similarly rewarded with the *Ehrenpreis* (Honor Prize).[60]

Silver goblets and trophies constituted only the beginning of the Kaiser's reward system. The German federation that came into being in 1870 assembled a large mix of kingdoms, principalities, grand duchies, duchies, and free cities, each with its own complex array of military orders and decorations. The various award statutes divided along class lines with military orders for officers and, lesser, associated decorations for non-commissioned officers and the other ranks. Though unified for more than forty years prior to the First World War, Germany failed to establish any official "empire" awards. In the absence of such rewards, and in acknowledgment of Prussia's primacy among Germany's collection of jurisdictions, Prussian decorations were commonly presented to deserving officers and enlisted men of all the Kaiserreich's component parts.[61]

The Prussian *Orden Pour le Mérite* (often known by the nickname *Blauer Max*, or "Blue Max"), was the highest award available to an officer not related to the royal family, and became the most prestigious German military award of the First World War. Because the statutes governing its bestowal required the recipient to have rendered a long period of meritorious service to the crown or to have been personally responsible for winning a battle, prior to the First World War only senior officers were eligible for the small blue-enameled cross hung around their necks. To make it available to junior officers, senior commanders developed criterion favorable to officers at any grade who distinguished themselves in battle. Consequently, between 1914 and 1918 successful U-boat commanders and fighter pilots made up the two groups most often favored with the Blue Max. While criteria for the former involved enemy tonnage sunk, fighter pilots met their standard with "kills," or shooting down enemy aircraft.[62]

Maintaining the Blue Max's prestige required periodically raising the bar. The first German fighter pilots awarded the order for combat with the enemy were a Prussian, Oswald Boelcke, and a Saxon, Max Immelmann. Throughout the second half of 1915 and until January 16, 1916, when each scored his eighth victory, Boelcke and Immelmann alternated the lead in the number of Allied planes shot down. The timely deadlock offered the high command a way out of appearing to show preference for one kingdom over another by making a simultaneous award (as well as providing the threshold for aerial victories that a fighter pilot must cross to be eligible for the *Pour le Mérite*). As the year 1916 progressed and more young fighters achieved their eighth victories, authorities interested in maintaining the *Pour le Mérite*'s exclusivity changed the rule, doubling the minimum number of aerial conquests required for admission to the order. One year after Boelcke and Immelmann had earned their Blue Max, Manfred von Richthofen became the first pilot to receive his *Pour le Mérite* under the newly raised standard of sixteen victories.[63] Richthofen's outstanding success (during April 1917 he would surpass Oswald Boelcke's final score of forty victories) led directly to the number being raised again later that year, this time to twenty victories.[64]

Excluding senior officers and members of the royal family, whose influential positions and impressive connections dictated a political award of the *Pour le Mérite*, some 174 junior officers earned the most prestigious decoration for combat service.[65] An overwhelming sixty-two of the seventy-six aviation awards went to fighter pilots.[66]

German medals authority Neal O'Connor suggests the neglect shown to reconnaissance pilots might be explained by the fact so many were non-commissioned officers or enlisted men and, therefore, ineligible for the officers-only *Orden Pour le Mérite*.[67] The Prussian awards system did, however, provide two highly prestigious decorations for NCOs and the other ranks: the *Goldene Militär-Verdientzkreuz* (Golden Military Merit Cross) and the *Kreuz der Inhaber mit Schwertern des Königliche Hausordens von Hohenzollern* (Member's Cross with Swords of the Royal Order of the House of Hohenzollern). The decorations were considered equal to an award of the Blue Max and the Golden Military Merit Cross became known by the nickname "the *Pour le Mérite für Unteroffiziere*" (the NCOs' Order of Merit).[68] The distribution of the Golden Military Merit Cross, while somewhat more favorable to reconnaissance crews, does not support the notion authorities intended to make up for the imbalance in awards of the *Pour le Mérite* by making the lesser medal available preponderantly for reconnaissance work.[69] No greater hope was offered to the reconnaissance crewmember when it came to chances of his winning the Member's Cross of the Royal Order of the House of Hohenzollern. Of the ten aviation awards of the order's Member's Cross, no more than two were won for reconnaissance missions.[70] Three Member's Crosses were awarded to fighter pilots, three to bomber pilots, and two for ground-attack work.

In contrast to the victory-total standard it set for fighter pilots, the German high command does not seem to have promulgated any clear-cut criteria for awards to German reconnaissance pilots or observers. Despite aerial intelligence's vital importance to the success of the war on the ground, the high command clearly expected an exceptionally long record of successful service before awarding the *Pour le Mérite* for reconnaissance work. The only Blue Max-winning reconnaissance pilot, *Leutnant* Wilhelm Griebsch, flew 345 long-distance reconnaissance missions on the Western Front and in Macedonia between 1915 and the last year of the war before finally receiving the order on September 30, 1918.[71] Precise records are only available for five of the eight observers awarded the Blue Max for distinguished reconnaissance work, but those indicate a range from 160 missions flown to somewhere between four and seven hundred operational flights before their awards arrived.[72] Beating the nearly astronomical odds required to remain alive in a hostile aerial environment long enough to compile such records ensured the number of reconnaissance awards remained low. By comparison, while accumulating the eight, sixteen, or twenty combat kills eventually required for a fighter pilot's *Pour le Mérite* certainly required extraordinary combat and survival skills, the feat did not always require a great deal of time. The Red Baron's brother, *Ltn.* Lothar von Richthofen, scored the mandated twenty victories in less than two months. The younger Richthofen reported for duty as a brand-new fighter pilot on March 6, 1917, scored his first victory twenty-two days later, and brought his score to twenty less than six weeks later, on May 7.[73] The implicit message became clear. A German flier in a hurry for recognition needed to wangle an assignment to single-seat fighters.

Unlike their German counterparts, the British high command did not require a long record of achievement, but merely an impressive one, before awarding their highest valor medal, the Victoria Cross.[74] The small bronze cross suspended from a red ribbon generally came in recognition of a single act of bravery, one that at the risk of the recipient's own life inflicted significant loss on the enemy or saved the lives of British forces. William Leefe Robinson was awarded the Victoria Cross in September 1916 in appreciation for his downing of the first German airship destroyed over England; a spectacular feat achieved in front of thousands of grateful British witnesses.[75] In the closing days of the war, William George Barker captured the last Great War Victoria Cross bestowed on an airman when he single-handedly fought off a large group of German Fokker D.VIIs, likely destroying four in the process.[76] Frank Hubert McNamara's service in landing to rescue a squadron-mate shot down in the Palestinian desert merited his Victoria Cross.[77] In all, the British government awarded some nineteen of its highest bravery award for aerial actions.[78] Fighter pilots received eleven of those decorations. Of the remaining eight, seven were awarded for attacks on German airships or for various other bombing or ground-attack missions. John Aidan Liddell earned the single Victoria Cross awarded for actions during a reconnaissance mission.[79] However, the citation did not actually mention the reconnaissance, but rather the wound Liddell suffered and the fact he successfully returned a badly damaged aircraft despite his injury.

Records of awards of the premier French decoration, the *Légion d'Honneur*, for reconnaissance work have not been discovered. The liberality with which the French issued their highest award to fighter pilots renders irrelevant any consideration of its value as an incentive to exceptional valor, at least in the sense understood by German, British, and American aircrew in pursuit of their own supreme awards. One hundred eighty-nine French fighter pilots scored the requisite five victories necessary to claim "ace" status. Comparing French award criteria with those employed by the other belligerent powers, considering who within the group *failed* to receive the *Légion d'Honneur* makes more sense than asking who won it. The French high command left only thirty-one of their aces without the *Légion d'Honneur*. And while twenty-five of those thirty-one were non-commissioned officers or rankers, the lack of officer status did not eliminate a man from consideration for the award, as it did in the case of the Prussian *Orden Pour le Mérite*. Nor did his death, as French high command regularly made posthumous awards. Rather, the French appear to have considered the *Légion d'Honneur* an award for repeated acts of good service, in a way similar to the manner in which the Germans treated the Blue Max but without the rigid specific criteria required by Prussia's award statutes.[80]

The short record of the United States in active combat led to a mere eight awards of the Medal of Honor for aviation service. In conferring the Medal of Honor, American award criteria resembled the British more than the French or the Germans. Authorities conferred the medal more frequently for a single outstanding act of bravery than for a repeated record of exemplary service. Two fighter pilots received this recognition. 2/Lt. Frank Luke, Jr., received his award for his brief, glorious, and ultimately fatal career as a destroyer of German observation balloons during the St. Mihiel and Meuse-Argonne offensives in September 1918. The second went to "ace of aces" Capt. Edward V. Rickenbacker. The remaining six awards went to members of Army and Navy two-seater crews, two for life-saving actions, two for a bombing operation, and the final pair for a dramatic infantry contact mission. Ens. Charles Hammann and CMM Francis Ormsbee, Jr. received their awards for saving airmen whose airplanes had crashed from drowning off the coasts of Italy and Florida. The Army crew, Lts. Erwin Bleckley and Harold Goettler, earned their medals on October 2, 1918, for a sortie during which the pair sacrificed their lives while dropping supplies to troops of the 307th and 308th US Infantry—the famous "Lost Battalion." Like Luke's medal, Goettler's and Bleckley's Army awards were posthumous. Two Navy Medals of Honor went to Lt. Ralph Talbot and Gunnery Sgt. Robert Robinson for a bombing mission of October 8, 1918. Robinson died immediately following the flight as the result of some thirteen wounds suffered while defending their airplane. Talbot died in an unrelated crash only a few days later.

Whether earned for spectacular acts of gallantry or for prolonged service, men who took direct actions that led to instant results were far more likely to receive awards than those who performed reconnaissance or observation missions that brought later military successes. Assuming they lived to enjoy those orders and medals the perks that accompanied wartime glory greatly benefited military men. Awards enhanced social status, chances for military promotion, and in some cases income.[81] If an airman died as a consequence of his act of bravery, as had several of the Medal of Honor and Victoria Cross recipients, the recognition allowed his countrymen to believe he had not died in vain. Bravery awards further afforded incentives to the mass of common soldiers and sailors who were expected to follow in the hero's footsteps. Creation of a body of heroes, surviving or dead on the battlefield, supplied useful propaganda and laid the foundation for the subsequent history of the conflict. During the war heroic sacrifice provided an inspirational example to civilians who built support at home for the military's efforts at the front. After the war their stories contributed to construction of a national mythology that increasingly valued adventure, glory, and stunning feats of heroism over the mundane daily work required by the entire population to win the war. In the case of military aviation in the First World War, the glorious myth that overtook the ordinary work was found mostly in the stories of fighter pilots. Those who took photographs or called in the location of friendly or enemy troops from the back seat of an airplane or from the basket of a balloon found themselves largely excluded from the story. Historians writing the story of the First World War have yet to fully acknowledge their service.

CHAPTER 3

The Forgotten Air Service

*For, as ubiquitous harbingers of the weapon most feared by groundlings,
they were at all the Sommes, Caporettos, Belleau Woods, and Tannenbergs.
Nothing and nobody kept them down for long and in the nightmares of
thinking Staff their persistence had the excruciating effect of the Chinese
Water Torture. Because of them countless attacks were forestalled, foiled, or
crushed. Because of them millions of tons of merchant shipping voyaged in
safety. Together with their aeroplane confreres they did, however belatedly,
convince the Army that aviation held the solution to artillery registration and
short-term Intelligence.*

—Alan Morris, *The Balloonatics*

*But when you look up at the "sausage" shining in the sunshine three or four
miles away, and know that there are eyes in it which can see you and report
your movements to the nearest battery, you begin to be uncomfortable. They
have so much advantage of you, those eyes in the sky.*

—Adelaide *Register, 16 October 1916*

Though the world quickly became fascinated with the heroic and
romantic alternate view of the war it found in the stories of fighter
aces, the real value of military aviation lay elsewhere. During the war's
opening movements the airplane proved its value as a reconnaissance
tool, providing critical information to both sides. Once fighting settled
into the trenches the tactical situation changed. Then balloonists ree-
merged as an essential part of the observation chain.

The balloon is the oldest military aircraft. On June 5, 1783, more
than a century before the Wright brothers flew at Kitty Hawk, the
Frenchmen Joseph-Michael and Jacques-Étienne Montgolfier accomplished the first successful balloon flights.[1] The first war-related flight
took place on June 26, 1794 when forces of the Army of the First

French Republic under Jean-Baptiste Jourdan raised a balloon named *L'Entreprenant* (Enterprise) during the battle of Fleurus to observe the movements of Dutch and Austrian troops at Maubeuge, near the Belgian frontier.[2] *L'Entreprenant* was operated by the *Compagnie d'Aérostiers*, a new French military unit formed under the command of Jean Coutelle.[3] The *Compagnie d'Aérostiers* remained in service for five years until the French government dissolved it, possibly because the balloons proved insufficiently mobile to keep up with Napoleon's units during periods of rapid advance due to the difficulties of producing hydrogen while on the move.[4]

From that time until the American Civil War, balloons saw only limited military use, and then in small campaigns. Scientific experiments on them did continue, and balloons became popular attractions at American county fairs.[5] In the United States balloons served both sides during the Civil War, providing general reconnaissance to the armies and spotting assistance for the artillery.[6] Balloonists John LaMountain and Thaddeus Lowe began operations early in the conflict, LaMountain making his first reconnaissance flights in July 1861. Lowe followed shortly thereafter, ascending near Washington, DC, in the balloon *Union* on August 28, 1861 and again on September 24, 1861 near Arlington, Virginia. The Union's balloon group grew to number seven balloons before the government disbanded the organization due to lack of funds, but not before the aeronauts showed the potential of aerial reconnaissance. At Fair Oaks, reports from the Union balloon proved critical to the favorable outcome of the battle.[7] The Confederacy responded with their own small aeronautical investment, eventually constructing three balloons that operated for a period of fifteen months from April 1862 until the summer of 1863.[8]

These pioneering efforts in the United States offered sufficient promise to revive interest in ballooning among European military circles. Lieutenant George Grover, Royal Engineers, became the first member of the British military to ascend in a tethered balloon when he began experimenting in 1862. Six years later, the French used free-floating balloons as a means of escape when Paris came under siege during the Franco-Prussian War. The British Army established its first balloon school at Woolwich in 1878, and began making technological improvements to the fledgling aeronautical science aimed at developing mobile hydrogen storage containers that enabled balloons to be quickly inflated.[9] The accuracy of observations provided by balloonists during the army's 1889 maneuvers caused British military commanders to begin to take the balloon seriously. General Sir Evelyn Wood proved sufficiently impressed to recommend relocation of both the balloon factory and school to Aldershot so it could work more closely with the rest of the Army.[10]

Subsequent to the first successful powered flights, fixed-wing airplanes and motorized lighter-than-air dirigibles had begun to compete with balloons for the right to fulfill British Army and Navy aerial requirements. A white paper outlining British Army estimates for 1911–1912 reported the reorganization of the Aldershot balloon factory to handle airships and airplanes, and the transfer of the Balloon School to an air battalion. At the same time, British authorities expanded opportunities for those interested in aviation service to allow officers from branches other than the Royal Engineers to serve in the air and men with compatible skills to become enlisted members of the new Royal Flying Corps.[11] By the time war broke out in Europe in the summer of 1914, further refinements to the British aviation program had brought about a formal division between the Air Battalion's Army and Navy Wings, giving birth to the Royal Flying Corps and the Royal Naval Air Service. Balloons also became a casualty to the myriad changes brought on by the fascination with heavier-than-air powered flight, captive balloons all but vanishing from British as well as French Army arsenals. Military necessity would force both nations to resurrect the balloon before the war's first anniversary.[12]

Prior to the First World War, the spherical shape of early balloons kept them from achieving their full potential as the eyes of the artillery. Observers bouncing around in any wind stronger than a gentle breeze often became airsick and regularly found it impossible to remain focused on enemy targets.[13] This stability problem caused the spherical balloon to nearly vanish from military service by the outbreak of the First World War. In 1896 *Maj*. August von Parseval and *Hptm*. Rudolf Hans Bartsch von Siegsfeld successfully floated the first *Drachen* (Dragon) balloon, an engineering advance that quickly replaced the older spherical balloon.[14] The *Drachen* differed in several respects from its predecessor, with design refinements aimed at improving the stability of the observer's platform. The most important—as well as the most visible—differences in the *Drachen* lay in the elongated shape of the balloon and in the addition of a stabilizing lobe to the rear of the craft. French construction of *Drachen*-type balloons began in October 1914 and completed balloons began arriving at the front that December. Germany had nine of the improved kite balloons in the field on the Western Front in February 1915 and by the end of the year the number of German balloon sections had increased to forty, each with two balloons.[15]

Because the Parseval-Siegsfeld *Drachen* balloon had an extremely low ceiling—around 1,500 feet in an average wind—it offered limited usefulness as a reconnaissance and artillery-observation platform. German designers dealt with the low ceiling issue by making the balloon bigger, increasing its volume first to 800 cubic meters and later still to 1,000.[16] Floating it higher in the sky did not entirely cure the *Drachen*'s problems. Contrary to its designer's initial hopes, the addition of the lobe did not completely solve the stability issue and too many observers still became airsick as their craft pitched and yawed violently in moderate-to-high winds. This led to further fundamental improvement in observation balloon design, but the French engineer Albert Caquot beat the Germans to the next advance. Caquot tackled the pitch and yaw problem by adding two fins to the side of the envelope to supplement the lobe on the balloon's underbelly, giving the tail section an appearance similar to the feathers on an arrow. These additional surfaces allowed the Caquot to ride the wind in a much calmer fashion than earlier balloons, contributing to greater crew comfort, improved morale, longer stays aloft, and better quality photographs than those taken from *Drachen* and the more primitive spherical types.[17]

This ability proved itself in an account of a "free balloon" flight taken by Capt. F. H. Cleaver, commanding officer of the RFC's No. 1 Kite Balloon Section on October 27, 1915:

> The speed and direction of the wind was tested and found to be 15 m.p.h. by the air meter. The balloon was then let up and marched for 300 yards to the winch; it was easily controlled by the balloon party. The winch was shackled on and I and Lieut. Beaufort ascended; the wind appeared to be increasing, the speed was again taken from the balloon and found to be 30 m.p.h. The guy of the right sail carried away, which caused the balloon to oscillate considerably, thus increasing the strain on the cable and rigging. On this an order was immediately given to haul down. The winch, whose power is only 6 horse failed; the wind was rapidly increasing in strength and on again being tested the speed was found to be 40 m.p.h. Fortunately for the occupants of the balloon the cable then parted, had it not done so the rigging most certainly would have gone. The valve rope was immediately pulled and as soon as the end of the cable or any part of it touched the ground, the balloon in spite of the loss of gas naturally was lightened owing to being relieved of the weight of a portion of the cable, and ceased to descend and at times rose; this coupled with the heat of the sun causing the gas to expand and the balloon to become still lighter, was responsible for what might appear to be a long flight, which owing to the speed of the wind was carried out at 40 m.p.h. A perfect landing was effected in 45 minutes without any damage to the balloon, occupants and instruments.[18]

These qualities quickly proved the Caquot to be the best balloon design on the Western Front and all the combatant nations eventually adopted it.[19] *General* Ernst von Hoeppner, commander of the German *Luftstreitkräfte* freely admitted that German balloons put in service after 1916 were patterned after a captured British example.[20] Caquots and their German copies eventually served on all fronts and with naval forces operating in the Atlantic and Mediterranean.

Balloon crews on both sides of the lines shared more than the stability problem. Suspended by ropes in a basket underneath the bag and tethered anywhere from a few hundred to around seven thousand feet above their station, balloons were connected to a horse-drawn or a motorized winch that allowed the craft to be raised or lowered quickly. Lowering the balloon in a hurry proved essential in response to an attack by hostile aircraft. Generally balloon sections were stationed a few miles behind the front line near one or more of the artillery units with which they worked. When the balloon company needed to relocate in response to changing battle conditions, if time allowed, the bag could be deflated and moved by truck, but if the situation did not allow that, the crew could "walk" the inflated balloon to its new base. Walking the balloon was difficult at best, involving dodging trees and temporarily moving telephone wires. In the war's final months relocation became a regular feature of the lighter-than-air units' daily activities. Between August 8, 1918, when No. 6 Balloon Section, RAF, arrived at Boves Wood for the last Somme battle, the section "moved forward almost daily keeping about 5000 yards behind the Infantry" until the unit made its final move to Avesnes the day before the armistice.[21]

While balloon mobility had certainly improved by the First World War, artillery battery commanders believed the telephone in the basket constituted the most important enhancement. Telephone lines ran directly through the cable connecting the balloon to the winch. Balloonists, like observers in airplanes, were initially limited to dropping message bags or sending light or sound signals to communicate with the artillery. German balloon observers also experimented with wireless transmission both from the basket and from stations erected adjacent to the winch.[22] The successful use of kite balloons equipped with telephones by the Royal Naval Air Service in its 1915 campaign in the Dardanelles demonstrated the advantages of a direct link between the artillery and the aerial observer.[23] Army commanders learned that the balloon observer's ability to talk directly to the battery commander made him at least the equal of ground-based forward observers. His ability to more clearly communicate also marked his chief claim to superiority over his counterpart in an airplane, who frequently found his work hampered by the lack of a reliable direct link to the batteries. Telephone-equipped British balloons were reported on the Western Front for the first time on January 9, 1916 when No. 2 Kite Balloon

Section, RFC, registered fifteen targets and maintained "constant communication ... with the 2nd Army heavy artillery group."[24]

The advantages of voice communication being obvious, commanders on both sides sought to develop the same capacity for their airplanes by equipping them with radios. Weight restrictions dictated transmitters only for artillery aircraft. Wireless sets also required a trailing antenna rolled up on a spool that had to be reeled out behind the aircraft before transmission could begin. Several feet of trailing wire did nothing to enhance the already minimal performance of most early two-seat observation aircraft and presented a definite hazard if the airplane came under enemy attack prior to the antenna being retracted or if the crew neglected to reel it in prior to landing. German observer Hanns-Gerd Rabe recalls feeling "a jolt to the aircraft, as if it had grazed an obstacle," just before his LVG C.VI touched down following his last wartime mission, a consequence of having forgotten to take in his antenna.[25] Two-way communication would have to wait for the next war. Airplane observers could send corrections to batteries, but the receipt of follow-up requests or other instructions required flying back to the battery to look for signal panels on the ground, a process that took them away from the target. With fuel supplies dictating two- to four-hour missions, the constant flight back and forth to the target area limited the aircraft's usefulness. Balloonists, on the other hand, could remain focused on their targets for hours at a time, spending all day in the service of a particular battery or working with two or more artillery crews throughout their long shift.[26] Captain Alastair Geddes, commanding officer of No. 13 Balloon Section, RFC, won the Military Cross for what must have been an exhausting fourteen-hour stint in his balloon observing for the artillery over Fricourt Wood during an attack on Thiepval.[27]

Whether from prescience or strictly by accident, German forces went to war ahead of the British and French in their lighter-than-air observation capability. When the German Army took to the field in the summer of 1914 it did so equipped with balloons. From the German perspective, maintaining balloons prior to the war might have been a simple outgrowth of the nation's pride in its position as the world leader in airship development. Since Count Ferdinand von Zeppelin launched his first rigid airship at the turn of the century, Germany had competed with France for the lead in lighter-than-air technology.[28] Keeping pace with both heavier- and lighter-than-air developments made sense given the infant status of military aviation. No contemporary army or navy commander in 1914 could have done more than guess whether the airplane, airship, or balloon would emerge as the most important form of aerial weaponry. Of course the airplane would eventually triumph, though even in the early twenty-first century at least one nation's military has retained the balloon as part of its forces.[29] But a sense of the balloon's status as transitional technology in most countries' military arsenals, a link between a romantic age of lancer units engaged in cavalry charges and the hard reality of modern warfare, can be found in the equipment list of Germany's 1914 balloon companies: German balloons were pulled to their stations behind the battlefield in horse-drawn wagons.[30]

Through the war's opening weeks, as German troops quickly maneuvered for position in compliance with the Schlieffen Plan, their balloons kept pace with the advance, but did not see much action. The opposing forces moved in a series of thrusts and parries throughout France and Belgium, fighting their way to the North Sea by October 1914. Out of room, they began to dig the first of a complex network of trenches in which they would remain largely stalemated until March 1918. In an effort to break through their opponents' defensive network of trenches, machine-gun emplacements, and barbed wire both sides made heavy use of artillery.[31] Observation from the air became critically important.

Once part of the action, balloon crews constituted the second tier of a three-tiered artillery-observation process. They offered a more elevated oblique view than that enjoyed by battery spotters stationed on high ground but not as close or vertical as the view from an airplane.[32] Throughout the war, German forces occupied most of the high ground along the Western Front.[33] Consequently, German artillerists frequently had the benefit of ground-based observers, more so than their Allied counterparts. But when visual observation by both sides' ground spotters proved inadequate because of insufficient range or exposure to enemy fire, commanders in search of intelligence turned to the balloon.

When the war on the Western Front settled into the trenches, indirect artillery fire began to dominate the battlefield and artillery commanders needed a view of the target to verify the distance at which the long-range fire became effective.[34] Distant barrages softened up the enemy prior to infantry attacks, broke the barbed wire in front of enemy trenches so that friendly forces could advance, and kept opposing troops pinned down during assaults and in bunkers during quiet periods.[35] The prospect of a protracted artillery duel quickly made apparent the advantage of possessing balloons. French commanders reinstated their balloons almost immediately, fielding a dozen companies by the end of 1914, each with three balloons.[36] German forces put twenty-three balloon sections in the field upon mobilization.[37] The commander of the British Expeditionary Force, Sir John French, requested the addition of kite balloons to observe for the artillery in March 1915. Because the Army had abandoned its balloons, the Royal Navy, which that same month had begun balloon training with equipment received from the French, offered to loan a kite balloon section that arrived at Boulogne under the command of Major Brabazon on May 8, 1915 and went into action with the V Corps near Poperinghe on the 25th.[38] Naval balloons continued to make up a significant part of the Army's balloon support until March of the following year.[39] Over the next three and a half years, balloon units formed an integral part of the artillery registration systems on both sides of the Western Front.[40] The Royal Flying Corps' 2nd Balloon Wing report of a record 286 targets ranged during one week in 1917 illustrates the strength of the bond that came to exist between the artillery and its aerial partners in the second half of the war.[41] Their effectiveness sometimes made balloons unpopular with neighboring units due to their tendency to attract artillery fire.[42] Troops very much liked to dish it out, but taking it proved to be another matter entirely.

The German approach to organizing its *Balloonzüge* (balloon sections) illustrates the strength of the partnership achieved between observation balloonists and ground units. As part of the reorganization of Germany's aviation program in the last months of 1916, balloons became the joint responsibility of the *Kommandierende General der Luftstreitkräfte* (commanding general of the Air Force, abbreviated *Kogenluft*) and the *Inspektion der Luftschiffertruppen* (inspector of Airship Troops, abbreviated *Iluft*). Below this overall command structure, a *Stabsoffizier der Luftschiffertruppen* (staff officer of Airship Troops, abbreviated *Stoluft*) provided balloon staff support at each German Army headquarters. Within each army, balloon detachments at the division level managed three to five individual *Balloonzüge*, each with an active and a reserve balloon working with artillery units assigned to the corps.[43]

Despite their key role in the evolving war, historians have paid little attention to the work of balloonists. Segregating lighter-than-air operations from those that took place using heavier-than-air equipment, several sources have noted the different characteristics, capabilities, and uses of balloons and airships. Technical books especially have narrowly focused their profiles of wartime aircraft, frequently detailing the design, development, and operational career of a single type.[44] Apart from being unsuited to fighter operations, lighter-than-air craft performed much the same reconnaissance and observation activities as their heavier-than-air counterparts, simply operating under different conditions and frequently in different venues. Within these broad categories, balloonists performed a variety of valuable tasks. In addition to ranging the artillery, army balloons provided photographic reconnaissance, mapped enemy and friendly positions, and relayed signals from the front lines, while naval balloons located mines and submarines, and performed general scouting duties; in one incident a British balloon observer relayed a request for rifle grenades from a group of British troops engaged with a German bombing party.[45] Balloon observers regularly proved their worth to ground commanders during important operations and by spotting significant targets of opportunity.[46] Suspending a balloon proximate to the front lines offered advantages that airplanes could not always match.

By focusing on heavier-than-air operations (and even more narrowly on fighter operations or bombing campaigns), historians have minimized the importance of reconnaissance and observation by failing to capture the valuable contributions made by those manning lighter-than-air craft. When lighter-than-air units are included in assessments of aviation strength the proportion of aviation devoted to observation and reconnaissance becomes demonstrably weightier and the contribution aviation made to the overall war effort expands as well. The status of the US Air Service at the time of the armistice, for example, is commonly reported as forty-five squadrons on the Western Front, with twenty pursuit squadrons, seven day- and night-bomber units, and eighteen corps- and army-observation squadrons (including the single night observation unit).[47] Considering these airplane squadrons alone makes the USAS appear slightly top-heavy in fighter units. Add in the seventeen balloon companies serving on the Western Front on November 11, 1918—units devoted solely to observation—and that perspective changes dramatically in favor of observation.[48] Include the twenty-seven US Navy air stations sprinkled around the French and British coastlines, nineteen of which were engaged primarily in the search for U-boats, and the conclusion that commanders counted on their airmen for aerial intelligence more than anything else becomes inescapable.[49] The same point applies to the French Aviation Militaire, which boasted seventy-six *compagnies de aérostiers* serving alongside its 364 airplane *escadrilles* by the armistice in 1918.[50] The British Expeditionary Force included forty-nine balloon sections in its order of battle at the end of the war, along with ninety-nine airplane squadrons.[51] The Royal Air Force organized these sections into balloon companies, each company controlling two or three sections. Three or four companies made up a balloon wing.[52] One hundred eighty-four German *Balloonzüge* (more than double Germany's ninety fighter squadrons) opposed these Allied units in support of their own artillery.[53] Omitting balloons from the count of aerial units or isolating those units into a separate category makes it easy to dismiss their contribution to the air war.

Between the outbreak of war in 1914 and the American war declaration in 1917, US Army and Navy officers, serving as neutral observers, attempted to acquire access to Allied aviation information, including data on balloons.[54] The officers detailed on these assignments were not given all the latest information and regularly denied permission to go to the front.[55] They did learn enough, however, to realize that the United States had surrendered the lead it once enjoyed in aviation technology and capacity and now seriously lagged behind the European powers both in heavier- and lighter-than-air technology. In the year prior to American entry into the war in Europe, the punitive expedition against Mexico presented the War Department with reason to build up the US Army. This beginning provided a small foundation for the more massive increases that war in Europe would require. In November 1916, the balloon school at Fort Omaha, Nebraska, closed since 1913, reopened under the command of Commandant Charles D. Chandler.[56] The school taught free-balloon piloting, captive balloon handling and maintenance, and the techniques employed in observation, photography, and artillery regulation.[57]

Despite the strides made during 1916, the United States entered the European conflict seriously behind its German enemies, as well as its French and British associates.[58] American aviation did not possess a single aircraft suitable for service on the Western Front or even in any of the less active areas that made up the war's sideshows.[59] The United States lagged behind the European powers in part due to the uncertainty over whether Americans would enter the war and, if so, on which side. Not sure they could trust their American counterparts, British and French military leaders had denied them access to information about progress in military aviation made during the war. This included pertinent information about balloons.[60] When the United States did get involved in the war domestic balloon production capacity amounted to no more than two to three per month.[61] Although the 1st Aero Squadron, an airplane unit, had seen service in the Mexican campaign, the single balloon the US Army took along on its chase after Pancho Villa made the trip largely by accident.[62]

In addition to coming late, the US Army's realization that balloons were necessary to its war preparations also lacked completeness, enthusiasm, and any sense of urgency. Evidence of this lack of purpose can be found in the organization of the Bolling Mission during the summer of 1917. In July 1917, in the flurry of activity that followed the American declaration of war, Congress passed the largest single appropriation up to that point in its history: $640 million for military aviation.[63] Also in July, VAdm. William Sims, on duty in London, informed Josephus Daniels, the Secretary of the Navy, that the British needed one hundred kite balloon sections.[64] While Congress debated the appropriation, the group charged with responsibility for recommending what types of aerial equipment the nation might manufacture or purchase with its expected funding organized an expedition to Europe to survey the Allied air forces. Colonel Raynal C. Bolling headed the mission. In civilian life Bolling served as chief counsel at US Steel and was considered one of the nation's foremost corporate lawyers. Bolling also had experience as a pilot, but the Army selected him for this assignment not for his aviation savvy but rather for his expertise in drafting and negotiating complex international contracts.[65] The Army intended to bolster the mission's depth by assigning personnel who possessed the background to make informed judgments about all America's aviation needs. Yet, when the Bolling Mission left for Europe they departed without anyone in the group who had any knowledge of balloons.[66] In summarizing the history of the Balloon Section following the war, Col. Charles D. Chandler wrote to the chief of the Air Service that the Bolling Mission had specifically requested the services of a balloon observer, but this request had been denied.[67] Without an expert as part of the mission, Bolling assigned the task of reporting on balloons to Edgar Gorrell.[68]

As the Army's chief balloon officer, Charles D. Chandler had a huge task in front of him. The reactivation of balloon operations at Fort Omaha had not immediately borne fruit. Training at the school had yet to begin when the United States entered the war in April 1917. On the plus side, when the United States became an associate power of the Allies, Army requests to the British and French for information and assistance were given the attention not previously accorded American neutral observers. In the autumn of 1917, British and French advisors with sample balloon equipment arrived in the United States.[69] For the US Army's part, following the receipt of Gorrell's report on Allied ballooning from the Bolling Mission in September, Maj. Frank Lahm traveled to Europe to tour British and French units as part of a more extensive study. Lahm's report included a recommendation for the construction of an American balloon school in France, near the French school at Vadenay.[70] The Army established this school in January 1918 under the command of Maj. Max C. Fleischman.[71] Unfortunately, the school had just been completed and was ready to get underway training students in March when the German offensive forced its evacuation to a safer location at Camp Souge, near the French southwest coast.[72] At Souge the American school flourished and by the end of hostilities, 199 candidates had graduated from its observer and maneuvering-officer classes, and 623 soldiers had been trained in various specialties from the operation of winch trucks to how to handle a machine gun.[73]

Beginning with observer candidates selected exclusively from the Air Service, US Army commanders quickly learned what their allied and enemy counterparts had discovered in the winter of 1914–1915, that maximizing the value of the balloon demanded a close liaison with the artillery. Officers serving in German *Balloonzüge* generally had prior service with the artillery and, in January 1918, the US Army decided to divide the number of new officer trainees selected for balloon duty equally between the Air Service and the artillery.[74] To a casual observer considering the Balloon Section at the armistice, it might have seemed as if the organization was run as a partnership between the Air Service and the artillery given that its 446 officers included 230 members of the Air Service and 216 field or coastal artillery officers.[75] This division of responsibility made sense given the Balloon Section's great need for observers with knowledge and appreciation of artillery operations and procedures.

The US Air Service's decision to recruit balloon observers from the artillery also reflected earlier British experience and illustrates the close connection between aviation and the success of ground operations. British artillery officers appreciated the work of their balloon observers so much they launched a takeover attempt. Following the battle of the Somme, the British artillery advisor, Maj. Gen. J. F. N. Birch, proposed that officers from the artillery be trained for service as balloon observers as a first step towards the artillery taking control of the RFC's balloons. British authorities approved his plan and just after the battle ended in November 1916 assigned a single artillery officer to each of the RFC's twenty-two balloon units. The RFC observers the artillery officers relieved were sent back to England to man and train new balloon sections. The proposed artillery takeover of the balloons never materialized, but once the precedent for cross service had been established more artillery officers did find themselves serving in balloons. In February 1918 the RFC doubled the number of artillery officers in each of its kite balloon sections from one to two.[76] In French service the *compagnies d'aérostiers* that handled the Army's balloons remained part of the *Aviation Militaire* throughout the conflict though they maintained close liaison with the artillery. Many French balloon companies remained assigned to work with the same *corps de armée* from their formation in 1914 or 1915 through to the armistice, no doubt achieving strong working partnerships with those units and perhaps minimizing the need for inter-service transfers.[77]

US Army leaders, in addition to adopting the British preference for experienced artillerists, also shared the British belief that only officers should train as observers. Effective artillery registration required ongoing liaison between battery commanders and the balloon and airplane observers adjusting their fire. Observers participating in planning conferences, generally held the day prior to the anticipated firing program, had to be able to communicate with battery commanders on an equal level to have their opinions respected. Furthermore, the observer required an understanding of the big picture in order to respond flexibly to changes in the tactical situation that necessitated alterations in the pre-set plan, a quality that developed with experience, talent, and with the wider spectrum of training given an officer. Finally, the observer needed to stand in position to assume command of his company should something happen to his commanding officer. Enlisted men, lacking in rank and trained only in specialties peculiar to their own branch, would not possess these advantages.[78]

France's impact on the development of the US Air Service is remembered primarily for the personnel and aircraft production recommendations contained in the Ribot telegram. On May 24, 1917, French Premier Alexandre Ribot sent a message to the United States suggesting an American aviation force large enough to field some 4,500 airplanes on the Western Front in 1918. French influence over the American aviation program eventually extended far beyond Ribot's early suggestions.[79] The French stamp can be seen on a broad array of US Air Service actions ranging from selection and production of aircraft types for use at the front to the choice of syllabus followed in American training centers. The proper conduct of aerial reconnaissance and observation figured prominently in French teachings. Official US Army procedures followed French guidelines in calling for three means of bringing artillery to bear during trench warfare: "direct observation from the observation post; by the map; by aid of aerial observation."[80] The tactical lessons American military commanders learned from their French advisors included the idea that the airplane should be reserved for reconnaissance missions either beyond the range of view available to the area balloon, or of portions of the front the local balloon could not see due to some obstruction.[81] American commanders came to tout this division of responsibility as official policy, though they did not always effectively translate it into practice.

The four-day battle to eliminate the St. Mihiel salient marked the first time the Allies entrusted the American Expeditionary Force with its own operation. Fifteen American balloon companies and six French balloon units participated in the brief campaign.[82] Prior to the battle, French balloon companies prepared a large-scale relief map of the sector that Brig. Gen. William Mitchell, overall commander of all Allied aviation units at St. Mihiel, used in planning the operation.[83] Adverse weather prevented balloon-assisted artillery registration during the first two days of the attack, but during its final two days at least three of the balloon companies achieved important results.[84] Weather did not prevent the balloons from maintaining a general program of surveillance, however, and John Paegelow, Mitchell's balloon commander, reported "in practically every instance," his balloons "were up at day break on the morning of the attack."[85] Furthermore, the balloons kept an eye on enemy activity at night throughout the attack, a capability shared by only a single American heavier-than-air squadron.[86]

Thirteen American balloon companies took part in the war's final campaign, the Meuse-Argonne battle, repeating the success the lighter-than-air sections had enjoyed at St. Mihiel.[87] The ability the balloonists exhibited in keeping pace with the advances made by the infantry during both campaigns marked something of a climax in the history of military ballooning. The existence of open warfare after more than three years of static trench fighting made the American balloon crews' wartime experience vastly different than that of their British and French colleagues. The 2nd Balloon Company, the first American balloon unit to arrive at the front, became operational a month prior to the last great German push, a point when the four-year stalemate in the trenches began to break up and opposing forces resumed a war of movement.[88] Over the first three years of the war movement on the Western Front represented the exception. During the 2nd Balloon Company's time in France, frequent and rapid relocations to more advanced points on the battlefield became the norm.[89]

The US Air Service solved the mobility problem that had beguiled Napoleon by crafting detailed battle plans which laid out specific routes along which its balloons might advance or retreat prior to the attack's anticipated zero hour. Balloon crews surveyed the actual route along which they might retreat prior to the attack and studied maps and aerial photographs of anticipated routes along which the advance might proceed.[90] Advanced planning succeeded to the point that balloon companies detailed for the US Army's September 12, 1918, attack on the St. Mihiel Salient were able to maintain their position in the line while walking their inflated balloons behind advancing infantry.[91] During the Meuse-Argonne operation "balloons operated during the day and advanced at night."[92]

As impressive as the Balloon Section's record appears, postwar efficiency assessments of the US Air Service's Balloon Section suggest much room for improvement. While the balloon units solved their mobility challenges, communications presented another problem. During the fast advances of the late summer of 1918, many balloon companies were not able to keep in communication with combat units in their area using the regular telephone systems because the troops were moving quicker than new telephone lines could be added. The US Second Army found a solution in the temporary connection of a test box phone at a forward post of command with communication from there by courier.[93] Faced with the same problem, the RAF's No. 22 Balloon Section found a more dramatic answer to its communication challenges. The commander of the artillery battery with which the balloonists were working positioned himself at the bottom of their winch and shouted corrections to his crew using a megaphone.[94]

American commanders occasionally asked their balloon crews to take oblique photographs. Equipment shortages prevented those requests from occurring more often, shortages so acute the government resorted to appeals through the media. Wartime newspapers and magazines in the United States carried pleas from the War Department for patriotic citizens to turn their cameras over to the war effort, particularly those with superior German lenses.[95] A lack of qualified photographers to develop pictures also plagued the balloon companies, so much so that individual units could not set up their own photographic operations. When taking photographs proved absolutely necessary, a nearby photo section took up the task and the photographer would travel to the closest balloon to get his pictures.[96]

A more serious challenge involved the lack of liaison between balloon companies and the corps Air Service airplane squadrons brought on by regular disputes over which targets belonged to whom. These disagreements affected the effectiveness of both balloon and airplane operations. Balloon company commanders took the position that their colleagues in the corps squadrons did not appreciate that targets visible to balloons should be assigned to balloons and airplanes should register only those targets that were more distant or hidden. Official records indicate that target assignments were supposed to be made nightly at conferences between artillery and Air Service commanders, but that such matters were generally omitted.[97] During periods of open warfare, many targets were fugitive and thus impossible to anticipate or assign. This, as well as the general debate over the different visual perspectives of the airplane and balloon observer, likely accounted for this omission.[98]

With the ability to reflect afforded by the armistice, Air Service senior commanders reconsidered their decision to recruit nearly half of their wartime complement of observers from the artillery due to the reluctance some artillery officers exhibited for aviation service.[99] The preference these officers expressed for working with their batteries over watching the war from a balloon basket did not reflect an unfavorable opinion of the value of balloon observation. Army commanders valued the contribution balloon personnel made to the artillery's destructive capability to such an extent that, in the postwar struggle over the future of aviation, some Air Service officers believed if they conceded control of balloons to the Army and Navy they might prevail in the contest for the Air Service's more aggressive functions.[100]

Evidence that the enemy respected the assistance balloons gave the artillery can be deduced from the number of attacks German airmen and artillery batteries made on balloons. American balloon observers made a total of 116 parachute descents during their relatively short time on the Western Front. Thirty-five of the balloons from which they jumped burned during the attack.[101] While these numbers illustrate the continually escalating nature of aviation operations and aerial combat on the Western Front, as well as the value accorded balloons, British balloonists serving in France prior to the Americans' arrival had also been subject to regular attacks. The 2nd Balloon Wing's observers serving during the summer of 1917 bailed out of their baskets on an almost daily basis, reporting twenty jumps during one week, including one day on which eleven observers descended simultaneously.[102] USAS balloon crews were in action for only 259 days on a small part of the Western Front. In comparison, the *Luftstreitkräfte* reported 135 German balloons lost to aerial attack and artillery fire for the whole of 1917 and on the whole of the front.[103]

Balloon observation had woven itself so extensively into the artillery regulation process that, had the war continued to June 1919, the Air Service planned to expand its Balloon Section from 69 to 139 companies. Expansion required production and, while American manufacturers had achieved only minor results in their efforts to blacken the European skies with airplanes, their balloon construction program proved successful beyond expectations. In April 1917, American looms could turn out enough rubberized cloth to construct no more than two balloons per week.[104] Enlisting the aid of the Goodyear and Goodrich companies, along with United States Rubber, Firestone, Connecticut Aircraft, and Knabenshue Manufacturing, enabled the Air Service to boost output to an impressive ten completed balloons per day by the November 1918 armistice.[105] Further, Benedict Crowell, the US Assistant Secretary of War, in his comprehensive postwar report, *America's Munitions*, estimated that American manufacturing would have reached fifteen completed balloons per day in 1919, sufficient to supply not just American needs, but the "whole anti-German balloon program."[106] While throughout its time in the war the United States had to rely on France, Great Britain, and Italy for most of its airplanes, within those same nineteen months it positioned itself to become the Allies' chief supplier of balloons had the armistice not intervened. Just as the omission of balloons creates a misimpression of the size of the American investment in aerial reconnaissance, historians' failure to consider American lighter-than-air manufacturing during the war tilts the scale toward a picture of a complete production failure. When the record of American balloon manufacturers is considered the record does not look nearly as dismal.

The Balloon Section's achievement in getting its units trained and deployed also compares favorably with the heavier-than-air portion of the Air Service. Standing alongside the forty-five aero squadrons that made it to the front lines by the armistice were seventeen balloon companies. Twelve more were in various stages of training with the artillery at one of the American firing centers located throughout France or at the balloon school at Camp Souge, and another six were en route to the front. The 2nd Balloon Company had the longest record of any American aerial unit at the front, having served from its arrival at Toul in February 1918 to the armistice and with only one week out of the lines following the battle of Chateau Thierry.[107]

After the war, an American military analyst assessing the balloon's contribution, estimated balloon units provided an astounding "93 percent" of all observation at the front.[108] US Assistant Secretary of War Benedict Crowell wrote the balloon "had practically displaced the airplane as a director of gun fire," becoming "the very eye of the Artillery."[109] For its part, Crowell added, the artillery "reciprocated with an efficiency beyond anything known before in the history of warfare."[110] The Balloon Section's statistical summaries confirm that American balloons made 5,866 ascents for a total time in the air of 6,832 hours. Of those ascents, 1,642 had been flown at the front for a total of 3,111 hours spent observing the line. American observers made 116 parachute jumps in response to eighty-nine aircraft attacks. Operationally, 12,018 enemy shell bursts were reported, four hundred enemy batteries were observed firing, and 1,113 instances of traffic on roads and railroads controlled by the German Army were reported.[111]

The advent of an elevated observation platform had forever altered the nature of artillery operations. Gunners moved out of the front lines they had occupied in the wars of the past and switched from looking their enemies squarely in the eye to shooting at targets entirely invisible to them. Engaging in "deep battle," by firing at points well into the enemy's rear area enlarged the size of the battlefield and added targets previously impervious to attack. For the first time those manning a military's rear areas had to live with the threat of attack as railroads, ammunition dumps, and manufacturing facilities all became vulnerable to regular, sometimes constant shelling, made more accurate by eyes in the sky.

Map 1: France and Belgium. © *Sydney Barth*

CHAPTER 4

"Art. Obs.": Spotting for the Army's Big Guns

The development of the Air Service is a matter of general knowledge. The combining of their operations with those of the other arms, and particularly of the artillery, has been the subject of constant study and experiment, giving results of the very highest value.

—Field Marshal Sir Douglas Haig, *Despatches of Sir Douglas Haig*

One could read reports daily about the successes of our fighter pilots. The activity of the observation fliers was thought of only seldom, and then it was only slightly touched on. And yet it was the observers alone to whom the difficult reconnaissance work was assigned and who actually made possible the effective firing of our artillery.

—Arthur Pfleger, *Franz im Feuer*

The combination of aircraft, modern artillery techniques, and static warfare made the First World War battlefield different than any before. Balloon observers extended the range over which artillery batteries could fire effectively using only ground-based spotters. Airplane crews extended the range farther still, allowing battery commanders to put a pair of eyes directly over targets invisible to both ground and balloon observers.[1]

Army leaders of all nations appreciated the value of effective artillery fire. Converging artillery fire properly observed and ranged offered one army great advantages over another.[2] Commanders could further enhance this benefit if their artillery shells could reach the other force's rear areas where the enemy had its troops assembled and its munitions and supplies stored. Elevating the observation platform made possible the delivery of long-range artillery fire and led to development of the deep battle, an expanded form of warfare that encompassed more than just the front-line battlefield. The days of generals placing their artillery batteries near the infantry to exchange line-of-sight fire with visible targets had ended.

The heavy artillery duels that developed on the Western Front in the autumn of 1914 forced combatants to settle into opposing trenches and made apparent the importance of the airplane as an instrument of the deep battle. A report on aerial activity dated September 6, 1914, the opening day of the first battle of the Marne, indicates that the German First Army used reconnaissance aircraft in cooperation with its artillery.[3] A British intelligence summary of events on September 25, 1914, complimented the early work of the Royal Flying Corps (RFC), noting "the aeroplanes attached to Corps are directing the fire of our artillery with great success."[4] Appreciation of the aid artillery commanders received from their aircraft began to spread beyond the command level. German front-line troops who suffered Allied shelling shared the high opinion of the RFC's work. A letter confiscated from a member of the 242nd Reserve Regiment (XXII Reserve Corps) captured in October 1914 characterized as "wonderful" the British ability to shoot. "I don't know whether the information is obtained through their aeroplanes, which are always hovering over us," he speculated, "or whether they have telephones behind our lines."[5]

Despite such assessments of the British artillery's accuracy, the earliest attempts to use airplanes to regulate artillery fire suffered from an inefficient communications system.[6] Initial communications practices required pilots and observers to fly away from their observation points to return to the artillery battery or to a command post to drop weighted message bags containing written reports. Time delays proved problematic. Weighted message bags gave way to visual signals— namely light flashes, smoke signals, and wireless messages sent from the airplane—to which batteries responded by displaying cloth panels laid out in pre-arranged patterns.[7] Battery commanders in receipt of signals sent from an airplane vertically over the target computed the target's position using a clinometer, sextant, or a pair of theodolites.[8] As airplane crews improved their efficiency, artillery officers' demands for their services increased.[9] Over the winter of 1914–1915, pilots and observers in the RFC's No. 9 and No. 16 Squadrons experimented with wireless transmitters as part of a continuous effort to improve communications between the artillery and aviation.[10]

While the British Army was learning the basic techniques of artillery regulation in France, their naval colleagues attempting to force the Dardanelles learned from the bitter experience of having effective aerial observation used against them. In March 1915, *Hptm.* Erich Serno, who later held overall command of the Ottoman Empire's aviation units, flew the first reconnaissance against the combined British-French naval force that had been assigned to the ill-fated campaign. Serno's reports aided in the successful artillery defense that kept the Allied ships from getting through the straights and contributed to the British failure at Gallipoli.[11]

Air power historians remember the first major Western Front engagement of 1915, March's battle at Neuve Chapelle, primarily as the first engagement to make widespread use of aerial photography. Aircrews performed these missions largely for the benefit of the Royal Engineers who used the photos as the basis for up-to-date maps.[12] British forces also used the photos and the maps produced from them in planning the artillery barrage that preceded the battle, a barrage characterized as "the strongest concentration of guns per yard ever assembled, giving an intensity of fire that would not be equaled again until 1917 at Ypres."[13] Once the active phase of the battle opened, aircraft worked directly with the officers commanding both First Army Artillery Groups, quickly strengthening the relationship between aviation and artillery.[14]

The British high command anticipated that artillery and aviation officers would establish this close working relationship. War Office Memorandum A-1802, issued in February 1915, called for officers at artillery headquarters to issue instructions every evening to airplane observers with whom they were assigned to work the following day in

order to outline potential targets identified by that day's aerial reconnaissance missions. Artillery battery commanders pinpointed potential
objectives on a map of the area and then ranged those targets with
bracketing fire until their shells fell directly on the mark. For their
part, airborne observers signaled corrections to assigned batteries while
watching the effect of the fire. When spotting moving targets, such as
columns of troops, airplane crews flew over the target and fired smoke
signals. Battery crews, in turn, computed their target's range based on
the airplane's position and altitude.[15]

In the wake of the Neuve Chapelle attack, the Royal Flying Corps
updated instructions to its squadrons in the field, issuing more detailed
procedures for cooperation with artillery.[16] Experience had taught the
RFC that line and range corrections were best made simultaneously.[17] The
most significant change in protocol lay in the increased emphasis on the
use of wireless, a technological upgrade intended to enhance communications between airplane crews and artillery batteries. Wireless-equipped
aircraft could communicate far more quickly and effectively than with
previous signaling methods, making it possible for the RFC to change
earlier protocols that limited aircraft to working with a single battery.
Now, manuals instructed units that, "a highly trained observer in a
wireless machine can probably range two batteries on the same target."[18]
Artillery observation crews improvised throughout the early months of
1915 and added valuable experience that informed instructions coming
from RFC headquarters. No doubt prompted by that experience, an
unknown editor redacted the word "probably" from No. 4 Squadron's
copy of the aforementioned April 1915 manual, removing any uncertainty from the idea an observer could range more than one battery. The
British soon upgraded the quality of their artillery maps, marking them
with lettered squares inside of which they identified targets by number.
Referring to these new maps, battery commanders could direct fire onto
target "A-17" or "B-3" further simplifying the communication process
between their crews and those manning airplanes.[19]

The most unusual innovation announced by the RFC came in
the form of a clock code. Introduced in April 1915, the clock code

introduced a new system of communication intended for use between airplane crews and artillery batteries. Using the target as dead center, the pilot or observer directing an artillery shoot affixed a small celluloid circle to his map. The celluloid circle now overlaying the map contained a series of concentric lines marked off in intervals from 50 to 500 yards from the target: circle "A" lay at the 50-yard mark; circle "B" was at 100 yards; circle "C" was at 200 yards, and so on, until one reached circle "F" at the 500-yard mark. Around its perimeter lay numerals corresponding with those on the face of a clock, the numeral twelve representing due north and six due south. Using the clock code, aircraft crews could speak to the artillery battery in shorthand, informing the battery officer that his shot had fallen at "C3," indicating that the shell had landed two hundred yards due east of the target.[20]

More than two years later, in December 1917, the Royal Navy's Monitor Spotting Committee considered adoption of the clock code for use at sea by the other half of British aviation, the Royal Naval Air Service. Naval officers endorsed the change because the clock code involved short, easy signals and could be employed for water missions at short notice without the necessity of prior photographs. They too found the clock code offered greater precision than the grid system then in use and, conceding the Royal Flying Corps had more experience in artillery spotting than their own officers, decided to recommend adoption of the Army's method with some refinement. The Navy's aerial spotting experience on the Belgian coast demonstrated the clock code's superiority over the grid system. As members of the Monitor Spotting Committee found, the grid system required preparation of a specific grid for each target where the clock code could be used on any target. Moreover, the clock code required calculation of only one distance as opposed to the grid system that needed two computations. Furthermore, a Navy committee concluded the advantages of systematic uniformity should the two British flying services merge. Seven weeks after its initial meeting, the committee approved changing to the clock code and communicated the new procedures to the Vice Admiral, Dover Patrol, in a letter dated February 21, 1918.[21]

The clock code worked well for airplane crews, but not so well for others involved in the artillery ranging process. Balloon observers and those stationed at high points on the ground could achieve at best an oblique view of the target rather than the near-vertical vantage point necessary to use the clock code. Consequently, British ground and balloon observers continued to use the grid system, necessitating familiarity with both ranging systems for those manning the wireless sets at the artillery batteries. Perhaps preferring to keep artillery ranging as simple as possible, French, German, and American military forces, stuck strictly to the grid system for their own air and artillery crews.[22]

The early months of 1915 saw significant advances in many areas of aerial observation. In addition to wireless transmission coming into general use, enhancements in aircraft, notably the appearance of the French Caudron G.3, improved commanders' ability to acquire information from close reconnaissance sorties. During these same months pilots and observers on both sides of the lines took the first aerial photos and flew the first successful infantry contact patrols.[23] The wide variety of work performed during artillery observation missions is illustrated by a September 28, 1915 entry in the Royal Flying Corps' *War Diary*:

> In spite of the unfavorable weather and the difficulties of observing fire, useful work was done by aeroplanes of the 1st Wing on the 1st Army front. Wire cutting by the 21st Heavy Bty ranged by No. 2 Squadron appeared to be successful. No. 3 Squadron ranged the 35th battery on to a heavy gun. Direct hits were obtained by the 33rd Siege battery on a hostile battery ranged by No. 3 Squadron. No. 3 Squadron also ranged the 111th battery on to a hostile battery which was silenced. The 34th Siege battery was successfully ranged on a hostile battery. Numerous explosions appeared in the hostile battery.[24]

Advances in the employment of aviation technology in Europe during 1915 forced skeptics in the US Army to acknowledge its potential importance to battlefield success. Despite having first purchased aircraft in 1909, American army leaders failed until 1916 to confirm their acceptance of the incorporation of aviation strategy into European military doctrine. In a document entitled *Military Aviation*, the War College Division of the General Staff Corps recommended equipping each American Army division with a twelve-aircraft squadron. The squadrons were to be assigned reconnaissance, artillery observation, bombing, and aerial combat duties.[25]

Aviation's value to ground operations, particularly the artillery, revealed itself as much when the fliers could not operate as when they could take the air. By the spring of 1915 those planning ground operations understood their plans were likely to suffer when inclement weather prevented aviation operations. A British War Office report written on the Neuve Chapelle battle noted that mist clinging to the ground prior to the battle had prevented air observation for a few days allowing the enemy to take advantage of the situation by concentrating artillery for a counterattack.[26] A similar report on the battle of Festubert noted the start of the battle had to be postponed a day because the weather prevented artillery observation.[27]

As the war neared its first anniversary, commanders continued to refine artillery observation techniques by use of aerial operations. Establishing and maintaining real-time communication between aircraft crews observing the firing and the artillery battery conducting it remained one of the key obstacles to success of the new system. Early approaches involving panel and light signals or written messages dropped from the aircraft, as first practiced at the battle of Festubert, proved inefficient at best.[28] On January 10, 1915, Capt. E. Hewlett and Sgt. Dunn of No. 3 Squadron, RFC, used a signal lamp to correct fire for the 1st Division before being forced to land in the 2nd Division's area due to engine trouble. The day before, Capt. Hewlett had added a pencil sketch to his report of enemy trenches on the road to La Bassee.[29] In most cases, the ideal of two-way voice communication between the men in the cockpits and those firing the guns was not possible because the combined weight of a transmitter and receiver adversely affected the performance of contemporary airplanes. Under the circumstances, the Royal Flying Corps settled for installing only wireless transmitters.[30] Using their transmitter, airplane crews could signal coded corrections to battery crews. When battery crews wanted to communicate with their partners in the air they used lamp or panel signals. The system worked well enough on June 19, 1915, for Maj. Gen. Hugh Trenchard, general officer commanding the Royal Flying Corps in France, to write to the Deputy Director of Military Aeronautics: "In view of the rapidly increasing use which is being made of wireless telegraphy in connection with the observation of artillery fire from aeroplanes, it has been found convenient to attach an officer having special qualification in this branch of telegraphy to Wing Headquarters."[31]

Trenchard might have taken a cue from German artillery observation procedures in making his decision to station a wireless officer at wing headquarters. A captured German document, circulated as part of the regular Royal Flying Corps Intelligence Summary a month prior to the announcement of the British air commander's action, outlined a well-considered protocol for pilots and observers working with the guns, one that incorporated the use of aerial photographs for advance target organization as well as a system of wireless signals. The German procedures called for the air and artillery crews to fix and number their targets in advance using information culled from aerial reconnaissance photographs. Once aloft the pilot and observer signaled "ready to observe" and the number of the first target. After firing commenced the airmen transmitted shorthand Morse code signals indicating "right" or "left," "long" or "short," coupled with an estimate of the distance the shell had fallen from the target. No agreed-upon signal existed for targets of opportunity, so if the pilot or observer sighted such a fleeting target he signaled its presence in the clear, e.g. "Hostile battery at 1 km East and 0.5 km North of Marly." As soon as battery crews located the target on their map and began to fire, the airmen resumed using the established list of signals.[32] The system proved its worth at the end of the first week of the Somme battle, on July 6, 1916:

> An aeroplane of No. 9 Squadron reported one Battalion of infantry and a
> motor transport proceeding from Bois de Leuze to Guillemont. A heavy
> battery was ranged on this target and seven direct hits were obtained on the
> column. A number of men were seen to fall and the rest scattered in disorder.
> A direct hit was also obtained on one of the lorries. The infantry was watched
> for some time, but were not seen to reform.[33]

The parallel development of aerial observation procedure and wireless technology stimulated each other throughout the war. As spotting became more effective and its use more a routine part of operations, efforts to inhibit the enemy's artillery became an imperative. The evolution of the fighter aircraft is intimately tied to the need to destroy reconnaissance and observation machines.[34] But while fighters constituted the most glamorous method of limiting the effectiveness of the wireless-equipped artillery spotter, both sides developed other means as well. The German army routinely attempted to jam British, French, and American wireless transmissions and to deceive aerial observers by setting off dummy flashes in the hopes of drawing fire onto non-existent targets.[35] The need to prevent jamming in turn led the British to develop techniques that allowed them to identify enemy wireless stations attempting to jam their signals by both the direction of their transmissions and the musical note of their signal.[36] British air commanders, acting out of fear the Germans might break their codes, also developed alternating groups of signals that aerial observation crews employed during operations.[37]

Friendly radio traffic interfered with artillery spotting nearly as much as enemy jamming. Working together to eliminate or reduce such interference, French and British air commanders developed a coordinated schedule of firing operations so that their transmissions did not overlap. The designers attempted to develop a system that considered every detail, down to the flight time of the artillery shell, which they estimated at 56 seconds.[38]

Wireless technicians found a scientific solution to the problem of friendly local interference in their development of the clapper break. The clapper varied the pitch of a wireless set's transmission. By the outbreak of the Somme battle in July 1916, reducing radio interference allowed the British to double the number of aircraft working on their areas of the Western Front to a ratio of one wireless aircraft to every 2,000 yards.[39] In a war where artillery had established itself as the primary killer, this proved critically important.

A year earlier, before the war's first anniversary, British heavy artillery officers were already reporting good results in correcting their fire with the help of aerial observation. In May 1915, they began combining air reports with those received from ground-based observers and intelligence data received from division headquarters. The results proved sufficient for artillery commanders to recommend expansion of the wireless network so that counter-batteries could have their own sections.[40] The organization that grew out of those recommendations tightened cooperation between aircraft, artillery, and the wire telegraphy stations assigned to its batteries, the latter issuing instructions based upon aircraft reconnaissance.[41]

As the war progressed both sides sharpened their artillery observation skills. By the battle of the Somme, army commanders had come to understand the principal value of artillery lay in counter-battery work, or the destruction of the enemy's artillery. An artillery battery commander's ability to knock out his opposite numbers depended on maintaining good observation that, as one report confirmed, "in many instances, could only be obtained from the air."[42] Paul von Hindenburg, part of the duo who replaced Erich von Falkenhayn as commander of all German armies on the Western Front in 1916, commented on the partnership between aviation and the artillery in the aftermath of the German campaign against the French at Verdun. "[T]o engage the enemy's artillery with the help of aeroplane observers," he wrote, "is the principal and most effective means of fighting a defensive battle to a successful conclusion. Should this succeed, the enemy's attack is absolutely paralysed."[43] In the summer of 1916, the British also took action to guarantee the steady production of well-trained observers by establishing an observers section at its Brooklands Wireless School. The school trained twenty new observers per month.[44]

Counter-battery work assumed such importance that by the launch of the battle of the Somme, more than 40 percent of the British Army's corps squadrons were committed to this type of work. From the last week in June 1916 until October 20, 1916, British artillery conducted 1,721 operations against hostile artillery, more than six times the 281 actions directed against German trenches.[45] Aircrews did not always have an easy time regulating the artillery. On July 29, 1916,

No. 2 Squadron's 2/Lt. J. B. E. Crosbee and Lt. G. W. Devenish, were working with the 140th Heavy Battery and 2nd Siege Battery, when the 140th refused to fire, likely because a hostile aircraft had been spotted "very high and a long way off." After the enemy airplane left, the 140th "still refused to fire," so Crosbee and Devenish tried the 2nd Siege Battery, which fired two shots that landed close, but not exactly on target. By that time, the No. 2 Squadron crew's B.E.2d was running low on petrol forcing them to return.[46]

The records of No. 34 Squadron, Royal Flying Corps, indicate that during the months of August, September, and October 1916 fully 50 percent of its attempted artillery co-operation missions failed either because of wireless problems or other miscommunications with their assigned batteries, or due to interference by enemy aircraft.[47] Despite these problems, including the growing strength and talent of the German fighter pilots who opposed them, by the end of the Somme battle artillery crews had amassed sufficient respect for the Royal Flying Corps to fight to take control over them.[48]

When the dust settled on the Somme battle, British artillery commanders began to covet direct authority over the aircrews that regulated their guns. Sir Henry Rawlinson, commanding officer of the Fourth Army, endorsed a proposal that would have given the Royal Artillery command of the corps squadrons in all matters except those relating to aviation technology.[49] Fleshing out the idea, Rawlinson suggested that if commanders could find no airmen qualified to serve as artillery observers they should train artillery officers to act in their place.[50] Trenchard vigorously opposed any scheme under which the RFC would lose control of its squadrons, pointing out that the corps squadrons performed more than just artillery observation. The RFC chief also noted that the corps squadrons were not, at that moment, equipped with the type of machines necessary to do all the work the artillery required, especially long-distance photography. Because of their poor livery, corps squadrons would have had to cede jurisdiction over photographic work to fighting units, an action Trenchard would not support. Trenchard also argued the problems the Artillery Corps sought to correct by grabbing control of aviation units were not entirely air-related, citing too frequent changes in the assignment of batteries to aircrews as the cause of much of the trouble.[51]

The inter-service political war over ownership of the corps squadrons soon expanded, drawing other senior officers into the fray and dividing them. Although he supported transfer of control of observation balloons to the Artillery, Maj.-Gen. James F. N. Birch, the artillery advisor at General Headquarters, sided with Trenchard when it came to RFC retention of corps aircraft. Yet Gen. Sir H. S. Horne, commanding officer of the First Army, sided with Rawlinson, maintaining that the Army would not realize artillery's full potential until "direction and control of artillery fire from the air is placed in the hands of the artillery."[52] Trenchard dodged the attempted takeover of his air squadrons, though the debate continued with respect to observation balloons.[53]

In the wake of his successful campaign to retain control of his airplanes, Trenchard proposed increasing the size of the RFC's corps squadrons and doubling their number. He backed up his recommendation with a request that the Army's brigade commanders estimate the number of airplanes they thought necessary to provide complete artillery coverage throughout days with favorable flying weather. Based on these opinions, Trenchard sought to increase the number of airplanes in a corps squadron from eighteen to twenty-four.[54]

The Royal Flying Corps finalized its evolving artillery regulation techniques based on its experiences during the Somme battle, making only minor improvements over the last two years of the war.[55] In December 1916 the British General Staff published those updated procedures in "Co-operation of Aircraft with Artillery (S.S. 131)."[56]

One of the minor enhancements made following the new guide's publication involved fine-tuning the zone call system. Since June 1916 pilots and observers noticing fleeting targets were empowered to broadcast a "zone call" to any artillery battery in a position to respond quickly. The zone covered a 3,000-square-yard area. Aircrews calling for fire in a particular zone identified their location by transmitting two letters, the first of which corresponded to the lettered square on the map over which they were flying at the time. The second letter narrowed the fire to a particular zone within the map square.[57] By the end of 1916 so many crews were taking advantage of the opportunity that confusion developed between neighboring batteries. Because adjacent corps used overlapping, identically marked maps and crews transmitted the map square (but not the map sheet) on which they were working, batteries did not always know where they were supposed to be shooting. To solve the problem, on March 24, 1917, General Headquarters issued an amended procedure calling for updated 1:40,000-scale maps printed in alternating sequences divided into squares marked "A" through "D" on one set and "W" through "Z" on the next moving from north to south.[58] On July 24, 1916, the Royal Flying Corps' *War Diary* reported "the system of area calls is working very well."[59] By October 1, the same source noted artillery in the 5th Brigade area cut wire and damaged trenches and that a "heavy accurate shrapnel barrage was brought to bear on enemy trenches during our attack by means of the zone call."[60] Four days later, No. 4 Squadron's Lieutenants Dickie and O'Hanlon, "whilst on contact patrol, called for fire on enemy in trenches N. of Thiepval by zone call. Shrapnel was seen to burst over them within two minutes."[61]

Major A. S. Barrett, commanding officer of No. 6 Squadron, further refined the science of aerial artillery ranging in late 1916 with development of the ringed photograph. Barrett provided his pilots and observers with air photos of their targets marked with concentric circles, marked "Z," "A," "B," and "C," and with the "N," "S," "E," and "W" compass points. This simple aid reduced distance mistakes crews frequently made in locating the fall of artillery shells. In an early form of battle damage assessment, crews marked on the photograph where the shots fell. Royal Flying Corps Headquarters endorsed the idea and recommended implementation in all British corps squadrons.[62] In an earlier example, on July 18, 1916, Lieutenants Bagot and Peach, on a flash patrol between Armentieres to Bois de Biez in B.E.2c 4162, reported "2 flashes at N.28.A.5.4. (7:40 p.m.) Photo 162," before having to give up the mission due to low clouds and mist.[63]

In terms of artillery observation, the United States entered the First World War entirely dependent on the French and British for preparatory operational assistance on the modern battlefield. The American Expeditionary Force came to Europe with outmoded battle doctrines that anticipated a war of movement rather than the stagnant state of trench warfare practiced on the Western Front.[64] Mobile warfare doctrine put artillery in an auxiliary role, subordinate to the infantry, rather than casting it in the lead and supposing it would help to achieve breakthrough.[65] In the years prior to the war, the US Army had failed to prepare its artillery any better than it had built up its air power. When the first American units arrived in France two months after the declaration of war, they came without artillery. By the armistice the US Army had nearly 3,500 pieces. As the nation eventually did with its Air Service, the United States solved its artillery problem by purchasing most of its equipment from the French.[66] The other element necessary to an effective artillery program, an observation system, also had to be built from scratch.

Possessing neither an air force nor an aerial doctrine, the United States had to act quickly to build an aviation organization capable of operating with its artillery units in France.[67] The Army and Navy used the nearly $640 million Congress provided both to build and buy aviation equipment. Most of the material the American Expeditionary Force acquired abroad came from French factories.[68]

American artillery officers realized how vital effective aerial observation had become and they attempted to address the problem quickly. They began training their own observers at artillery brigade training centers immediately after the arrival of the first US artillery units in France.[69] The Air Service also began to train observers, but the artillery refused to entrust its officers to the Air Service at this early stage of American participation in the war, citing the necessity of its personnel training with their own units so they might become versed in French artillery methods.[70] This arrangement proved unsatisfactory because the observers instructed by the artillery learned only how to work with the artillery without training in any other aircrew skills. In response the Army created an Air Service observation training organization. The basic course of instruction ensured the new observer finished training with at least elementary skills in the entire range of aerial observation topics, including reconnaissance, photography, infantry contact, and artillery observation. Subsequent advanced training in the finer points of artillery regulation took place in advanced schools placed next to the artillery training centers where artillery and aviation officers could train together in mock combat situations.[71] In September 1917 the Army designated Tours, France, as the location of the Observers' School and the first trainees began instruction there in January 1918. Sites for the advanced artillery aerial observation schools (AAOS), named in October, included: Coetquidan (1st AAOS), Souge (2nd AAOS), Meucon (4th AAOS), and LeValdahon (5th AAOS).[72]

In addition to the French airplanes the US Air Service purchased, American aviators also accepted French artillery-observation methodology.[73] American observer training in France generally followed French methods by employing instructional materials that were little more than translated French manuals.[74] The US Army's decision to follow the French in its approach to artillery regulation might reflect more than its intent to operate in closer contact to French units than to the British. When the United States entered the war the British conceded their French counterparts did better at artillery spotting than their own army, "owning chiefly to close co-operation between the officer commanding the French Artillery and the aircraft attached to it."[75]

Students in the advanced courses were expected upon their arrival to know the characteristics of the various artillery pieces then in use, including the French 75- and 155-caliber guns, and the differences in various types of shells. During the course the cadet observers practiced firing 8-second salvos in three-, four-, and six-round series. Instructors emphasized combining speed and accuracy when adjusting the 155-caliber gun, but were willing to sacrifice speed for greater precision when adjusting the 75-caliber. Of the 1,250 officers who commenced training over the course of 1918, just over seven hundred were serving at the front at the time of the armistice.[76]

The US Air Service recruited students for the observer courses from three sources: men trained in the United States, candidates furnished by the artillery, and volunteers from all other arms of the AEF.[77] The second and third sources became necessary because the stateside training program never yielded sufficient numbers. Air Service officials in France regularly complained that domestic trainers could not meet their personnel requirements and that the deficiencies had to be made up in Europe.[78] Late in the war recruiting efforts within the AEF started to dry up as well, prompting the Air Service command in France to suggest as an incentive that cadets be provisionally commissioned prior to leaving the United States, with their commission becoming permanent only upon successful completion of the observer's course.[79] Further, the American recruiting program suffered qualitatively as well as quantitatively. Observers who began their training in the United States frequently arrived in France either inadequately schooled or instructed in methods long out of use at the front, necessitating lengthy retraining.[80]

Beyond recruiting enough capable men to serve in the cockpits, the US Army faced the equally daunting challenge of convincing those designated for observation training that their work represented aviation's most valuable contribution to the war. Captain Harold Wilder, a US Air Service artillery observation trainer, told his students, "Observation comprises the Air Service which acts in direct connection with the other branches of the Army. Complete contact with these branches has been a primary object of the Service and its results have been in proportion to the success of this cooperation."[81] Regular training bulletins issued by the Air Service reminded the observation pilot of his worth, telling him that "it is a mistaken idea some flyers have that a pilot who has been sent to observation is a cast-off in chasse."[82] The Air Service's persuasive efforts put strong emphasis on the notion that "all aviation is built around observation."[83] The training bulletins touted accounts of observation's successes, including the story of an American crew credited with saving a division that compared the feat to the best a fighter pilot had ever achieved: "There should be more satisfaction to these two men for what they did than for the honor of bringing down six Hun planes in a day."[84]

When the nature of artillery observation began to change as trench warfare gave way to movement in the conflict's final months the Air Service used its training bulletins to instill the level of confidence observers needed to stand up to the battery commander. Articles in the bulletins reminded observers "the big trouble at present seems to be in the adjusting on fleeting targets. When an observer calls for an adjustment they must fire on that target or else send him 'No' and not adjust on a different target as some have done when given a target of importance by an observer."[85]

Convincing the aviation cadets of the value of their work and instructing them in the proper techniques of artillery observation represented only half the training equation. Building the relationships necessary between front-line aviation and artillery units in order to field an effective destructive force comprised the other half. Maximizing the potential lethality that artillery brought to the modern battlefield required that the men firing the shells understood the value of those observing for them in the sky and that the two branches communicated on an ongoing basis. To foster this appreciation for aviation within the artillery, Air Service instructors at the artillery schools designed a short course for artillery officers comprised of three lectures: a general introduction to artillery's role when using air observers, and two lectures that used stereopticon slides to instruct students in how to use aerial photos in planning artillery fire and designing camouflage.[86] Experience would prove that classroom instruction alone did not produce complete results. Only working together in the field would achieve the strong link between aviation and the artillery essential to victory in combat. Artillery officers needed to become fliers.

By the summer of 1918 the US Air Service had several months' experience training and using artillery officers as balloon observers when it decided to effect the same blend in its corps observation squadrons. The immediate shortage of qualified trainees arriving from the United States as well as the desire for observers with a broader technical knowledge of artillery work prompted the change in policy.[87] Training began so quickly that of the 193 observers who graduated from the Second Aviation Instruction Center at Tours in September 1918, the majority had come from the artillery.[88]

As important as good training might have been, indoctrinating artillery officers in the ways of aviation and aviators in artillery techniques constituted only the first steps towards building a successful artillery observation organization. The rest of the effort had to take place in the field. Meaningful liaison between the two branches had to become so much a part of the regular routine of both services that it permeated Army culture. The effort to build this new culture started at the top of the Army's organizational chart and flowed down to the level of the individual squadrons and batteries. To achieve this the Air Service stationed liaison officers at each divisional headquarters to work directly with the division's commanding general in the selection of each day's targets.[89] Artillery commanders notified the Air Service which of the targets had been allocated to terrestrial, balloon, and aircraft observers, and the Air Service assigned the appropriate units to the operation.[90] Their efforts were not always immediately successful. Commenting on their coordination with ground units, Air Service trainers remarked:

> Liaison between the Air and the Ground is very poor with new divisions, as these men have not understood the full value of the airplane. Artillery liaison is also poor, especially in the work with fugitive targets. In order to encourage liaison, these observers should be encouraged to visit the unit with which they will be working as often as possible so that they may secure this cooperation and show them by practical experience what the value of the aeroplane really is.[91]

If the Air Service hoped to become a truly effective battlefield asset its efforts to improve liaison between air and ground units had to reach down the chain of command to the level of the individual air squadrons and artillery batteries. As a start, squadron commanders attending the nightly conferences at which the next day's targets were arranged and allocated were instructed to bring along a few of their observers. While their commanding officer obtained the latest intelligence data from division headquarters the observers discussed target specifics with the artillery commander.[92] Success during the battle required at least a partial division of authority between air and ground units. Battery commanders had responsibility for the success [of the shoot] and the air observer generally acted in a subordinate role, but the observer had the ability to exercise his own judgment and intervene under limited circumstances.[93] The observer could suggest the use of precision or zone fire, but the actual decision belonged to the battery commander.[94] If the battery suffered a delay for any reason and could not fire within thirty seconds of the air observer's signal, procedures required that it hold its fire until it received another signal from the aircraft.[95] To facilitate cooperation to an even greater degree the Army developed forms for use in the field; an "objective card" which illustrated the location of the target on both a map and a photograph and, for occasions when wireless signals proved impossible, a form the observer could drop to the battery to convey urgent firing instructions.[96] Artillery observation thus became part of the US Army's bureaucracy.

The French can take credit for the centerpiece of systemization, which had been in place long before the American Expeditionary Force arrived on the Western Front. The *Plan Directeur*, a 1:20,000-scale map, pulled together every bit of intelligence data available to the Army and verifiable by aerial photograph to depths of 10 kilometers inside German lines and 5 kilometers inside Allied territory. French Army Intelligence updated the map daily and issued it as the basic artillery map. Mapmakers supplemented the *Plan Directeur* with 1:10,000-scale trench maps that included "wire, obstacles, dugouts, trails, and important details of trench organization," and 1:5,000-scale infantry maps that detailed both the German and Allied sides of the lines.[97] Throughout its stay on the Western Front, the AEF used these French maps as its basic day-to-day artillery guide.

Conducting an effective artillery firing session required more than the development of trust between aircrews and their gunners and designing a well-organized system. It also required regular practice. When a sector of the front went quiet and the artillery did not need regular adjustment, the Air Service's squadrons devoted their time to general reconnaissance and photography duties in preparation for the next rounds of heavy fighting. Valuable as this preparation proved to subsequent operations, the downtime frequently resulted in diminishing skills in both airmen and gunners. Operations officers encouraged observers to avoid this problem by insisting they call upon the artillery to engage fugitive targets during their routine reconnaissance flights.[98] Air Service trainers advised the operations officer to resort to shame if necessary to stave off the possibility of his teams falling into a "live and let live" philosophy, reminding them, "It is a very mediocre observer who cannot pick out some target of immediate value during a reconnaissance."[99]

Practice paid dividends both in terms of the artillery's accuracy and in the development of new techniques. From its rudimentary beginnings in the summer of 1914 the science of artillery observation had developed by the last months of the war into a highly organized and destructive program practiced by all the warring powers. The German *Luftstreitkräfte* felt sufficient confidence in its techniques and its artillery fliers to begin experimenting with night ranging during 1918 on the French and British fronts.[100] The observer could establish his location through the use of natural landmarks or be pointed towards the target with flares set up by the battery. Darkness required that he guard against his vision being dazzled by the fire and that he identify bursts by their "circular form" and flash discharges by their "bright semi-circular glow."[101] Apart from these special instructions, work proceeded along firmly established lines laid out in the *Manual of Position Warfare for All Arms*.[102]

Not satisfied with simply fine-tuning daytime techniques for use after dark, German artillery fliers began experimenting with ranging their guns with photographs rather than human observers. The new method required more cooperation between aviation and artillery than any simple pre-fire conference. The process began with an artillery battery taking a few ranging shots, after which a reconnaissance crew would photograph the area shelled. Mathematicians would use shell holes visible on the photographs to calculate a datum point for use in ranging the guns, eliminating the need for an observer to be present during the actual shoot. The US Air Service Chief of Staff Col. Thomas D. Milling proposed an easy, if rather ludicrous-sounding, countermeasure to this German experiment, suggesting that if the enemy's practice firing occurred late enough in the day that the reconnaissance flight might not appear until the following morning troops would spend the night filling in the real shell holes and replacing them with fakes in other locations.[103]

The US Air Service and its partners in the artillery began learning these lessons during the spring of 1918 when the first corps squadrons arrived at the front. During July and August the AEF engaged in its first real battle at Chateau Thierry. For that campaign the 1st Aero Squadron found itself assigned to corps reconnaissance and artillery adjustment duties while the 12th and 88th Aero Squadrons handled divisional work, which included regulating the divisional artillery as well as providing for general and special reconnaissance, infantry contact, and special command missions.[104] The artillery sorties performed by the three units penetrated enemy lines to a depth of 1,000–2,500 meters, shorter-range observations being handled by ground spotters or balloon crews.[105]

Valuable and sophisticated as Allied artillery adjustment techniques had become over the four years since the start of the war, the doctrines the French and British had formulated and passed along to the AEF focused on principles that applied to stationary, not open, warfare. When the German lines finally began to give way to Allied attacks and American, British, and French forces started advancing, those principles broke down. Artillery regulation became a difficult proposition during a war of movement.[106] In a rush to follow up on their breakthroughs, and hampered by habits acquired over long years of not needing to communicate with aviators, American artillery batteries did not always let their corps squadrons know where to find them. The US Army did not have the time to resolve these communication problems in the few weeks that remained in the war. As a short-term remedy, artillery officers reverted to ground spotters and balloons during open warfare, reserving airplanes for circumstances where observation would have otherwise been impossible.[107] Another method of dealing with fugitive targets was to assign to patrol duty an aircrew familiar with the zones of the various regiments. The crew would call down the various targets available and the regimental commander would decide which ones to attack.[108]

Though hampered by the same communication problems, their lengthier experience allowed the British and French air forces to adapt more quickly than their American colleagues to the return to mobile warfare. By late September 1918, British historian Hilary St. George Saunders boasted, "the Royal Air Force was everywhere, and this time so carefully had the system of signaling to the artillery been devised and rehearsed, that, despite the swift movement of the battle, its Corps squadrons were enabled to direct the guns again and again on to suitable targets."[109]

Though American aviators' and artillerists' relative inexperience in the art of modern warfare hampered their ability to make the rapid changes frequently necessary to effective inter-branch cooperation, the achievements of French and British forces did succeed in convincing the Army that a strong aviation program constituted an element essential to victory in modern combat operations. Outlining the requirements for an army of one million men in 1918, the War Department proposed that the Army's Air Service component consist of twenty-four observation squadrons, fifteen pursuit units, five bomber squadrons, one photographic section, twenty-four balloon companies and six air parks.[110] Nearly two-thirds of these units (the observation squadrons, balloon companies, and the photographic sections) provided direct assistance to the artillery, the balloon companies doing almost nothing else.

The composition of the US Air Service by the time of the armistice demonstrated that strong emphasis on artillery regulation. Of the forty-five airplane squadrons that made it to the front lines by November 11, 1918, twelve had corps reconnaissance as their exclusive duty. Including the seventeen balloon companies at the front on the last day of the war, the number of Air Service units devoted to artillery observation rose to twenty-nine within a total of sixty-two (46.7%) heavier- and lighter-than-air units.[111] Those numbers put the

US Air Service in line with the French aviation program from which its leaders took their primary example. During the last seven months of the war the French had 230 *escadrilles* on the Western Front, 107 of which worked with the artillery.[112] By contrast, on the war's last day the British Royal Air Force had ninety-nine heavier-than-air squadrons, seven independent flights, and nineteen balloon companies on the Western Front. Although the RAF devoted more effort to aerial combat and bombing and comparatively less to reconnaissance than did its American and French counterparts, corps observation units still made up twenty of those ninety-nine squadrons and the RAF's official history boasted that British aviators had registered the fall of twelve million shells.[113] Another historian estimated that 80 percent of the British artillery's targets had been obtained from the RAF.[114]

Assessing lessons learned during the war after the armistice, US Air Service trainers formulated techniques to use during future periods of static and open warfare. Looking back they noted that good liaison work had become even more important while troops were on the move due to the large number of fugitive targets available. Acknowledging the problems artillery battery commanders had keeping in touch during the Meuse-Argonne offensive, the trainers suggested that battery commanders not make adjustments in open warfare using the customary battery-target line, but instead by using as reference points the old signaling panels laid out by each battalion station. They further recommended that observers then pinpoint shots in a manner similar to zone fire by signaling whether the shell landed to the right or left of the panel. Acknowledging these suggestions would yield imprecise results the trainers proposed that the artillery revert to the more established principles that had proven successful during the fighting once ground movement slowed down or stopped long enough for squadrons to reestablish contact with individual batteries.[115]

Whether fighting from the trenches or on open ground, the days when the artillery had to rely on the cavalry to capture the high ground in order to see its targets had ended. Using aerial observers in airplane cockpits and balloon baskets, the big guns could hit targets previously thought impossible to spot. The range of the guns now constituted the only limitation to the size of the battlefield. The major air forces that served on the Western Front and in the other theaters of war, even those that took a more aggressive approach to the conflict, considered it their primary job to assist their counterparts on the ground in taking the fight to the enemy. Aviation had become an integral part of all armies and a vital component to military success on the ground. Air power provided the ability to see what happened "on the other side of the hill" and held the key to making the artillery more deadly than it had been in any previous war.

CHAPTER 5

Infantry Liaison: Keeping Track of the Attack

During mobilization for the Spanish American War US Army Chief Signal Officer Adolphus Greely linked Washington with the Atlantic, Gulf, and Pacific coasts by multiple telegraph and telephone lines and, in his report for 1898, proclaimed that the age of strategic military communication had arrived.
—Daniel R. Beaver, *Modernizing the American War Department*

The quiet work of the pilots and observers who flew in direct co-operation with the infantry is apt to be obscured by the more spectacular attention which attaches to air fighting. They, alone, were the witnesses of the whole titanic struggle, and through their eyes the army commanders could follow the fortunes of their troops.
—Walter Raleigh and H. A. Jones, *The War in the Air*

Aerial reconnaissance exists to gather, process, and disseminate information to battlefield commanders and troops in real time, or in as close to real time as is possible. Artillery observation aircraft provided this service for the big guns positioned behind the trenches. "Contact patrols," or "infantry liaison," as infantry commanders sometimes termed the mission, developed due to the need for a communication method that would not break down when attacking troops advanced beyond their own front lines.

The state of early-twentieth-century communications necessitated involving airmen in maintaining contact with attacking troops. Shortly after the war on the Western Front settled into the trenches, troops on both sides of No-Man's-Land established elaborate communications networks consisting of dispatch riders, communications trenches, and miles of telephone lines that linked their battlefronts with their command posts. The system worked well enough until commanders ordered an attack. But when the troops went over the top they immediately ran beyond their hard-wired communication systems, making difficult if not impossible generals' remote command. In the absence of lightweight mobile wireless communication equipment, aircraft offered the fastest and most logical method of maintaining touch with the extent of any advance. No specific date has survived for the first contact patrol, but one historian has credited early French success with the method as having inspired the British to experiment with the practice in March 1915.[1] Sound in theory, contact patrols worked well when ground troops were extensively trained in how to work with aircraft, but otherwise frequently broke down.

From the war's earliest days, ground troops were suspicious of anything that flew overhead. Afraid an airplane in the sky meant they would come under artillery fire any second, infantrymen generally shot at anything they saw before taking cover.[2] Airmen regularly reported being fired upon by jittery friendly troops, as well as the enemy.[3] Attempts to remedy this problem by training at least some troops in aircraft identification and by the adoption of distinctive national insignia failed to significantly cut down the ground fire.[4] By the end of 1914 the Royal Flying Corps had replaced its original insignia, the British Union Jack, because from a distance it too closely resembled the Iron Cross emblem used on German aircraft. (Friendly fire from British troops resulted in the loss of at least two of their own airmen.[5]) In its place the British decorated their aircraft with a red, white, and blue cockade similar to the roundel used by the French.[6] The other Allied air services also employed roundels, the Belgians using red, yellow, and black, the Russians, red, blue, and white, and the Italians, red, white, and green. In the last months of the war, American forces replaced the star-in-a-circle identifier used on airplanes in the United States with their own red-blue-white roundel.[7]

The airplane represented a potential solution to commanders' communications problems during an attack that made the risks brought on by ground fire worthwhile. Fliers could operate above the fighting unhampered by shell holes, barbed wire, *chevaux de frise*, and other obstacles that slowed or altogether prevented the movement of dispatch riders. Aerial observation offered significant potential benefits to those managing the attack in real time, despite the absence of two-way voice communication with airplane crews. Aviators flying infantry-liaison missions faced the same challenges to wireless transmission and reception as aviators engaged in artillery regulation missions, but instead of communicating with the commander of a single battery, aircrews had to get an entire line of soldiers in the vanguard of an attack to understand their instructions and respond. The problems inherent in infantry-liaison work never went away and affected both sides of the lines equally throughout the remainder of the war.

In their attempts to make the system work, air and ground commanders adopted a variety of sound and visual signals for airplane crews to use in locating the front line. Generally, airmen would sound a Klaxon horn, due to its "distinctive note, which could be readily heard on the ground," or fire a flare to attract the attention of the infantry.[8] To mark their position, soldiers were expected to respond by firing their own flare or by laying out a white cloth panel (in winter the reverse side was black).[9] Viewed from the air, the series of flares or panels would form a line that staked out the attack's forward-most point of advance. The British began using contact patrols as a means of regular infantry liaison at the battle of Festubert (May 15–27, 1915) after severed telephone lines had adversely affected communications with the front during the earlier attack at Neuve Chapelle.[10] Sir William Robertson, chief of the General Staff during the Neuve Chapelle battle, predicted that future engagements with the enemy would face the same problem. The British lieutenant general wrote in a memo dated March 14, 1915, that "telephone and telegraph lines are almost certain to fail during a successful advance."[11] Attempting to remedy the broken link in the communication chain, the RFC's No. 16 Squadron conducted experiments between the two battles at Aire working with infantry in the First Army's training area.[12] Although results of the practice missions were described as "good," details suggest otherwise. Airmen flying at 6,000 feet saw troops well enough as forces moved across dry ploughed ground, but distinguishing friend from enemy became problematic when the fighting moved to grass or through crop fields and once forces of the two sides had actually joined in battle.[13]

No. 16 Squadron personnel continued their experiments under actual battle conditions. On the first day of the Festubert battle, pilots flew three wireless-equipped Maurice Farman two-seaters with orders to transmit their reports to four wireless receiving stations set up especially for the test. Infantry commanders ordered their own attacking units to display their seven-by-two-foot white strips when they reached several predetermined points. The airmen kept an eye out for advancing troops.[14] When the infantry failed to progress on schedule, not reaching the locations where they were to display their panels, the RFC's observers still accurately transmitted their advances.[15] Aerial observation earned high marks generally, artillery spotters receiving credit for helping the guns drive back the enemy along a four-mile front "to an average depth of 600 yards."[16] Even in the face of this impressive performance, No. 16 Squadron's real achievement was its establishment of the "practicability" of contact patrol work, judged by one observer as the "outstanding feature with regard to the work of the Royal Flying Corps."[17] Provided the ground troops performed as planned, the RFC remained optimistic about the future of contact patrols.

Aware of many potential rewards, despite the challenges, senior infantry officers came to see value in cooperating with aircraft. In a letter written in July 1915, shortly after the battle of Festubert, Brig. Gen. Reginald John Kentish, a battalion commander who went on to head the Third Army Infantry School at Flixecourt, recommended the addition of training in aircraft and infantry liaison to the syllabi of all senior command instruction centers. Unfortunately, owing to heavy demands on the RFC, whose commanders could not then spare the airplanes or crews necessary for training activities from active duty, the instruction had to wait. Kentish repeated his recommendation on November 8, 1916, just ten days prior to the end of the First Somme battle, by which time he was serving as commanding officer of the Senior Officers School at Aldershot. By the time he wrote his second letter, Kentish had been in touch with the RFC's Gen. Sefton Brancker to work out details for the training he favored.[18] Kentish's efforts bring into question the argument that infantry commanders had little if any awareness of the potential benefits of military aviation.[19]

Proper training of infantry-liaison techniques remained an issue throughout the war. Prior to battle of Loos in September 1916, aviation and infantry commanders arranged for troops to cooperate with infantry-liaison missions, but nothing suggests the infantrymen followed the plans. The British official air historian suggested that soldiers under fire became preoccupied with more immediate survival issues and could not bother with "what at the time may have struck them as of academic interest to the staff rather than as a vital precaution for their own safety."[20] Frequently enemy fire killed the men detailed to lay out the signal panels before they completed the work leaving the task to other troops who had not been trained in the procedure.[21] American forces arriving on the Western Front in 1918 encountered the same challenges and, in advance of the Chateau Thierry battle, attempted to solve their problems by conducting practice exercises.[22] American aviators soon discovered their infantrymen responded more readily to signals for the display of panels or flares after their attack had calmed down allowing them time to rest. While the attack progressed the infantry remained too busy to be bothered with communicating with airmen.[23]

As for the French, by the autumn of 1915 they too realized the need for more effective infantry liaison and tested various techniques during attacks in the Western Front's Champagne region. French observers followed the progress of attacking troops waiting for signals to come from infantrymen equipped with signal lamps, flares, small rockets, and cloth panels. Airmen plotted the location of the front line on a 1:50,000-scale map then dropped the map in a message bag on various reporting stations established prior to the battle. In a follow-up memo dated February 10, 1916, a member of the French Second Army Corps staff stated his belief that, in addition to the divisional balloon, French divisions needed a wireless-equipped airplane to signal the beginning of barrage fire in the event of the attack's failure or the appearance of targets of opportunity.[24] Once begun, other aircraft would regulate the artillery fire.

British and French military commanders soon found that contact patrol work differed significantly from artillery regulation. Effective infantry liaison could only be performed with airplanes. Balloon observers in stationary baskets could not adequately follow troops on the move or spot infantry working in remote locations.[25] On August 3, 1916, Gen. Henry Rawlinson, commander of the British Fourth Army reported that balloon observers had not been trained effectively to follow the progress of attacking troops. Rawlinson complained further that balloons were situated too far behind the lines to observe the location of the front line, and that no information of value had been received from his balloon observers during recent operations.[26] In notes written at the end of August 1916, French aviation commander Paul-Fernaud de Peuty, who would assume total control of the French Aviation Militaire in 1917, built on Rawlinson's observations. He reflected that, "the airplane observer is the only one in the position to see," and posited that aerial observations might "bring about a saving or wastage of a number of lives amongst the infantry."[27] De Peuty further acknowledged the close connection between contact patrol missions and the infantry's needs, writing "the duties of an observer working for the infantry are based on the information required by all formations of the Corps."[28]

As with all other aspects of aviation, airmen applied or developed infantry-liaison techniques in places other than the Western Front. In April 1916, Geoffrey Salmond, commander of the RFC's Fifth Wing in Egypt, issued a report on cooperation techniques with ground forces. Cognizant of the many differences between positional warfare on the Western Front and the desert warfare conditions his aviators faced in the Middle East, Salmond cautioned that the techniques "might prove useful to Royal Flying Corps detachments employed in Mesopotamia, India, and East Africa."[29] Salmond accepted the RFC's responsibility for protecting infantry columns against surprise during good daylight weather conditions, but in a more aggressive tone added that, "the enemy once located should never be allowed to get away so long as he is within the reach of aeroplane reconnaissance."[30] Even more hampered by less-than-stellar communications than his colleagues in France, Salmond suggested that ground officers in need of real-time aerial reconnaissance could request the assistance of a flyer by firing a flare to attract the pilot's attention and then sending a man carrying a white flag running two hundred yards in the general direction of the requested reconnaissance.[31] On the Western Front such a signal would have almost certainly meant sacrificing the runner to enemy fire, but in the open desert opportunities for creative cooperation were more plentiful.

After its initial thrust into France in 1914, the German Army adopted a far more defensive posture on the Western Front than did the Allies. After the early war of movement slowed and then stopped during the last months of 1914, German forces dug in. With occasional exceptions, such as their attack on Verdun in February 1916, German commanders appeared content, until their spring offensives of 1918, to hold on to territory gained, repulsing French and British attempts to evict them. In March 1917, *General* Erich Ludendorff organized a stronger defensive stance on the Western Front by pulling German troops back to a string of heavily fortified positions that became known as the *Siegfried Stellung* or the Hindenburg Line.[32] As a byproduct of this strategy, German two-seater crews performed contact-patrol duties on fewer occasions than their Allied counterparts, focusing more frequently on visual and photographic reconnaissance, artillery regulation, and bombing missions.

When German fliers did perform infantry-liaison missions they faced the same problem encountered by their Allied counterparts. *General* Ernst von Hoeppner remarked that German soldiers did not regularly display their signal panels when called upon to do so by infantry fliers, forcing crews to fly almost at ground level to distinguish troops by the color of their uniforms.[33] However aircrews obtained the information, German commanders did come to value the battlefield intelligence provided as highly as their Allied opponents. Hoeppner reported the infantry fliers' reports "were deemed more reliable than all other means of information" and were "of the utmost importance in reaching decisions."[34]

While German airmen practiced the art of infantry contact when necessary, real interest in using aircraft in ground-support roles began following a contact patrol crew's decision to take an aggressive part in the fighting. During a small operation in the neighborhood of Arras on April 24, 1917, the *Schutzstaffel 7* (protection flight) crew of *Vizefeldwebel* (Sergeant Major) Josef Schleiffer and his commanding officer, *Hauptmann* (Captain) Eduard Zorer, after locating panels laid out by the infantry in response to their flares, flew ahead of the attack strafing the British defenders.[35] Their initiative prompted a mention in the official Army communiqué and a message of appreciation from *Kommandierende General der Luftstreitkräfte* Ernst von Hoeppner in the weekly *Nachrichtenblatt*.[36] Over the summer of 1917 more ground-attack operations took place, either because of this early success at direct battlefield intervention, or the potential for force multiplication it implied, or the lack of frequent need for contact patrols owing to the defensive nature of German Western Front operations, or all in combination. *Armee* (Army) and *Luftstreitkräfte* (Air Force) commanders were impressed by the results and at the beginning of 1918 formalized the new reality by converting the *Schutzstaffeln*, initially formed to provide protection to reconnaissance and artillery flights, into *Schlachtstaffeln* (battle flights) with direct ground-attack responsibility.[37] The reorganized units proved effective in the last major German push, "Operation Michael," which began on March 21, 1918.

The resumption of movement on the Western Front brought about the need for closer cooperation between infantry and aircraft on both sides of the lines. By May the commander of the British 23rd Army

Corps considered the matter of liaison with aviators sufficiently pressing to write to headquarters, "I consider it very desirable that the whole scheme of aeroplane co-operation within this Corps should be put into effect at an early date."[38] Later in the year, as changes in position on the Western Front became still more rapid, he wrote again recommending an increase in the number of flares issued to cyclist regiments and infantry battalions to 1,000 flares each.[39]

When US forces joined French and British units at the front they mimicked the communication methods the Allied powers had constructed for use in positional warfare, relying on telephone lines and exchanges, radio relays, carrier pigeons, motorcycle dispatch riders, and airplanes. American aviation units began arriving on the Western Front just at the time of the 1918 German spring offensives. US Air Service squadrons preparing for infantry-liaison missions equipped themselves with air-to-ground radio and a variety of visual signaling devices, including rockets, flares, and weighted message bags to use when dropping detailed reports to command posts.[40]

With a few months' experience US Air Service corps observation crews came to share their British colleagues' faith in the powers of infantry contact. The 50th Aero Squadron began operations on September 12, 1918, the opening day of the St. Mihiel offensive, just eight weeks before the end of the war. The unit flew the Liberty-engine powered American DH-4 on divisional observation duties. The squadron's historian described infantry liaison as "the reason for having aviation in modern warfare" and noted that infantry contact patrols "are the only means of communication in many cases during a battle."[41] The official record of the unit's activities also included a strong statement lamenting the general lack of appreciation for the work aviators performed in support of infantry:

> The general public knows little about this end of aviation even though this is the most important branch of aviation. Its proper or non-functioning can save or destroy thousands of lives of our own troops and it also can be the means of the success or failure of an offensive. This is not known by the general public because of the notoriety given the "chasse" planes when they bring

a Hun plane down. No mention has ever been made when the observation planes saved hundreds or even thousands of our own troops. It is the most constructive work in the combatant arm of the army.[42]

For their part US Army commanders had issued clear instructions to infantry for the first day of the St. Mihiel attack, ordering that, "the front line will indicate its position to the planes (a) on reaching the 1st Day Objective (b) on reaching the Intermediate Objective (c) whenever requested by the planes."[43]

The ability of ground-based units to cooperate in this plan proved inadequate. On the second day of the battle the 50th Aero Squadron attempted liaison with the 90th Division. Their missions did not succeed because the infantry failed to show panels or fire flares when the aircrew fired their signals. Crews from the squadron made another attempt two days later. This sortie only succeeded because the crew descended low enough to identify the American troops by the color of their uniforms. The infantry had again failed to display their panels. On the same day the squadron's attempt to spot for a local artillery unit also failed because the battery refused to display its panels when signaled.[44]

The chief of US Air Service answered the need for training American ground troops to work with their aviators with the establishment of an infantry contact school for front-line soldiers. The three-day course taught the use of signal panels, rockets, and flares.[45] The school worked and contact patrol work improved somewhat, although there were still too many incidents in which the aircraft had to descend to a danger-ously low level to identify troops because the infantry did not display its panels.[46] Some of these instances had less to do with training than they did with the failure of US Army Service to supply front-line units with the necessary signal panels.[47]

Despite the continued failures to establish contact with soldiers in the line, units flying infantry-contact missions established firm personal and communication connections with the Army's senior command structure. The 50th Aero Squadron stationed officers at both the 82nd and 90th Division Headquarters who kept in touch with the squadron and the chief of Air Service, 1st Army Corps. The unit's crews checked with corps headquarters for updated requests prior to heading for the lines at the start of each mission and at its conclusion dropped written reports to the division and corps command posts.[48]

The war's last major offensive, the Meuse-Argonne campaign, brought signs of hope that American forces might succeed at infantry-contact work as well as a possible explanation for some of their earlier failures. On September 28, two days after the offensive opened, the infantry finally came through by putting out its panels in response to a signal from a 50th Aero Squadron DH-4. The Gorrell report's official account of this operation remarked that the long-awaited display "did much to further the enthusiasm for this work and to bring about a closer approach to the theoretical but unobtainable perfection."[49] A later mission the same day revived the unit's doubts about the strength of its partnership with the infantry. Lieutenants McCook and Lockwood put their aircraft down in No-Man's-Land during a contact patrol over the 77th Division. French forces picked up the pair and sent them walking back towards an American command post "under the guidance of some American negro troopers."[50] Talking to his escort along the way, McCook learned that his unit had never received training in how to cooperate with aircraft and, in fact, had no idea what flares shot from an airplane meant.[51]

In spite of lackluster responses from the troops, the 50th Aero Squadron's infantry-liaison fliers continued to make bold attempts to prove the value of the contact patrol. Their most audacious venture came during the Meuse-Argonne campaign while trying to locate and supply the famous "Lost Battalion." By early October the state of infantry-liaison work in US military forces had improved somewhat. The infantry occasionally showed flares, although 50th Aero Squadron crews learned that ground forces had received orders to fire flares only at night. Consequently, the squadron had to continue its low-level flights in order to come close enough to identify uniforms, a method that drove the unit's success rate up to 50 percent.[52] On October 5, the squadron received orders to attempt to establish contact with the 1st Battalion of the 308th Infantry Division, which had become cut off and surrounded by German forces. The stranded infantry force, under the command of Maj. Charles Whittlesey, sent a carrier pigeon back to American lines with information on its position and the squadron responded by dispatching two DH-4s in the morning and two in the afternoon to carry messages, chocolate, and cigarettes to the "Lost Battalion." The planes also carried propaganda leaflets to drop on German troops passed en route and copies of the latest issue of *Stars and Stripes*.[53] Whether Whittlesey's troops displayed their signal panels or the white cloth strips were simply obscured by battlefield smoke has been disputed, but the 50th Aero Squadron's patrols returned without having located the trapped soldiers.[54]

The squadron record characterized the continuing aid effort as the "outstanding feature of the day's work" on October 6. On that day the unit lost several aircraft as a consequence of low-altitude operations. German forces brought down two crews uninjured, a third severely injured, and Lts. Harold Goettler and Erwin Bleckley killed in action. Goettler, the pilot, and Bleckley, a former artillery officer serving as his observer, lost their lives while barely skimming the treetops, well within range of deadly German ground fire.[55] For this sacrifice the two later received posthumous Medals of Honor, the only crew to win the nation's highest award for an infantry-contact patrol.[56] Two days after Goettler and Bleckley lost their lives, the Lost Battalion displayed a panel east of the location recorded on their earlier pigeon message. Knowledge of their true location led to the realization that many of the supply bundles the 50th had dropped over the preceding three days had fallen on positions either held by German troops or inaccessible to the American infantry due to their proximity to German forces and consequent vulnerability to sniper fire.[57]

Weather and contests for aerial supremacy interfered as much with infantry-liaison sorties as they did with every other aspect of military aviation. Bad weather and an increase in enemy aerial activity in the week following the squadron's work with the Lost Battalion forced the

50th Aero Squadron to assign a protection plane to each contact patrol mission, primarily to guard the low-flying aircraft against German fighters, but also to increase reconnaissance efficiency at the front.[58] German forces facing American units had provided this same kind of protection for their own two-seaters engaged on photography, reconnaissance, and artillery-regulation missions for nearly two years. In the spring of 1918, *Luftstreitkräfte* commanders assigned *Schutzstaffeln* to direct ground-attack duties in anticipation of their return to the offensive. Escorted infantry-contact missions continued throughout the remaining weeks of the war, American results improving somewhat as the 78th Division's troops learned to use its flares when called upon. In October, the war of movement forced the 50th Aero Squadron to concentrate on infantry-liaison missions almost exclusively. On October 19 the unit's record book noted that contact patrols "constituted the entire endeavor of the day" and that infantry-contact had become "the premier duty of the squadron."[59] Three days later, the immediate need for infantry-liaison patrols had slowed down, offering the 50th Aero Squadron an opportunity to practice their skills with French soldiers at Nairlieu.[60] Contact patrols resumed in November as American troops advanced rapidly across France, with ten more flown between November 1 and 6, the squadron's final days of operations.[61]

After the war ended, 2/Lt. Joseph E. Eaton assessed the effectiveness of various contact-patrol methods.[62] Eaton characterized the primary method taught to American forces—the display of panels—as "unreliable with the Fifth Corps, seldom working at all, and when it did, giving false information."[63] He complained that the infantry "would seldom respond, almost never in attack; and in lulls, if panels were shown, they were generally misleading."[64] Eaton attributed the soldiers' lack of willingness to cooperate to the common complaint that during an attack they were afraid enemy aircraft would also spot the panels and immediately respond by bringing artillery fire down upon them. Misleading information provided during less active periods he blamed on troops putting signal panels in convenient places rather than at the actual location of the front line. He noted that, "in a sheltered place, usually rolling country, one or more panels might be shown in the first line or several hundred yards to the rear. The rear panel, if in a more exposed position of the line might be set a quarter or even half a mile from the front line."[65] During operations conducted over a two-week period in October, Eaton asserted that the infantry never once gave exact information identifying the location of the front line.[66] He rated a second method of locating the troops—flying up and down the line in an effort to attract machine-gun fire—only slightly better than looking for panels. Airplane crews were frequently unable to precisely locate the machine gun firing upon them. Furthermore, just as many friendly as enemy troops fired upon airplanes and the obvious danger of losing aircraft and crews when one or more of the machine guns found its mark, rendered this method largely ineffective.[67]

Flying low enough to identify the troops by their uniforms, the third infantry-liaison method Eaton examined, proved "generally successful." This, of course, echoed the experience of the 50th Aero Squadron during the war's two final offensives and several years of Allied experience, but Eaton's report provided more exact detail. "Depending on visibility," he wrote, "brown uniforms were to be clearly distinguished at 300 meters, indistinctly at 400, and doubtfully at 500 meters or above."[68] Eaton inadvertently complimented the German military's choice of *feldgrau* (field gray) uniforms, observing their troops "were much more difficult to see on account of the superior blending qualities."[69] Furthermore, German troops occasionally fired rockets in an effort to confuse American aircrews trying to locate the line, particularly if the American aircraft fired on them and a false signal offered the prospect of relief from attack.[70]

Eaton's report on the mixed effectiveness of infantry-liaison techniques reflected not only American but British wartime experiences. In July 1915, based on the success of experiments conducted the previous May, the British ordered flares for the infantry to use when contact-patrol aircraft signaled for the location of the line.[71] Use of flares in combat proved effective when troops *actually* fired them, but early on those occasions proved sporadic at best and British fliers reported, just as the Americans had, that their best results came when they descended low enough to identify troops by the color of their uniforms.[72] With training and experience, the British situation improved and, over August 23 and 24, 1916, No. 3 Squadron observers reported that infantry using flares had allowed them to locate the front line "with almost perfect clearness."[73]

> At one point, north of Delville Wood, an observer (Second Lieutenant F. E. S. Phillips) saw that at 6:40 P.M. the line of our infantry, marked by the blazing of fourteen flares, was still under shrapnel fire from our own artillery. He flew back at once and dropped an urgent message giving the information to corps head-quarters. The barrage was ultimately lifted a hundred yards. The pilot returned to the fighting, and the observer completed his map and dropped this and a further message which were received at Corps head-quarters at 8:00 P.M. The map showed that a part of the 14th Division was held up on the right of Delville wood. The wood was finally cleared of the enemy by the division next morning, August the 25th, and the forward progress of the troops to their various objectives was once more forwarded and reported from the air, step by step.[74]

Later in the Somme battle, on September 15, 1916, Canadians advancing on Courcelette reported the capture of the town by lighting a semicircle of flares around the village.[75] Similar news came from troops firing flares on October 23, 1916, to indicate extension of the British position around Le Transloy.[76]

The imaginative commander could also use his infantry fliers to deceive the enemy. During the battle of the Somme, the possibility of the German lines breaking, thus allowing British cavalry to operate prompted British planners to attempt to send false information to the enemy. Knowing German front-line troops would hear and retransmit the message, a British aircrew flew along the line sending the wireless transmission: "Enemy second line of defence has been captured on a front of 6,000 yards. British cavalry is now passing through in pursuit of the demoralized enemy."[77]

The lack of a workable two-way, real-time method of interaction between front-line troops and their generals in the rear during the rapid movement of an attack made aviators a critical link in the communication chain. *General* Ernst von Hoeppner, commander of German aviation during the war's final two years, remarked that, "infantry aviation had become the most valuable means of liaison between the commander and his infantry."[78] The British official air historian agreed, characterizing infantry liaison, "one of the most important roles of aircraft," adding that, "contact patrol had given results which made it clear that this new demand on the air would be a feature of all future ground operations."[79] Americans, who had come to the air war late, set out to learn the art of infantry liaison early in their time on the Western Front. By the November 1918 armistice the work had become "a matter of the day's routine," though "it had not been perfected."[80] Infusing ground troops with the necessary discipline to look for and cooperate with air observers remained a challenge for aviation and ground-based commanders at the conclusion of hostilities. When troops did respond the technique worked well, providing vital battlefield intelligence in as near to real-time as was possible to commanders in the First World War. And they were grateful for the help.[81] The ultimate solution to the battlefield communication issue, two-way voice communication between troops in the vanguard of the attack and command centers in the rear, would have to wait for the next war.[82] Without radio, military forces did the best job possible with the technology available to ensure a regular flow of information. As well as aviators did keeping track of the infantry during attacks, they excelled to an even greater degree in assisting battle planners with up-to-date maps and aerial photographs.

CHAPTER 6

"Two Men and a Darkroom under the Stairs": Aerial Reconnaissance and Aerial Photography[1]

In aerial matters, the first requirement is an adequate supply of efficient artillery, photographic and contact patrol machines.
—Sir Douglas Haig, "Comments on Meeting of *Col.* Bares, French *Aviation Militaire*, with Members of British Air Board, November 1, 1916"

Never mind if the Boches do get the pilots in the chasse planes— the camera must be saved.
—Granville Pollock, "He was Lost Far Up in the Air," *Muskogee Times-Democrat*, April 16, 1918

Although artillery observation accomplished much tactically, aerial reconnaissance successes during the early weeks of the war demonstrated that airplanes and balloons possessed strategic worth as well. Its reconnaissance function put aviation at the forefront of intelligence gathering and intelligence officers came to rely heavily on aerial reconnaissance. As reconnaissance squadrons matured by adding photography to their duties, and as the skills of photo interpreters sharpened, aerial photography wove itself into the fabric of the war deeply enough to nearly dictate the nature of the conflict. From the first day of the war, fliers integrated themselves fully into the information-gathering system. The information that they provided to senior command officers became part of a complex collection process that included interpretation of statements made by prisoners of war, spy reports, captured documents, telephone and wireless intercepts, and a host of other sources. Aerial reconnaissance soon became a starting point in the daily quest to determine what lay in the army's front. Immediately following the war's outbreak, airmen proved their worth to both sides, on the Western Front when aerial reports provided French and British troops with the opportunity to halt early German advances at the Marne River, and on the Eastern Front when German reconnaissance fliers spotted oncoming Russian forces in time to prepare for the battle of Tannenberg. Indeed, *Gen.* Walter von Eberhardt wrote on the function of the aerial observers:

> The reconnaissance flier is the command's most important resource in clarifying the location of the adversary. By virtue of his great radius of action and his considerable speed, he is in the position deep inside enemy territory to recognize early the intention of the opponent by determining the transport movements and assemblies.[2]

The key role aerial reconnaissance played in the outcome of these critical early engagements did not immediately reveal itself. The British Royal Flying Corps' first wartime reconnaissance report nearly confirmed the opinion of Ferdinand Foch, the supreme Allied commander during the war's last months, who characterized aviation as militarily "worthless."[3] Filed on August 19, 1914, by No. 4 Squadron's Lt. G. W. Mapplebeck, the summary certainly did not inspire confidence in the role aviation might play in the war. Taking off from Maubeuge, site of Napoleon's first-ever military balloon reconnaissance flights, Mapplebeck appears to have been lost much of the time. Intending to "branch off on arriving at Nivelles," he missed his objective and flew instead over Brussels, which he did not recognize. Using a small-scale map Mapplebeck eventually located himself over Ottignies and then Gembloux, where he reported "a small body of cavalry moving faster than a walk in a south-easterly direction." Reporting that he had "great difficulty reading the large scale map ... [but] very little with the small," Mapplebeck rated the small-scale map "simpler to use for cross country flying, though not so good for detailed observation."[4]

Much to the relief of his commanders, Mapplebeck and other fliers honed their flying and reconnaissance skills as the war progressed. They accustomed themselves to the landscape and no longer found themselves lost. Although the basic science of "observe and report" reconnaissance remained relatively static throughout the war, aviation commanders did introduce some minor refinements. British and French armies and their aviators had practiced aerial reconnaissance in prewar maneuvers, but had not developed either the tools necessary to wartime operations or a coordinated system designed to maximize the value of the information they gathered. Within a week of Mapplebeck's August 14 narrative, No. 4 Squadron introduced a more uniform aerial reconnaissance report form. Initially prepared by hand, the form's header assigned a number to the reconnaissance sortie, noted the date, plane number, the hour the mission started and ended, and the names of the crew. Below the header the form contained columns showing the time, place, and things observed, such as the number of trains visible, the various railroad stations in operation and the status of important military objects, e.g. bridges, and the reference map used during the reconnaissance.[5] Royal Flying Corps Headquarters ultimately standardized the reconnaissance report initially developed and refined at the squadron level for use throughout the service.[6]

The condition of maps presented the British Expeditionary Force with a far more important challenge than standardizing the RFC's aerial reconnaissance report forms. The Army had yet to print and distribute the highly detailed maps necessary for military operations in the field. In the absence of that level of specificity, aircrews rudimentarily noted their observations by locating enemy troops or hostile targets as "immediately N of the first 'U' in FLEURUS," or "¼ mile S of E in FLEURUS."[7] Fliers gave their commanders an idea of the number of troops they observed by calculating the length of the unit, e.g. "mounted troops (about 800 yards long)."[8] Pilots and observers also frequently included small sketches of the enemy's positions as part of their reports.[9] Redesigning the maps began with the basic step of coloring in the roads to provide at least minimal detail.[10] By the end of September 1914, with the aid of aerial scouting reports, the British were issuing situation maps revised nearly daily.[11]

The early British reconnaissance reports also reflected the lack of any organized system of communication between British and French units during the war's first month. In those early weeks British fliers devoted as much time and attention to locating friendly Belgian and French units as they did the enemy.[12] Sometimes a pilot benefitted simply by finding himself in the right place at the right time. Lieutenant Bonham-Carter, of No. 4 Squadron, for instance, reported landing during an early August mission and having a chance conversation with the "GOC XVIII Corps," in which he learned "that the French Cavalry encountered hostile infantry [the previous] afternoon and evening N. of Mons and Charleroi Canal."[13] As they gained confidence in their own ability to assess the tactical situation on the ground, aircrew members began doing more than relaying facts, adding to their reports informed opinions about outcomes and conditions.[14]

Demand followed the development of capacity, and as military leaders began to appreciate the need for the very specific level of detail modern warfare generated and the value of information provided by their airmen, ground troops clamored for more. Commanders began requesting general aerial reconnaissance assistance, in the form of aircraft assigned to perform tactical work for the corps, as well as specific missions aimed at obtaining detailed information about particular objectives, e.g. the number of trains entering or leaving a specific station.[15] The need to collect information on an ongoing and systematic basis next led the RFC to develop a standard set of instructions designed to maximize the value of its observer's report. The new orders detailed the kind of things pilots and observers should look for on a mission, with specific attention paid to details concerning railways, columns (infantry and cavalry, especially), transport, barges, and aerodromes. The instructions were printed on a card crew members could carry with them during flight. The RFC began by ordering five hundred cards.[16]

Though the organization of uniform reporting methods marked a step in the right direction, an intelligence system that relied on human memory and written messages could never provide the level of detail necessary to effective military planning. The constant maneuvering of troops on the Western Front during the war's first weeks had masked the need for anything more than the simple details and appraisals that fliers brought back for their commanders. When forces on the Western Front dug trenches late in 1914 they changed the military situation dramatically by preventing cavalry from fulfilling their traditional reconnaissance role.[17] Immobility on the ground enhanced the value of aviators' reports. Even those commanders whose careers had long been associated with the cavalry, no longer had any choice but to rely on aerial reconnaissance missions as their primary source of real-time intelligence.[18] The additional time offered to digest knowledge about the enemy brought with it the need to verify and expand on the reconnaissance crews' reports more reliably than with human eye and memory. If senior commanders were to develop the reconnaissance material to its maximum worth, they required a medium capable of recording and reporting everything visible, not just the high points considered important by junior officers with limited training and appreciation of the strategic picture. Wartime airmen thus began photographing what they reconnoitered.[19]

The need for photographs brought with it a need for a better camera. Prior to the war, the Royal Flying Corps possessed a single fuselage-mounted box camera.[20] By the time the fighting started they had broken it.[21] When the British Expeditionary Force left for France, the RFC possessed six Airplex cameras with 12-inch lenses.[22] In addition to their issued equipment, several pilots and observers furnished their own cameras. According to its official historian, No. 3 Squadron engaged in aerial photography experiments early in 1914; indeed, historian Nicholas Watkis contends that a lieutenant in this unit, George Pretyman, took the RFC's first wartime aerial photographs during a September 15, 1914 sortie. (Squadron records do not substantiate the claim.)[23] The unit's war diary does confirm the assignment of British aerial photography pioneer Sgt. Frederick Laws to the squadron immediately upon the outbreak of war, although whether Laws performed such duties while with the unit is unclear.[24]

Regardless, by the end of 1914, the Royal Flying Corps' senior commanders and their Army counterparts began to show interest in aerial photography. French successes in this new branch of military science in the war's early months had attracted their attention and No. 3 Squadron's commanding officer, Maj. William Geoffrey Hanson Salmond, received an order to study French methods.[25] Based on that examination, Gen. David Henderson, the former director of Military Intelligence who headed the Royal Flying Corps in the field, ordered the establishment of an experimental photographic section. The RFC's handful of photography enthusiasts made up the new unit assigned to design a practical aerial camera.[26] Within sixty days they introduced the Type A, which No. 3 Squadron used for the first time over the lines on March 2, 1915.[27] In the next week, as the British Expeditionary Force prepared for the battle of Neuve Chapelle, Nos. 2 and 3 Squadrons photographed German-held territory in front of the First Army, to a depth of 700–1,500 yards.[28] The photographs provided the basis for a new set of 1:8,000-scale maps, each one marked with the trench lines visible on the RFC's photographs. These maps allowed First Army commander, Sir Douglas Haig, to position his forces and assets in preparation for the attack and to anticipate what his German opponents might do in response. Each of Haig's corps received 1,000–1,500 copies of the newly annotated maps to use in planning its infantry and artillery attacks.[29]

For the first time since the war opened, the British attacked with a thorough understanding of what lay in front of them.[30] This detailed aerial view of the ground on which the battle would be fought marked a transition in organized warfare, a momentous step forward from mounted cavalry patrols whose ground-bound reconnaissance missions were incomplete at best, limited to geography not occupied by the enemy and comparatively slow. Airmen, on the other hand, could cross the lines and penetrate the enemy's back areas daily in search of data and deliver their reports in close to real time. Army commanders soon began to schedule or postpone operations based on the availability of aerial reconnaissance.[31] The effective use of aerial photographs at Neuve Chapelle apparently convinced the commander of the British Expeditionary Force in France, Sir John French, to take a personal interest in the quality and accuracy of the views he and his officers received.[32] The stagnation and frustration inherent in trench warfare thus gave birth to the mass production of military intelligence, a signpost on the road to the information age.[33]

Commanders on the Western Front were not alone in their appreciation of the potential value of aerial reconnaissance and photography. At the same time that John French and Douglas Haig were preparing the attack on Neuve Chapelle, Allied forces deployed in the Mediterranean were attempting to implement Winston Churchill's overly ambitious and ultimately ill-fated plan to achieve victory in the east by forcing the Dardanelles. Considering the possibility that the desired naval solution might not be enough and that an Army invasion of the Gallipoli peninsula might become necessary, British Secretary of State for War Lord Horatio Kitchener telegraphed Gen. William Birdwood instructing him that he "should not commit (himself) to any enterprise of this class without aerial reconnaissance and ample covering fire by the Fleet."[34]

Tactical aerial reconnaissance and supporting fire from the sea, while valuable aids in a successful landing, could not completely direct how and where to proceed once ashore. Neither the British nor the French had surveyed the geography of the Gallipoli peninsula since the Crimean War in the 1850s.[35] Frustrated by the inadequacy of the only map available to him, Maj. W. V. Nugent, Royal Field Artillery, set out to draft his own by using an early and very incomplete set of aerial photographs and tracing the images onto drawing paper using a flèche.[36] No. 3 Squadron, Royal Naval Air Service, led by Commander Charles Samson, arrived in March and began to supplement these photos using the single Goertz-Anschutz folding camera they had brought from France.[37] Samson eventually upgraded his equipment with the addition of a camera borrowed from a French unit that arrived in the area in May 1915.[38] Using this equipment, Samson's squadron achieved "wonderful results," enough for Samson to suggest that an officer in each unit "should be properly trained to take, develop and print photographs properly and quickly."[39]

Like their counterparts on the Western Front, the aerial photographers operating over Gallipoli soon discovered that photogrammetry, the science of pinpointing the exact geographic location of an object from its position on a photograph, involved more than simply taking pictures. The infantry needed reasonably accurate information about where to find the enemy and the strength and depth of their defenses. The artillery required even more precise detail to pinpoint targets hidden from the gun crew's line of sight and located at a variety of distances and elevations. Aerial photographers had the potential to provide this information more completely and accurately than any other source, provided the crews could achieve the requisite degree of precision. Responding to this need, reconnaissance pilots learned the vital necessity of maintaining their aircraft straight and level at 6,000 feet in order to keep the resulting photos in proportionate scale to one another.[40] The photographer had to shoot a set of reference points in order to put in a vertical plane those and all other places recorded on the picture, after which the primary reference points required triangulation to fix their exact positions on the resulting map.[41] Neophyte interpreters initially had problems locating the same location on different photos owing to the variety of angles produced by bobbing aircraft even when the photos were taken from the same altitude. They overcame this problem by means of overlapping images, and eventually with use of the stereoscope.[42] Ground technicians aided interpretation of images by developing an "adjusting camera" that projected images directly onto a piece of tracing cloth, from which they could extract desired details from photos and print them on maps.[43] RNAS aircrews eventually amassed enough photos that surveyors were able to produce a 1:10,000-scale map that became the basic view of the Gallipoli peninsula on top of which regularly updated overlays showed changes in enemy defenses and dispositions.[44]

The British Army supplemented its store of diagrams produced locally by aerial photography with a series of 1:25,000-scale maps captured from the Turks. While these represented an improvement over what had been available prior to the arrival of the RNAS in the region, planners regarded maps produced from aerial photographs as superior in detail and they distributed them throughout both British and French forces operating in Gallipoli.[45] Colonel Frederick Sykes, who had headed up the Royal Flying Corps in France during 1914, inspected the aerial units in the Dardanelles in July 1915 and recommended the expansion of their work through the addition of six photographers, each equipped with what had by then become the "standard RFC camera and material."[46]

These pioneering efforts on the Western Front and at Gallipoli, impressive though they were, represented a late start for the British who lagged behind the French in developing either an appreciation for the possibilities of aerial photography or the capacity to take and interpret photographs. The French had begun experimenting with aerial reconnaissance and photography prior to the war and by the end of 1915 Maj. Robert Brooke-Popham, commander of No. 3 Wing, noted their use of "magic lanterns" [an early form of projector] to interpret aerial photos.[47] By this time the French were also equipping each *escadrille* attached to a corps with a photo lorry in which technicians developed and printed photos immediately upon receipt from the crews as they returned from their missions. Aircrew delivered finished photographs to commanders at headquarters who scrutinized them for potential targets and any other useful information and then used them to continually update their maps.[48]

The German *Luftfahrtruppen* (aerial troops) also led the British in development of aerial reconnaissance capability and in building a photo capacity.[49] As early as 1911 German airmen began practicing with the artillery to fix the location of opposing batteries on aerial photographs, and aerial photographs dating from the war's opening weeks survive in German archives.[50] Photos taken at German airfields early in the war show crews about to depart on reconnaissance sorties equipped with cameras, and members of an *Artillerie Flieger Abteilung* (artillery aviation section) standing outside the unit's mobile darkroom in October 1915. Such evidence demonstrates that the Luftfahrtruppen organized facilities for the rapid acquisition and reproduction of aerial photographs at the same pace or earlier than the Allies.[51] Germany refined its photo reconnaissance capacity to a high standard, working out, among other issues, precise tables for aperture settings that changed depending on light conditions at different times of day and during different seasons of the year.[52] By January 1917 the office of the commanding general of the Air Force (*Kommandeur General der Luftstreitkräfte* or *Kogenluft*) had compiled sufficient data to issue complete aerial photography manuals for its lighter- and heavier-than-air branches.[53]

Advances in techniques and equipment continued throughout the war, spurred on by increasing demand for aerial photographs.[54] Though slow at first to appreciate the significance of aerial photography to operations in the field, British staff officers, once convinced, "maintained an unswerving loyalty to air photography and pressed the RFC for more and more photographs."[55] *General* Joseph Joffre, commander of the French forces, also requested a constant supply of British aerial photographs in addition to those he received from his own airmen.[56] Senior officers already recognized the need to print and distribute air photos and the maps drawn or updated from them while their air arms were still struggling to deliver even the smallest supply. The British General Staff initially organized a small staff of draftsmen to analyze what came in from the RFC's squadrons.[57] They distributed copies of the photos even to the smallest units in the field, including artillery observation posts, so they might have a better idea of the position and nature of potential targets.[58] In a report to Gen. Sefton Brancker dated April 16, 1916, photographic expert Charles Campbell made camera equipment recommendations for each squadron and further recommended the creation of a photographic section within each RFC wing. Campbell concluded his report by suggesting "as photography has assumed such importance in the work of a pilot, that the practical examination for flying officer[s] include taking a good photograph of a given area."[59] Germany also put photography on its pilot tests, requiring the cadet to take successful photos from 6,600 feet.[60]

In addition to educating its aircrews in photography, the Royal Flying Corps introduced organizational refinements to ensure proper systematic photographic coverage of the entire front. British corps squadrons were given responsibility for the area within five miles of the front line on which their corps operated. Army wings received responsibility for areas within enemy territory beyond the five-mile line.[61] By the end of 1916, aerial reconnaissance and photography staff had seen their influence spread throughout the Army to such a degree that Lt. Col. Lionel Charlton, General Staff for Division of Air Organization wrote to the general officer commanding Training Brigade, advising that there would soon be "a very large increase in the (RFC's) personnel for photographic duties."[62] At the same time the Royal Flying Corps updated its official manual, *Notes on the Interpretation of Aeroplane Photographs* (the original of which had been translated from France's manual), to reflect the latest developments only to revise it again just four months later.[63] The March 1917 edition treated the work of reconnaissance and photography crews as a routine part of the military process, recommending that the manual's contents should be read in conjunction with another official publication that analyzed German Army doctrine.[64] In addition, the manual's intricate examination of the data analysts could extract by considering light and shadow and by comparing the appearance of an area over time illustrated the degree of sophistication the science of photo interpretation had achieved. After just two and a half years of war, and just on the eve of the American entry into the conflict, the airman's role as an intelligence gatherer had become thoroughly embedded in military procedures. Aerial reconnaissance reports and photographs had attained a level of usefulness unforeseen at the outbreak of hostilities and were now an integral part of the war planning process.

To support their planning, the progress of attacks once underway, and their artillery fire, military commanders came to expect regularly updated maps. The multiplicity of maps conceived and published nearly on a daily basis illustrates the variety of needs to satisfy.[65] The French and the Belgians had a slight initial advantage on the Western Front as the fighting took place on their territory and their armies took the field armed with prewar survey data, though the information was not always reliable.[66] The French used the 1:2,500-scale cadastral plan of the communes made between 1830 and 1850 as their foundation and from that rendered a 1:80,000-scale *Carte d'État Major* (Major State Map) for use as their most common topographical map. The entire map covered some 274 sheets, each one numbered and named for the principal town included and marked on its four borders with the names of the adjacent sheets. Likely in anticipation of a general European war, the French had revised the *Carte d'État Major* between 1912 and 1914. Paris served as the map's center. Cartographers laid out the sheets using five-meter interval hachures to provide relief. Prominent geodetic points, such as church steeples and water towers, were located by existing surveys to a maximum location and elevation error of two meters. It took only months of war for both sides' artillery to destroy many of these landmarks, a development that made aerial reconnaissance updates all the more important to all the combatants.

Building on the *Carte d'État Major*, which the French had prepared under conditions of peace, the 1:20,000-scale *Plan Directeur* (Plan Director) provided the trench, machine-gun, and artillery battery locations, and other specific battlefield detail military commanders required. American forces eventually used the *Plan Directeur* as well. The British military issued its own 1:10,000-scale trench map, which imitated the *Plan Directeur*, and the two regularly updated guides became vital aids to the Allied artillery. British infantry units kept abreast of the same information through a 1:5,000-scale version of the trench map. Both renderings of the trench map bore a date of issue and were color-coded with geographic detail in black and brown, with German trenches highlighted in blue and Allied trenches in red.

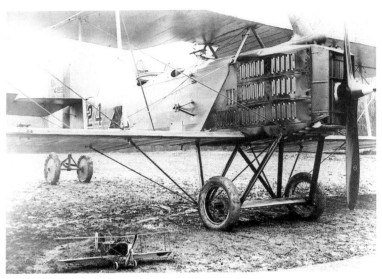

Above: Breguet 14A2 4891 of the USAS 96th Aero Squadron sets alongside an early scale model of the same. The Breguet 14A2, along with the Salmson 2A2, formed the mainstay of French and American reconnaissance squadrons during 1918. The number "24" aft of the squadron insignia is a unit number. The letters "JAS," possibly the initials of one of the crew members, appear beneath the pilot's cockpit. *(San Diego Air & Space Museum)*

Below: Another 96th Aero Squadron Breguet 14A2, this one carrying the unit number "7," climbs out on takeoff. This angle provides a good view of the USAS red-blue-white national cockade. *(San Diego Air & Space Museum)*

An American 88th Aero Squadron Salmson 2A2 crew loads a 50 cm camera into the observer's cockpit prior to a photo mission. The Salmson, like the Breguet 14, provided a rugged photo platform capable of withstanding considerable combat damage while putting up a substantial defense using its observer's twin Lewis guns and the pilot's single,

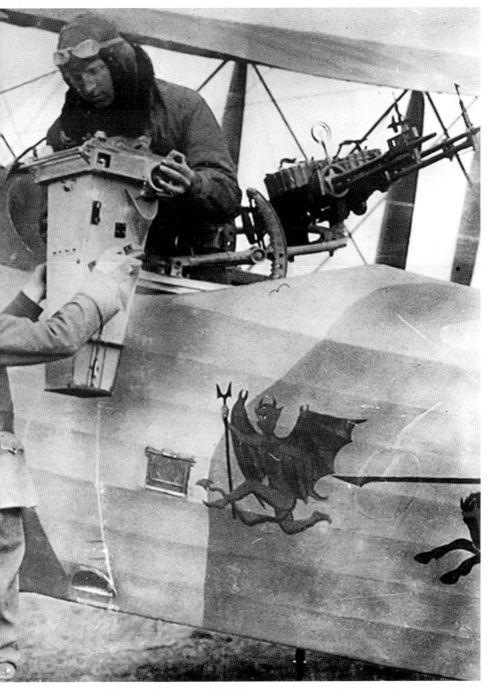

synchronized Vickers. The letters "TSF" (transmission sans fibre = wireless transmission) on the lower wing root indicate the Salmson also carried a radio transmitter *(Gorrell Report, NARA, via Terrance J. Finnegan)*

Above: As is evident in this photo of a USAS Balloon Section Caquot balloon blowing up, hydrogen-filled balloons were highly flammable. Balloons were frequently targeted both by German fighter planes and artillery. Their tendency to attract enemy artillery fire, in particular, made balloons unpopular neighbors among infantry units *(Al Zakrzewski via Aaron Weaver)*

Below: A 96th Aero Squadron members and visitors pose beside one of the unit's Breguet 14A2s. The word "Photo" beneath the cockpit indicated the aircraft was equipped with a camera *(San Diego Air & Space Museum)*

Above: Salmson 11A of the 91st Aero Squadron, USAS, mounts its camera on the observer's scarf ring usually reserved for one or two Lewis guns *(Photo via Colin Owers)*

Below: A Salmson 2A2 flies past a Caquot balloon. Although the dark quality of the photo makes it impossible to identify the Salmson's wing markings, the order of the rudder striping is French. That, however, is inconclusive as many French aircraft sold to the USAS still carried their original markings. The cockade on the balloon appears to be French as well *(Photo via Colin Owers)*

Above: This cutaway provides an excellent view of the camera installation inside the observer's "office" of this Salmson 2A2 *(Photo via Colin Owers)*

Below: German 70 cm, 50 cm, and 25 cm focal length aerial cameras *(Photo via Neal O'Connor)*

Above: The ARI (Avion Renault) served in both French and American reconnaissance squadrons until replaced by the far superior Salmson and Breguet *(Photo via James Davilla)*

Below: A balloon crew gets ready to go aloft. Note the maps in the basket's front pocket and the parachute cone container attached to the side *(Al Zakrzewski via Aaron Weaver)*

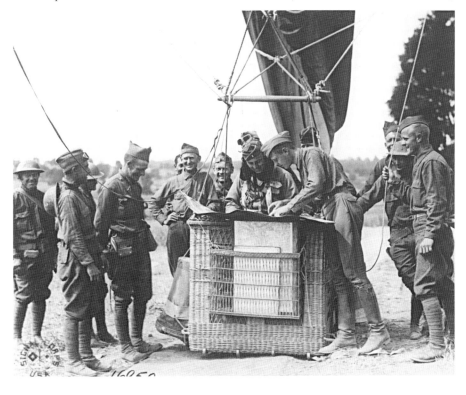

Left: Ltn. Wilhelm Griebsch, the only German pilot to earn the Pour le Mérite for aerial reconnaissance, flew 345 long-distance reconnaissance missions in France and Macedonia between 1915 and 1918 before finally receiving his Blue Max on September 30, 1918. The eight observers who won Prussia's highest award also flew hundreds of missions prior to being recognized for their achievements. *(Photo via Neal O'Connor)*

Below: An 8th Balloon Company crew holds down its Caquot balloon as a French officer appears to supervise. When aloft the elephant ear stabilizers inflated and pointed the gasbag in the direction of the wind. *(Photo via Cross & Cockade Journal)*

Above: Balloons were frequently bedded down in spaces surrounded by trees taking advantage of the natural camouflage to protect them from hostile artillery fire. *(Al Zakrzewski via Aaron Weaver)*

Below: A fine profile of a Breguet 14 in French service. *(Alan Toelle via Aaron Weaver)*

The ubiquitous R.E.8, nicknamed "Harry Tate" by its crews in honor of a popular music hall comedian of the day, formed the mainstay of British reconnaissance, photography and observation units after it replaced the B.E.2c beginning in the late

spring of 1917. Harry Tates soldiered on until the armistice, way past their "sell by" dates. In the last weeks of the war Bristol Fighters began to replace the R.E.8 in some units. *(Photo via Les Rogers)*

Left: An American Brequet 14, unit number 10, flying over the lines. *(Photo via Steve Ruffin)*

Below: The extensive damage done by the war: an aerial photo typical of the conflict's last years showing trenches, barbed-wire entanglements, and lots and lots of shell holes. Photos like this one were used by both sides to plan attack and defensive moves, target the artillery, and as the basis for the millions of maps printed during the war. *(Étude et Exploitation des Photographies Aériennes via Terrence J. Finnegan)*

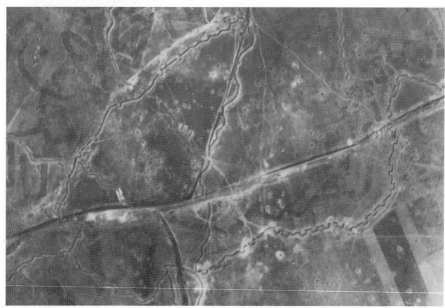

Above: Salmson 2A2 5247, no. 3. *(Photo via Colin Owers)*

Above: A Salmson 2A2 taking off on a mission. *(Photo via Colin Owers)*

Above: The Sopwith 1½ Strutter, a British design that served not only the RFC and RNAS, but also extensively with French reconnaissance and bombing escadrilles and, briefly, with the US Air Service before more modern and superior equipment became available in the form of the Breguet 14 and the Salmson 2A2. French manufacturers built most Sopwith 1½ Strutters that served with French units, as well as those that later equipped American squadrons. *(Photo via James Davilla)*

Above (L–R) British aerial photography innovator C. D. M. Campbell. *(Photo from Roy Nesbit, Eyes of the RAF. Phoenix Mill, UK: Alan Sutton Publications, 1996, via Terrence J. Finnegan);* One of France's early aerial photographers, Eugene Pepin. *(Pepin Papers, MA&E, via Terrence J. Finnegan);* Paul-Louis Weiller, France's leading advocate for using deep-penetration aerial photography to plot strategy, commanded a group dedicated to that purpose in the war's final months. *(SHAA via Terrence J. Finnegan)*

Above (L–R): British and American aerial photography colleagues, Frederick Laws and Edward Steichen. After organizing much of the US Air Service's aerial photography efforts, Steichen went on to become one of the twentieth century's best-known photographers. *(Gorrell Report, NARA, via Terrence J. Finnegan)*; J. T. M. Moore-Brabazon, aerial photography pioneer and later Member of Parliament. *(Gorrell Report, NARA, via Terrence J. Finnegan)*

Above (L–R): Another camera-equipped Spad, this one a model 13 assigned to the US Air Service's 1st Pursuit Group's 94th Aero Squadron. *(USAFA McDermott Library Special Collections (SMS57) via Terrence J. Finnegan)*; Pursuit units were frequently drafted into aerial photography service when commanders needed photos in a hurry as is evidenced by this camera-equipped Spad 7. *(SHAA, 87.2859, via Terrence J. Finnegan)*

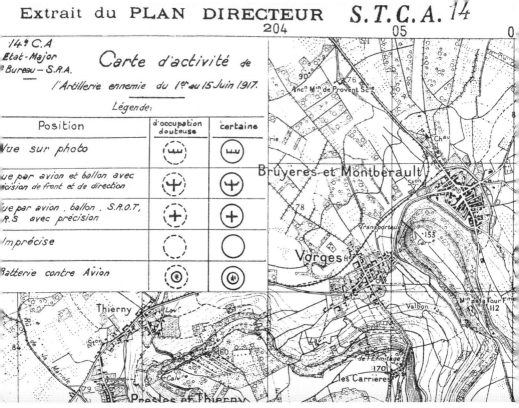

Above: An extract of the French Plan Directeur documenting enemy artillery activity June 1–15, 1917. Aerial photos provided the basis for regular updates to the Plan Directeur, the basic planning tool used by the French military throughout the war. *(SHAA via Terrence J. Finnegan)*

Right: This American war bond poster depicted the horrors of a hypothetical combined aerial and sea attack on New York City. Aircraft circle overhead while a U-boat passes the Statue of Liberty into New York Harbor. After the war, General Billy Mitchell used similar imagery in attempts to frighten the American public into pressuring their Congressmen into organizing an independent air force. *(George Marshall Foundation)*

Enlist Your Lens in the Air Service

IF you have a powerful photographic lens, put it to work for our men "over there;" let it disclose from the skies of France hidden machine-gun nests waiting to spread death among advancing American troops; let it save hundreds of American lives from being snuffed out in the trenches by shells from concealed batteries. An official report calls the situation "critical," brooking no delay.

What is especially desired at the present time are lenses of from 7 inches to 24 inches focal length and with speeds of from F 3.5 to F 7.7. Practically all lenses of this type will be purchased as soon as they can be found. The following are some of the foreign makes wanted: Carl Zeiss Tessars, Bausch & Lomb Tessars, Voigtlander Heliar, Euryplan, Cooke, Goerz, Bush, Ross, Ross-Zeiss, Krauss, Krauss-Zeiss, Steinheil-Isostigmar, Rodenstock. In addition, matched pairs of stereoscopic lenses, with speeds of F 4.5, focal lengths of 4½, 5, 5½, 6, 6½, and 7 inches, are needed.

If you are in doubt as to the value of your lens, ask the nearest photographer.

Remember that you can probably replace your Anastigmat lenses with others just as serviceable for you but not adaptable for the army. If you have a lens such as your army needs, send at once its description and the price you think fair to

SIGNAL EQUIPMENT No. 33
WASHINGTON, D. C.

This page contributed to the U. S. Army by the National Geographic Society

"Enlist Your Lens in the Air Service." Prior to the start of the First World War the best photographic lenses were made in Germany. When the United States entered the war the Air Service asked Americans to donate those superior German lenses for use in aerial photography. This ad originally appeared in the January 1918 issue of *National Geographic*.

The *Plan Directeur* covered an area five kilometers deep within Allied lines and ten kilometers deep within German-held territory. German troops took to the field equipped with 1:25,000- and 1:100,000-scale contour relief maps. Within Allied lines "sappers" (members of engineer corps trained in fortification or siege works) surveyed the ground, but aviators were responsible for surveying inaccessible geography behind the German front. In order to keep the maps up to date the latest vertical aerial photographs were projected onto a recent *Plan Directeur*, which the analyst then moved until the details of the photo matched the ground depicted on the map. The photo would then be drawn to scale and a new *Plan Directeur* produced. Using the latest aerial photos in conjunction with prisoner statements and other intelligence reports allowed cartographers at the French *Groupe de Canevas de Tir* (Artillery Survey Group) and the British Ordnance Survey to annotate the *Plan Directeur* and the equivalent trench maps with extensive detail on barbed wire, dugouts, machine-gun emplacements, communication trenches, and many other pieces of information that shed light on the disposition of the enemy's units and future intentions.[67]

Artillerists became accustomed to selecting target reference points using aerial photographs. As a routine part of the fire preparation process, they refreshed their maps with the latest pictures then transposed pertinent information onto target grids.[68] Using squared maps, French and American pilots and observers controlled artillery shoots by calling longs and shorts and rights and lefts to the batteries. British crews utilized their clock code for this purpose with the clock face laid over the same type of squared map, the target serving as the center point of the clock. From the German side of the lines two-seater crews flying at altitudes that made them nearly impervious to Allied interception provided their artillery batteries with similar data. During the war's last two years, American observers, learning from the Allied experience, were instructed that "aerial photographs are the basis for rough sketches in the air unit, provisional interpretation in the army corps and subsequent incorporation in the battle maps. The *destruction maps* are also made up from them."[69]

The inventory of maps by then available to the US Army command and US Air Service crews included:

- Special maps (1:50,000) used by the high command to track friendly infantry and artillery units with a separate series available in both 1:20,000 and 1:50,000 showing enemy artillery batteries
- General maps (1:20,000) of artillery objectives that combined information from aerial photographs, observation from the ground and statements made by German prisoners
- Maps of German secondary defensive organizations (1:10,000 and 1:20,000)
- Destruction maps (1:10,000) tracking daily progress in destruction of enemy objectives for use in attack preparation
- Aerial bombardment maps (1:80,000)[70]

Both sides coupled their attempts to obtain information about the enemy with extensive efforts at deception. Significant troop movements took place only at night when they would escape detection from reconnaissance aircraft, limited until late in the war to daytime operations, camouflage came into extensive use, and armies constructed fake gun emplacements, ammunition dumps, and airfields, complete with dummy aircraft, to entice the enemy into directing his artillery or bombers onto phony targets.[71] Occasionally the effort to hide came too late as when German artillery crews added camouflage to new batteries only after Allied aircraft had photographed the building work taking place.[72]

Countering attempts to hide from aerial reconnaissance crews necessitated the organization of aerial photo interpretation staffs. Analytical skills for this new branch of military intelligence, essentially nonexistent prior to 1914, sharpened considerably as a consequence of the war. During the first two years of the war, photographers' experiments included work on the first color aerial pictures and efforts to improve the timeliness with which aerial photos were received. Given the critical connection between the photo interpreter's work and the success of ground operations, the pursuit of real-time results became something of a holy grail in the development of aerial photography.[73] As important as commanders regarded the early receipt of intelligence, knowledgeable analysis counted for more. In May 1917, a British analyst demonstrated a high level of sophistication by picking up evidence of an upcoming German trench raid in a photo the RFC had taken showing what the interpreter determined to be a practice trench, identical to the aimed-for British trench. The Germans had dug the trench to rehearse the raid.[74] On another occasion a British airman photographed the interior of a German ammunition dugout under construction but not yet under roof, the kind of detail unavailable other than by aerial photography.[75]

Coalition warfare presented many challenges to British and French commanders, but in the area of aerial photo interpretation, it also offered an opportunity for the Allies to learn from one another. The British experience at the battle of the Somme revealed the need for a better system of analyzing and distributing information gleaned from aerial photographs. The RFC responded by largely adopting the system then in use by the French.[76] A joint study of aerial photographs conducted in the area of Dunkirk Command during the latter half of 1917 and throughout 1918 highlighted information that ranged from German attempts to camouflage artillery batteries by painting pictures of small shrubs over the sand dumps to opinions on the effect of ambient lighting conditions during the winter on the visibility of ground objects.[77] Analysts made use of photos to disprove unreliable intelligence reports.[78] They could also verify enemy inactivity by comparing new aerial photos to prewar local maps.[79] Information received that a new airfield had been constructed in a particular location could be confirmed or disproved by the examination of photographs.[80] Several missions flown during the study produced photographs aimed at aiding in the new science of bomb damage assessment.[81] By the final month of the war analysts were drawing important tactical and strategic conclusions from the photos they studied, such as those taken in October 1918 showing that the Germans had mined tracks around several railroad stations and ploughed the landing ground at St. Denis Westrem in preparation for a retreat from those areas.[82]

The long war and the new challenges presented by fighting deep battles offered new possibilities for combined arms operations, and aerial photographers played an increasingly important role in their collaboration with Allied artillery, intelligence, and senior command. *Capitaine* Paul-Lewis Weiller, one of the premier French aerial photographers, led the way. In 1918 Weiller organized a reconnaissance group dedicated to providing systematic photographic intelligence for strategic planning purposes. Three *escadrilles* soon operated on a regular basis at distances up to 100 kilometers behind German lines.[83] In the spring of 1918, as aerial photography organizations achieved new levels of sophistication, the US Air Service began operations on the Western Front. By then air reconnaissance had intertwined itself so tightly with ground operations that the newly appointed supreme Allied commander, Ferdinand Foch, could plan operations as much as a month in advance, anticipating what his German opponents might be planning by what he saw on aerial photographs.[84] For Foch, who before the war believed aerial reconnaissance useless, this reversal of opinion represented a substantial conversion.

Benefiting from lessons the Allies learned prior to its entry into the war, US Army leadership came to understand that modern warfare dictated that commanders obtain information from every available source and that aerial reconnaissance and photography constituted the most important parts of the information chain. Photographs offered the most reliable means by which one could study the battlefield.[85] By the war's final months the British expert Frederick Laws bragged that photos taken with a four-inch lens were able to distinguish barbed wire from 19,500 feet.[86] Objects as small as rifle stands could be seen in some photos.[87] Recognizing the intelligence value of air reports containing this level of detail, AEF commander Gen. John Pershing organized his subordinate command chain to maximize their distribution. Army G-2 (intelligence), G-3 (operations), the Army Artillery commander, the Air Service commander, or his equivalent at division or corps level, initiated most air missions. Aircrews returning with information from those missions reported to the group commanding officer through their branch intelligence officer, the army chief of Air Service, the group commanding officer or that officer's corps counterpart. Within this information-flow model, the collection, analysis, and dissemination of aerial reconnaissance reports became a regular part of the AEF intelligence organization.[88]

Before it could operate at levels compatible with allies and competitive with German adversaries, the unprepared US Air Service had, among other things, to solve supply problems and train reconnaissance and photography crews.[89] Patent litigation brought by the Wright Brothers in the fourteen years after their first powered flight had left the United States far behind major European nations in the development of military aviation. Without accurate aircraft inventories or existing reconnaissance and photography teams of their own or the training staff or syllabus to create them, those commanding the small US aviation program consulted both the French and British.

Beginning in the autumn of 1917, and meeting at regular intervals throughout the remainder of the war, an inter-Allied photographic conference met to discuss possible areas of joint action.[90] The group attending included many of the best aerial photography pioneers: Great Britain's Moore-Brabazon, Campbell, and Laws; France's Eugene Pepin; as well as American Edward Steichen. Reflecting the drastic need for coalition cooperation that had become apparent by late 1917 (and that would be brought home much more forcibly with the near success of the German spring offensive), the meetings concentrated on tighter organizational interaction and standardization and simplification of equipment. Representatives reached agreement on the common size for plate cameras (18 × 24 cm), for rollers on film types, and on a standard cone size for all 50 cm cameras. The group also reached accord upon the use of film for oblique photographs, saving the operator the difficult work of changing plates while flying in an open cockpit. Supplies of film, which Steichen agreed to arrange with the Kodak Company, would be shared among Britain, France, and the United States and distributed through the Paris office of the *Commission Technique Permanente Interalliée* (Permanent Inter-Allied Technical

Commission). The group conferred on stocks of gelatin, chemicals, paper, and glass, all of which varied by country, and on ways of achieving more equitable distributions among France, Great Britain, Italy, and the United States. Camera lenses offered special challenges. Prior to the war, German photographic lenses led the field in quality.[91] British glass production had fallen short of their need during the early years of the war, making lenses a particular problem for the RFC, and the French, though better situated, were not always in a position to cover the inadequate British supply.[92] The British requisitioned every lens in England to cover the shortage.[93] When the United States entered the war its Air Service faced the issue by making patriotic appeals to the American public to surrender their lenses, especially those of superior German manufacture.[94] Coalition warfare had not always proceeded along the most cooperative lines, but if victory was to be achieved at this late date those at the table were required to trust one another and work together to solve these common problems.[95]

Because its observation and reconnaissance squadrons utilized French reconnaissance methods in cooperation with French ground units on the Western Front, leaders of the US Air Service decided not to send any of their crews to train in Great Britain.[96] Yet, despite this decision to follow French principles at the front, the Training Section ultimately received much valuable assistance and material from the British as well as the French.[97] American reconnaissance crews trained using a mixture of French and British methods and materials, including the third edition of the British *Interpretation of Aeroplane Photographs*, and the *Illustrations to Accompany Notes on Interpretation of Aeroplane Photographs*.[98] Fledgling aerial photographers were instructed how to calculate the appropriate altitude for the camera in use on their mission and the interval between exposures necessary to get the overlap required for stereoscopic views. In the classroom, instructors using lantern slides taught their students photo interpretation techniques and how to properly coordinate aerial photography with other reconnaissance missions. Training classes employed French, British, and American camera equipment, including 26, 52, and 120 cm cameras, a mixture that reflected what the students would eventually use in the American zone of advance.[99] Once in the air the cadet observer flew five missions, progressing from the smallest to larger cameras. By his fourth mission his instructors expected the student to be capable of obtaining high-quality oblique photos.[100]

During May and June 1918, the US Air Service enlarged its instruction program to train 210 observers monthly at its Tours facility, graduating seventy observers every ten days. Expansion of the training program escalated throughout the remaining months of the war to meet growing demand for aircrews. Though personnel needs at the front at any given moment fluctuated with combat losses, estimates and training production throughout 1918 generally reflected the US Air Service's decision to favor observation and pursuit over bombing.[101]

Trainers had to update their syllabus in addition to increasing the numbers of new observers graduating from their programs. The resumption of movement on the Western Front after four years of stagnation in the trenches dictated new methods. American observers training in 1918 received instruction in low-level reconnaissance and operation of cameras in inclement weather.[102] Under the direction of Capt. Fred Place, students undergoing photography instruction exposed 92,288 negatives and made 184,756 prints in the school's laboratory during the course of their training.[103]

Bombing, which would become military aviation's *raison d'être* in the next war, developed early dependence on photography. Understanding the value of pictures of bomb blasts to commanders, bomber crews also received photography training. As their instructors taught, "next to bombing (photography) will be their most important work." Because such photographs offered evidence of the effectiveness of raids, commanders "must realize more and more there is a tendency on the part of Wing and Group Commanders to look for photographs to prove the value of bombing squadrons."[104] Aerial photographers working with artillery officers conceived a method of locating enemy batteries that aped the idea of bomb damage assessment. By the war's final weeks American artillery and photography skills had advanced to a point that aviation trainers were able to advise artillerists on a creative procedure. Artillery battery commanders who found themselves on the receiving end of a dud shell were to dig up the shell and read the fuse setting. Combining the fuse's timing with the angle at which the shell had fallen—determined from the angle of impact—gave the battery commander an approximate location of the German battery that had fired on his position. The Air Service then dispatched a reconnaissance flight that took photographs of the area and photo interpreters studied the pictures to locate the enemy battery and return fire.[105]

In the zone of advance, American units divided up their reconnaissance work similar to the organization of the Allied air forces. Squadrons belonging to the various divisions held jurisdiction over reconnaissance activities within and opposite their sector to a depth of five kilometers within German lines.[106] Corps squadrons managed adjustments of artillery fire, reconnaissance, and photographic missions to a maximum depth of ten kilometers within German territory, though as a practical matter they seldom ventured farther than six kilometers. Those units that generally regulated artillery fire fell back on reconnaissance and photography missions when their sectors quieted down.[107] Army squadrons did the deep reconnaissance work, sending photographic missions as far as 50 kilometers beyond the front line. Additionally, the Army squadrons had responsibility for providing aircraft and crews to perform special missions the army chief of Air Service might command, generally infantry-contact patrols.[108] Moreover, the Air Service categorized photography as "line, area and pinpoint work."[109] In accord with these categories, training officers suggested a graduated order of instruction that would have sent new observers to do simple reconnaissance work before going on to artillery spotting assignments and, as they sharpened their skills, to photography work.[110]

Reconnaissance and observation squadrons connected to ground units in their vicinity through their operations rooms, facilities staffed by the squadron's operations officer and a branch intelligence officer furnished to the unit by G-2 (intelligence) of the several corps or division general staffs.[111] The information flow began the minute the reconnaissance crew landed and reported the results of their mission to the branch intelligence officer.[112] Written reports traveled through the chain of command and the branch intelligence officer telephoned information of immediate importance to corps or division headquarters.[113]

Training in aerial reconnaissance and photography techniques quickly spread to the Army's other branches, particularly the artillery, whose leaders observed the benefits aviation brought to their operations. To cement those relationships, the US Air Service Training Section formulated a three-lecture course to instruct officers in every American regiment. Topics included artillery's use of aerial observation, the stereopticon, photo interpretation, as well as artillery fire preparation and camouflage.[114] Lecturing on resources that offered a "mass of detail presented with a maximum of accuracy," 1/Lt. Thomas Hibben, an experienced infantry officer, ranked aerial photographs as the number one source of information available to the infantry. Those officers who completed training skeptical of aviation's worth often found their opinions changed by subsequent experiences at the front.[115]

Fliers assigned to the dawn patrol frequently provided the information on enemy activities that turned skeptics into believers. Throughout the war, dawn reconnaissance missions held a special importance because of the massive amounts of enemy activity that took place at night. Aerial observers flying first thing in the morning could spot the results of nighttime activity as the troops finished their work.[116] By the spring of 1918, however, the combatants came to realize these fleeting observations were insufficient, and developed specialist units to handle night reconnaissance duties. Both the British and the French organized nocturnal squadrons, the British using F.E.2b pushers, by then obsolete for daytime use due to their relatively slow speed and poor defensive layout, and the French flying state-of-the-art Bréguet 14A2s. "During the offensive at Chateau-Thierry," trainer Thomas Box told students at the US Air Service's Second Aviation Instruction Center, "the work of [the French] squadron was considered so important that on the return of each machine the information at hand was reported directly to *Gen.* Foch's headquarters, and if anything of particular interest had been seen the observer reported personally."[117] US Army leaders attributed the success of German operations against its units prior to mid-July 1918 to the enemy's ability to move unobserved at night.[118] In response, the US Air Service designated the 9th Aero Squadron as a night reconnaissance unit. The squadron became active just before the St. Mihiel offensive in mid-September, operating initially as part of a French night bombardment group then joining the Air Service's First Army Observation Group in time for the war's last major offensive at the Meuse-Argonne.[119]

Systematic coverage of the front proved as important to combat operations as timely reconnaissance missions. Aiming for the same level of success in its photographic program that *Cpte.* Weiller had begun achieving on behalf of *Gen.* Foch, the office of the chief of Air Service Photo Section recommended that the American sector be completely photographed at regular intervals. The recommendation argued for the formation of photo flights, if not entire photo squadrons, and included an estimate that four photo aircraft, each equipped with a 26 cm camera, could completely reconnoiter the sector within two hours.[120]

American aerial observation on the Western Front had begun in February 1918 with arrival of the 2nd Balloon Company. The first heavier-than-air reconnaissance and photography units arrived in the spring. Until trained reconnaissance squadrons made it to the American zone of advance in numbers sufficient to provide the army with adequate coverage, single-seat fighter units were drafted into service for reconnaissance missions. The records of the 94th and 95th Aero Squadrons, which started operating at the front in March, contain frequent references to reconnaissance missions in the early months of their service at the front.[121]

By July, when the US Army participated in its first major action on the Western Front—the battle of Chateau-Thierry—the Air Service had three heavier-than-air units available for reconnaissance duties. The 1st Aero Squadron deployed for corps reconnaissance duties, both visual and photographic, as well as artillery adjustment, while the 12th and

88th Aero Squadrons performed divisional work, including the usual corps reconnaissance duties, infantry contact, and special command missions. Visual reconnaissance flights took place in the morning and evening at altitudes of 1,000–1,500 meters and flying five–ten kilometers inside enemy lines. Photo crews flew their missions at higher altitudes, 1,500–4,500 meters, and to depths 10–12 kilometers behind German lines. They performed their sorties on a regular basis prior to the attack and as needed once the attack started.[122]

At the battle of St. Mihiel, the professionalism and military effectiveness that aviation had achieved over four years of war revealed themselves fully. During the brief offensive that began on September 12, 1918, American Gen. William Mitchell commanded the largest aviation force yet assembled. Prior to the battle, American and French reconnaissance squadrons had been actively photographing the salient German forces had held since the war's opening days. Just as Haig had benefited from aerial reconnaissance and photography at Neuve Chapelle three years earlier, American commanders now learned the value inherent in effective aerial coverage of the battle front. Instructor Ralph DeCastro taught his student observers at the American Aviation Instruction Center at Issoudun that, "before the infantry went over the top each platoon commander knew from the photographs in his possession the exact nature of the terrain over which his men had to advance. The artillery in the rear knew exactly where to concentrate its heaviest barrage fire, and the HQ knew all the points that would be at all difficult to take."[123]

Airmen operating over the Western Front took a staggering number of photographs. By the war's midpoint, during the Somme battle, the RFC's *War Diary* reported its reconnaissance squadrons exposed over five hundred negatives on a single day.[124] Within six months the RFC shattered that number reaching a one-day high when it took 3,358 photographs.[125] British demand continued to accelerate to the point that between January 1 and November 11, 1918, more than 200,000 negatives were shot and nearly five million prints made from those negatives.[126] Over the entire war the British shot more than half a million photos.[127] Precise numbers of French and German aerial photos taken during the war are unclear, but the remnants that survive in European archives suggest totals equal to or exceeding the British results.[128] During its few months' service on the Western Front, the US Air Service operated ten photo sections that took some 18,000 photos and made 585,000 prints.[129]

By the armistice, reconnaissance pilots and observers had developed their branch of the air war to a high level of sophistication by advancing both technology and doctrine. Increasing use of the camera, enhanced photo quality, refinement of the photo interpreter's art, and the linkage of all these to military intelligence, mapping, and artillery regulation dramatically increased the demand for aerial reconnaissance. Moreover, its successes spurred increasingly creative efforts to overcome aerial reconnaissance through the use of camouflage and the night movements of armies. By 1918, reconnaissance pilots and observers operated in a far more complex environment than did their counterparts during the war's early days. Acknowledging the importance military aviation had taken on, Capt. Harold Wilder of the US Air Service Training Section, Observation Division, commented, "Observation comprises the Air Service which acts in direct connection with the other branches of the Army. Complete contact with these branches has been a primary object of the Service and its results have been in proportion to the success of this cooperation."[130]

Reconnaissance aviators did not merely connect with the rest of the army as Wilder put it. Their contributions to mapping the front, gathering intelligence on enemy intent, methodology, and operations, and their assistance to the artillery, meshed completely with the ground war becoming an essential factor in the success or failure of army operations. Furthermore, the value of aerial reconnaissance to the army began to make itself evident from the earliest weeks of the war. The belligerent navies took longer to learn the best ways to leverage their aircraft, but in the conflict's last two years aircraft also became an indispensible tool in dealing with the sea war's most important piece of new technology, the submarine.

Map 2: England, Wales, and Scotland. © Sydney Barth

CHAPTER 7

The Air War over the Sea

*When in August, 1918, I found on visiting France a complete chain of Naval
Aviation Stations engaged in a systematic patrol of the waters of that "neck
of the bottle" through which our troops and supplies had to pass, I had but
to examine the weekly charts of German submarine operations to realize how
much our aviators were doing to make these waters safe.*

—Franklin D. Roosevelt, *Flying Officers
of the United States Navy 1917–1919*

*The protection given to convoys by the presence of accompanying aeroplanes is
considerable and though attacks have actually been carried out when D.H.6
aeroplanes have been present, there is no doubt but that the enemy's submarines
have been seriously hampered in their operations by the constant fear of being
attacked or sighted by aircraft. In this connection it is of interest to note that
the day of greatest losses was one on which aircraft were unable to operate.*

—P. R. C. Groves for Director, Air Division, *Employment of
Aeroplanes for Anti-Submarine Work on North East Coast*

Although airmen's attempts to liaise with the infantry during the war
did not always achieve spectacular results, cooperative efforts between
aviators and sailors proved far more impressive. At the outset of the
war the British Royal Navy implemented a North Sea blockade to
prevent merchant ships from reaching their destinations and keep the
German surface fleet bottled up in port.[1] The military and geopolitical
effects of the blockade, though slow to show themselves, eventually
proved effective, slowly bleeding Germany of resources, sapping the
morale of the German people, and giving the United States a financial
stake in Allied success.[2] More narrowly, the blockade set the tone for
the war at sea and for the next four years German naval activity in the
Atlantic, the North Sea, the English Channel, and the air war over

these waters centered on efforts to either break the blockade or, failing that, to inflict similar damage on the Allies.

Naval aviation differed significantly from its land-based counterpart in the way it interacted with the non-flying forces it supported. Military aviators regularly separated their reconnaissance missions from offensive operations, observing or photographing enemy activities that bombers or the artillery dealt with at a later time. Naval flyers similarly reported their sightings to nearby cooperating surface vessels, but the fleeting nature of floating targets frequently forced naval aviators to attack the targets they spotted immediately.

An American, Eugene Ely, demonstrated what the future held for naval aviation when he successfully flew an airplane off the deck of USS *Birmingham* in November 1910 and then two months later landed one on the deck of the *Pennsylvania*.[3] The British created an Air Department within the Admiralty and began their own experiments in cooperation between aircraft and naval vessels in 1912, still more than two years before the beginning of the war.[4] The duties naval aviators anticipated performing included scouting for the fleet using aircraft carried aboard ships, patrol work along the British coastline, and cooperative missions flown alongside defending flotillas and submarines.[5] In January 1912, Lt. H. A. Williamson, a British submarine officer with an airplane pilot's license, first proposed using aircraft to patrol against submarines. He hypothesized that, even if unable to attack, the aircraft's presence would force a targeted submarine to stay completely submerged, thereby reducing its threat. Williamson noted the French were also experimenting with this idea.[6] Later developments would prove Williamson's predictions correct. Within six months early results of the British tests convinced the Royal Navy's Submarine Committee that aircraft showed "promise of providing a valuable anti-submarine weapon." On September 11, 1912, Capt. Murray Sueter, director of the British Royal Navy's Air Department, submitted an aircraft development proposal to the Board of Admiralty in which he listed potential duties that included "assisting destroyers to detect and destroy submarines."[7] Sueter's plan encompassed suggestions for a network of coastal air stations at various locations around the British coast, including Calshot, Dundee, Eastchurch, Felixstowe, Fort Grange, the Isle of Grain, Killingholme and Yarmouth.[8] The Admiralty adopted Sueter's scheme the following month and had most of the planned installations in operation prior to the outbreak of war.[9] In response to the first successful U-boat attack on a British vessel, HMS *Pathfinder*, on September 2, 1914, the Navy beefed up the stations at Dundee and Killingholme.[10] By the end of November the Navy implemented a revised plan specifically aimed at protecting the Straits of Dover, establishing bases to cover the fleet on both sides of the English Channel, in Dover, England, and on the French coast at Dunkirk.[11] Earlier that same month the British introduced an offensive element to its air operations when a Royal Naval Air Service (RNAS) seaplane took off from Dunkirk to mount the first direct air strike on a German U-boat.[12] Though the crew succeeded in locating the U-boat their attack failed when the submarine dived to escape. After this inauspicious beginning the Dunkirk crews devoted their attention mainly to reconnaissance and bombing of the German submarine bases at Zeebrugge and Ostend.[13]

Lighter-than-air vehicles also played a role from the beginning of British anti-submarine operations. Gas-filled airships operating over the water offered the same endurance advantage that observation balloons held in land battles allowing aircrews to remain over their patrol areas hours longer than airplanes. By the summer of 1914 the Admiralty had taken over complete control of airship development excluding the Army, and in February 1915 Sir John Fisher, the First Sea Lord, ordered the construction of the SS (Submarine Scout) airship, the first lighter-than-air type specifically dedicated to anti-submarine warfare.[14] The Admiralty's goal in ordering SS airships focused especially on keeping open the Straits of Dover and access to the Irish Sea. Their apprehension proved well founded. By the spring, U-boats of the *Deutsche Kriegsmarine* (German War Navy) appeared for the first time off the west coast of Great Britain threatening receipt of western hemisphere imports. To offer political cover for its submarine campaign, Germany declared the waters around the British Isles a war zone, seeking to prohibit the area to any and all traffic, even ships representing neutral nations.[15] Locating submarines in time to launch preemptive attacks required more speed and broader range than two-dimensional warfare offered, making aircraft crucial to defense. Submarines might be spotted cruising on the surface—time on the surface being necessary to recharge the U-boat's batteries—or, in clear weather and calm seas, the boat might be visible even while submerged. By the end of the year, British constructors had built twenty-nine Submarine Scouts.[16]

The amplified threat and the shift from two- to three-dimensional warfare required a broad reorganization of the entire naval defense system in order to incorporate the aerial component. As the war neared its first anniversary, RAdm. Sydney Freemantle, head of the Admiralty's Signals Committee, categorized reconnaissance as the airship's primary function, adding that its "duties are to locate enemy submarines and to keep them in sight as long as possible."[17] Successful communications between the airships and the Navy's destroyers were clearly essential; to guarantee the strength of that link the Admiralty established special transmission and reception stations and proposed instituting a dedicated radio wavelength.[18] The British Coast Guard administered the wireless stations reporting to each area's senior naval officer or the Naval Centre.[19] In August, in order to achieve tighter liaison between aircraft observers and the surface vessels whose attacks they would facilitate, the Admiralty removed all naval air stations from operational control of the director of the Air Department and placed them under the command of the various district senior naval officers.[20]

During 1915, the RNAS concentrated on lighter-than-air craft for anti-submarine warfare owing to the "unseaworthiness of seaplanes and the general lack of heavier-than-air equipment and personnel."[21] Most of the airplanes and aircrew still in England remained unavailable for anti-submarine work, reserved instead for Royal Flying Corps training facilities. Those not tied up with training duties the RFC saved for home defense missions, thus protecting a nervous British public against the threat of zeppelin attacks on military targets and cities in the British interior. This allocation of resources reflected a new strategic approach to the defense of the British homeland. During the first months of the conflict responsibility for aerial defense of the United Kingdom had rested entirely with the Admiralty. In June 1915, acting on the recommendation of War Office Director of Home Defence Gen. Launcelot E. Kiggell, the chief of the Imperial General Staff divided control of home defense responsibilities. The Royal Naval Air Service stood accountable for attackers as they crossed the English Channel, and the Army's Royal Flying Corps took charge once raiders had penetrated the coastline.[22] Though shedding accountability for aerial defense of the mainland should have made more naval aircraft available for the war against the U-boats, division of control between the Army and the Admiralty and the transfer of naval air station command out of the Air Department to senior naval officers later in the summer instead exacerbated competition for these resources. The situation became further complicated by an increase in reconnaissance work over the English Channel and the North Sea that prompted the British to expand their Dunkirk Air Command. During the spring of 1916 the RNAS divided the command "into three wings, one for aerial reconnaissance, photography and control of naval gunfire, one for bombing and one for aerial fighting."[23]

Provision of bombing and aerial combat capabilities ensured that British naval aviators did not have to rely solely on passive defensive measures to combat the submarine menace. The highly mobile nature of the war at sea meant that naval aviators did not always have time to return to base or signal for help before their target disappeared. The Dunkirk group had already demonstrated the potential value of direct interdiction by launching some of the first aircraft attacks on U-boats at sea.[24] Early in the war the Royal Naval Air Service organized an offensive capability, hoping to hit the enemy in his lair rather than simply waiting for his ships to appear. In its first month of operations, March 1915, Dunkirk crews launched bombing attacks on Ostend, Middlekerke and Hoboken, Antwerp, claiming (inaccurately, as it turned out) one submarine destroyed and two damaged.[25] The naval airmen organized a combined air- and seaplane force some thirty strong utilizing seaplane stations on England's east coast and a newly developed seaplane carrier, HMS *Empress,* with the aim of attacking German submarine pens across the English Channel. The group carried out several missions, but did not achieve significant success.[26]

By the end of 1915 improved German antiaircraft defenses and the relative ineffectiveness of the light bomb loads early air- and seaplanes could carry caused the RNAS to forego further heavier-than-air offensive activity. Initially, airships appeared to offer an alternative, given their more impressive carrying capacity, but ultimately lighter-than-air bombers proved no more successful in achieving measurable submarine destruction than their heavier-than-air counterparts.[27] Consequently, British airship crews returned to concentrating on reconnaissance, searching for submarines already at sea in conjunction with surface vessels rather than attacking the U-boats in their pens.[28]

Despite the considerable attention historians have devoted to its bombing attacks on London throughout the war, the German Naval Airship Division devoted substantially more of its resources to reconnaissance than to destruction. Of the 1,497 sorties German airship crews mounted during the conflict, 971 (65 percent) had scouting over the North Sea as their purpose, compared to the 306 missions (20 percent) flown to drop bombs on England.[29] The rather meager £1,527,544 total damage done to England during the German airship raids offers clear evidence that airship crews flying reconnaissance missions performed potentially far more valuable services.[30]

Throughout 1916 and into the following year the British developed the Coastal airship, a larger design capable of longer patrols, and added to the number of stations dotting the United Kingdom's shoreline. Between January and December, the RNAS constructed new facilities at Pembroke, Pulham, Longside, Howden, Mullion, and East Fortune, and opened an airship school at Cranwell. Reconsidering its earlier decision to abandon efforts to copy Germany's successful zeppelins, the Navy resumed construction of a project previously cancelled,

Rigid Airship No. 9, and built a large storage shed to accommodate the aerial behemoth at Howden. Anticipating further additions to its rigid aerial fleet in 1917, the Admiralty built more sheds at its Pulham, Longside, and East Fortune stations, and at the Cranwell training facility. Extending its reach off the British mainland the RNAS added an SS station at Caldale, in the Orkney Islands, for work with the Grand Fleet at Scapa Flow.[31]

Despite these preparations and its early appreciation of aviation's potential value in the anti-submarine war, not until the third year of the war did the Royal Navy give priority to the design and construction of heavier-than-air aircraft capable of directly attacking the U-boats.[32] Until then neither the British nor the French felt any pressing need to rush. Germany's desire to keep the United States out of the war had led the Kaiser to restrict the conduct of his U-boat commanders. This political strategy prevented submarines from achieving their full destructive potential and kept Allied naval losses within manageable limits during the war's first two years.[33] But by the second half of 1916 the German military and political situation had both eroded. Germany's attempt to defeat the French at Verdun had failed, ending in nearly as many German casualties as French, a situation made worse by hundreds of thousands further German, French, and British losses at the battle of the Somme.[34] In the wake of these setbacks, the Kaiser's high command reorganized its military, naval, and aviation assets hoping that, by bold measures, they might defeat the French and British in whatever time remained before the United States entered the war. As a key component of this new strategy, the imperial government stepped up U-boat activity permitting the *Kriegsmarine* to return to unrestricted submarine warfare.[35]

The lull in submarine activity in the Atlantic during the first half of 1916 had been prompted largely by American diplomatic protests. Germany's failure to bring about a favorable resolution to the war at Verdun and the heavy fighting at the Somme brought home the prospects of eventual defeat. Balanced against the possibility of losing the war the political risk of offending the United States seemed one worth taking. U-boats resumed hunting prey in British home waters in August 1916 and the new threat prompted the British to expand seaplane patrols in September. In response, Adm. Stanley Cecil Colville, commander of the Royal Navy at Portsmouth, requested installation of a four-machine seaplane base at Portland to supplement the existing facility at Calshot and two more SS stations, one for the Isle of Wight and one for Portland, each with ten airships.[36]

Actions like Colville's proved preliminary to a wholesale reorganization of the war against the U-boat and, on December 18, 1916, the Admiralty created the Anti-Submarine Division (ASD). The new organization took a special interest in aviation and vastly expanded both the number of heavier- and lighter-than-air craft available and the role of its aerial assets in the anti-submarine campaign. Creation of the Anti-Submarine Division centralized naval aerial activities that previously had been left to the individual prerogatives of each region's senior naval officer. The new division organized a coordinated system of coastal patrols and split naval aviation according to its offensive and defensive functions, much as the Dover Command had earlier divided its organization into reconnaissance, bombing, and fighting wings. Offensive assets included the airplanes and seaplanes patrolling Britain's waters actively hunting submarines, purely defensive reconnaissance missions being left to airships due to their endurance. Given these measures made areas near the coasts safer but left ships farther out to sea to their own devices, the director of the ASD further recommended enhancing direct protection of the fleet by equipping British vessels with kite balloons to improve their fields of vision.[37]

By January 1917 the British had built a massive naval aviation program that combined three seaplane carriers in service with more under construction, ships equipped with kite balloons, plans for rigid airships, coastal airships protecting the home waters, and large seaplanes able to patrol farther away.[38] Yet, despite this abundance of assets, Adm. Sir David Beatty, commander-in-chief of the Grand Fleet, regarded his air strength insufficient compared with his needs and recommended to the Admiralty that: "all naval officers who are engaged upon duties not connected with the fleet should be withdrawn and utilized for developing the Royal Naval Air Service."[39]

The early months of 1917 also saw Germany remove all remaining restraints from its U-boat commanders, resuming unrestricted submarine warfare that the German High Command hoped would bring the war to a successful conclusion within six months.[40] Instead, within just over two months the decision to escalate its cruiser war produced the outcome Germany most hoped to avoid. On April 6, 1917, the United States declared war on Germany. Ultimately, the resumption of unrestricted attacks combined with a botched German attempt to recruit Mexico into the war on its side, prompted the United States to enter the conflict.[41]

The U-boat war reached its peak coincident with the American entry into the war. The last half of April 1917 saw approximately 50 percent of the German submarine fleet at sea with five ships sunk on average each day. The 19th proved the worst single day of the month for the Allied merchant fleet, when U-boats and German mines sunk eleven ships and eight fishing vessels.[42] This spike in submarine activity pushed the average for the year 1917 to three ships sunk per day. As part of the British response the RNAS laid out formal areas for aerial patrols and categorized those missions as "routine," "emergency," and "contact," with contact flights reserved for its seaplanes. Beginning operations in late April, the new patrol system received formal Admiralty sanction on May 8, 1917.[43] Station commanders at Nore, Harwich, Yarmouth, Killingholme, South Shields, Dundee, and Houton Bay coordinated patrol hours and areas in systematic fashion to avoid overlap and to ensure that each district had at least one aircraft on duty in the air during all possible flight hours.[44]

The British further refined their naval aerial reconnaissance system in the spring of 1917 designing both the spider web system and Tracing U. The spider web created an imaginary octagon of chords radiating 60 miles out of the North Hinder light ship in the English Channel, an epicenter around which seaplanes could systematically patrol guaranteeing maximum coverage with a minimum supply of aircraft. Spider web patrols began on April 13, 1917, and in the first eighteen days five flying boats flew twenty-seven patrols sighting eight U-boats and bombing three.[45] Tracing U ("U" for U-boat) divided the southern portion of the North Sea into grids similar to those in common use by artillery units operating on the Western Front, allowing commanders of coastal air stations to quickly pinpoint submarine sightings, then dispatch attacking aircraft or communicate the information to nearby destroyers.[46]

Organizational refinements to the reconnaissance and patrol system proved effective and valuable, but the adoption of the convoy system in late April 1917 proved the most significant move forward toward defeating the submarine. To this point in the war many senior commanders in the British Admiralty opposed convoying merchant vessels believing that warships should be reserved for offensive action rather than escort duty. The large increase in sinkings that followed Germany's resumption of unrestricted submarine warfare in February, the success of an experiment in protecting French coal vessels begun the same month, and the entry of the United States into the war in April combined to reverse their opinions. Furthermore, America's enlistment in the Allied cause increased the number of ships available for convoy duty and opened US ports for use as convoy assembly points.[47]

The added naval capacity brought with it greater responsibility for Allied aviators. In order to protect the Atlantic courses over which the American Expeditionary Force and its equipment would travel naval aviation expanded its former role in protecting Anglo-French military traffic and neutral merchant shipping during the last half of 1917. Land-based airplanes and seaplanes could patrol the areas off the British and French coasts to the extent of their range covering the arrival of ships during the last leg of their travel from the United States. Kite balloons towed by warships could extend the effective field of vision of the convoy before the aerial escort picked it up, allowing crews a lifesaving early look at potential attackers throughout the journey. The British strengthened the new system further by completing construction of the network of airship stations the RNAS had begun organizing in 1916, the last becoming fully operational by the end of 1917.[48] The RNAS, of course, protected the British coast and that portion of the French shoreline most vital to arriving British traffic. The French Navy also vigorously defended its own ports, but paid more attention to the Mediterranean and the Adriatic, leaving the Atlantic largely to their British allies and later to the AEF.[49] The US Navy joined the effort within a few months of the American declaration of war and throughout 1918 expanded the network of protective air stations further still, taking over some British, French, and Italian coastal bases and constructing some of its own.

After the task of organizing an American army, an army that barely existed when the United States declared war, protection of that force as it crossed the Atlantic to fight on the Western Front represented the most important job facing American military and naval leaders in April 1917. In addition to the naval air stations they would build or take over in Europe, US Navy commanders faced the challenge of defending embarkation and receiving bases on their own side of the Atlantic, as well as a small number of less vulnerable installations on the Pacific coast. Even with aerial patrols fully operational the Navy would have to defend its ships against German submarines through most of the Atlantic crossing without the direct assistance of airplanes owing to the limited range of aircraft operating out of its coastal air stations. Taking their cue from British and French experience, American naval commanders enhanced the safety of the US fleet during that vulnerable period by equipping nearly every class of its ships with balloons to provide cover for the convoys.[50]

Building the aerial organization necessary to protect the fleet required putting US naval aviators on duty in France as quickly as possible. Within five weeks of the American declaration of war the Navy dispatched Lt. Kenneth Whiting to take charge of the first group of naval flight trainees sent to France.[51] Training preparations progressed well enough that by July the Navy reported to the French that two schools had been established within the French interior, one at Tours to instruct pilots and the second at San Raphael for prospective mechanics and observers. Plans had also been made for an additional school to teach naval artillery observation as well as an operational station at Moutchic-Lacanau.[52]

Once trained the Navy's aviators would serve at a network of stations in the planning stages or already under construction on both sides of the Atlantic. By July 1917 provisional plans existed for the organization of naval air stations at Dunkerque, Le Croisic, and St. Trojan in addition to the facilities at Tours, San Raphael and Moutchic-Lacanau.[53] Operations commenced at Moutchic-Lacanau on November 11, 1917 and within a week the naval air station at Le Croisic launched the first of an eventual 1,045 wartime patrol flights.[54]

By the following April another four stations had opened in Great Britain and France, at Killingholme, Ile Tudy, Dunkerque, and Paimboeuf, as well as a base at Bolsena, Italy. Patrols from these and the extant British and French air bases impressively demonstrated the value of aerial reconnaissance to the convoy system. In the spring, RAdm. Henry G. Wilson told the French press that cooperation between the French and US navies had substantially reduced sinkings in the waters along the French coast, comparing October 1917, during which thirty-four ships were torpedoed to February and April 1918, when no ships had been lost to the U-boats.[55]

Though submarine losses directly attributable to aircraft action are difficult to document, the mere presence of airplanes or airships frequently played critical roles in the demise of U-boats. Two incidents, both of which coincidentally took place on April 24, 1918, provide typical examples. In the first, airship SSZ 41, stationed at RAF Polegate received a report of a submarine operating southeast of the Isle of Wight. In response, the crew patrolled in the vicinity of the submarine's reported sighting for twelve hours in a dense fog, returning without having sighted the U-boat. A torpedo boat destroyer found and sank the German raider later in the morning. Official speculation held that the submarine had been forced to remain submerged in order to avoid detection by the airship and that by morning the desperate need for fresh air and recharged batteries forced the boat to the surface, putting it in a situation where it could no longer avoid detection.[56]

The second incident further demonstrates the potential of air-sea cooperation. Two American seaplanes patrolling off the French coast near Penmarch spotted what they believed to be a German submarine operating two miles from a convoy, responding to the opportunity with two bombs. Tracking the encounter, USS *Stewart* left its position in the convoy to investigate. While en route, the *Stewart* watched the aircraft mark the site with smoke bombs and, on arriving at the scene the American ship dropped depth charges after which the crew observed oil on the surface. Though no wreckage surfaced, other ships in the vicinity observed oil as late as two days later, providing strong evidence of a sinking.[57]

The success of the patrols and the convoy system firmly established what the world's navies had been learning throughout the war—that extending the vision of ships using aerial observers saved lives and material. Over the course of the war's remaining months the US Navy established a dozen stateside naval air bases, in addition to a pair in Canada, one each in the Azores and the Panama Canal Zone, and a total of twenty-seven air stations in Europe.[58] The stations on the American side of the Atlantic functioned primarily as coastal patrol stations protecting the convoy assembly points from the threat of German submarines.[59] The nineteen naval air stations on the European side of the Atlantic that conducted similar reconnaissance flights generally communicated their sightings to nearby ships but occasionally launched their own attacks on real or suspected submarines.[60]

Considering naval heavier- and lighter-than-air units along with the Army's airplanes and balloon sections makes it clear that American aviation had reconnaissance and observation as its main purpose.[61] Fifteen North American naval air stations and one in the Panama Canal Zone had reconnaissance as their primary duty, as did nineteen of the US Navy's twenty-seven European stations. In comparison, the French established a total of thirty-six coastal seaplane bases, as well as a half dozen balloon centers, and four dirigible bases.[62] Adding those thirty-five American bases to the forty-five US Air Service airplane squadrons and the seventeen American balloon companies working on the Western Front raises the total number of American aviation units that served during the conflict to ninety-seven, out of which seventy, or 72 percent, performed reconnaissance or observation as their primary function. Regardless of how military and naval air power developed over the rest of the twentieth century, during the First World War its principal and most valuable function lay in the aviators' ability to see and report what happened on the ground and water.

The numbers of aircraft acquired by the world's navies during the war further document the growing appreciation for aviation. The British Navy increased its heavier-than-air aircraft stock from fewer than one hundred to nearly three thousand, its airship strength from six to 111, and its inventory of captive balloons from two to 200. The *Deutsch Kriegsmarine* air fleet grew from twenty-four air- and seaplanes to nearly 1,500, and its lighter-than-air division worked its way through eighty-three airships, beginning the war with one and making it to the armistice with nineteen. The French Navy enlarged its heavier-than-air aircraft supplies from eight at the outset of war to 1,264 at the end, alongside fifty-eight airships and 198 kite balloons. Even the more limited resources of Austria-Hungary and Italy grew exponentially, the Austro-Hungarian air- and seaplane fleet expanding between eleven- and twelve-fold and the Italian inventory by more than twenty-fold.[63] For its part, over the relatively short time it spent at war the US Navy grew its aircraft inventory from fifty-four airplanes and seaplanes, one airship, and two balloons in April 1917 to over 2,100 heavier-than-aircraft, fifteen airships, and more than two hundred balloons at the armistice.[64] These figures reflect the same kind of progress the world's other warring powers made during the conflict.

Although these dramatic operational changes and numerical increases speak to how thoroughly aviation had been accepted into the world's navies, they do not begin to hint at the change in character the presence of aircraft brought to the war at sea. Although aircraft may have failed to live up to naval leaders' prewar expectations due to airframe and powerplant technological limitations, through its reconnaissance function naval aviation prevented many potential sea disasters.[65] History's failure to acknowledge this enormous contribution lies in the challenge proving a negative always presents to the post-event analyst. In evaluating the impact of the RNAS/RFC merger that created the Royal Air Force on April 1, 1918, one historian argued the demise of the Royal Naval Air Service "crippled Britain's credibility as a sea power."[66] During the First World War and afterwards the US Navy arrived at the same conclusion. The day had arrived when a modern navy seeking to project its nation's power around the globe could not hope to compete without its aircraft.

CHAPTER 8

Aerial Reconnaissance v. Air Power: Turning the Air Service into the Air Force

The development of air power affords the best and most rapid return for the expenditure of national resources of man-power, material, and money.
—Sir Frederick Sykes, *From Many Angles*

Starting out as a mere auxiliary in observing for armies and navies, within the four years of the war, air power fought great battles against opposing air power.
—William Mitchell, *Winged Defense*

Nearly as the Great War ended, and concurrent with US Air Service commanders' launch of a campaign to sever aviation from the Army and Navy, historians and aviation leaders began to ignore the valuable work performed by aerial reconnaissance and observation crews. The timing was not a coincidence. Establishment of an autonomous air force depended upon proving that aeronautics had worth independent of its relationship to ground and sea warfare, in other words, that aviation could exist as a "force," rather than merely as a "service." Discussion of how beneficial aerial reconnaissance or observation had proven during the war did not further the goal of establishing a new military aviation branch. In fact, introducing that evidence into the debate could prove counterproductive and actually strengthen the case Army and Navy commanders made for retention of control. To win their political contest against the older branches of the service, aviators had to create a more combative vision of air power than had existed during the war and sell the idea that future conflicts would not resemble those of the past.

As early as November 29, 1918, US Air Service Col. Milton F. Davis wrote a memo outlining a strategy to wrest control of aviation from the Army and Navy. Davis began by recommending that everyone in the Air Service organize to press Congress to create a cabinet-level Air Department. Davis's memo cut right to the heart of the burgeoning debate by claiming, "Future wars will be won by the nation, or nations, dominating the air." Davis pointed out that British aviation leaders planned to continue the progress they had made carving out a place for themselves during the war. He further invoked the painful memory of the American government's naiveté when it failed to invest in a strong military during the years between its own Civil War and its entry into the Great War. After asserting that "the costliest policy on earth is that of pacifism and unpreparedness," Davis concluded with an admonition to his colleagues that future control of aviation depended on "whether they [wartime Air Service organizers] wake up and do something, or whether they remain asleep and let the Navy, and the Post Office Department under the leadership of some live wires of German descent, do the organizing and carry off the plums."[1]

Within a couple weeks, US Air Service commanders were honing their arguments favoring an independent air force with an eye toward enlisting the support of specific prospective allies including "Congressmen, General Staff Committeemen, and other parties who have an influence in bringing about the separate organization which we all desire."[2] Going a step further than Milton Davis had done previously, an unnamed officer wrote to the director of Military Aeronautics in a memo styled "A Few Selling Points for a Separate Air Service." The communication laid out a sales strategy for separating aviation from Army and Navy control. This officer encouraged Air Service leadership to argue unequivocally that: "it would be possible in the future to carry on war without reference to armies or navies."[3] The memo predicted the next war would begin with an enemy aerial attack and would be won in the air. Perhaps believing a strategic concession to supporters of the status quo would soften resistance, the officer advised that Air Service commanders acknowledge that artillery observation and reconnaissance aircraft should remain a part of military and naval aviation. Explaining the logic of this calculated back step, the writer pointed out that the Army's occasional use of sea transport or the Navy's maintenance of the Marine Corps had never been used as justification for transfer of control of those functions away from their primary service.[4] In sum, the Army and Navy were welcome to keep a few aircraft for reconnaissance- and observation-related "service" functions, but the exercise of air "force" required a new department with an independent identity equal in status to the Navy and the Army.

Given his wartime position near the top of American military aviation and the course of later events that put him at the center of efforts to market Air Service independence, it seems likely Brig. Gen. William Mitchell authored the anonymous memo. On April 16, 1919, Mitchell put his signature on a far more detailed plan for a new Air Service that resembled the unacknowledged December 11 note in several particulars. For example, Mitchell suggested that, "Observation Squadrons should be assigned directly to the (Army) Units that they are to work with in war" and advocated "that the whole organization, i.e., both Supply and Troops, be called the AIR SERVICE, and that the tactical organizations and their immediate auxiliaries be called the UNITED STATES AIR FORCE."[5] Mitchell had come to the conclusion that in order to wrest bomber and fighter units from Army and Navy control to form an independent air force the Air Service had to surrender its reconnaissance functions. The general's father, John Lendrum Mitchell, had served in both houses of Congress and had apparently passed an understanding of power politics on to his eldest son.[6] Mitchell's strategy, designed to achieve the political end of Air Service independence, produced historical consequences that Mitchell may not have anticipated or simply may have considered insignificant. His subsequent efforts suggested to the public that aerial reconnaissance constituted the least important aviation function, rather than the vital part it had played during the war. Combined with the romantic tales about the more aggressive roles that circulated about flying throughout the conflict, the crusade Mitchell began would eventually erase from the public's memory the contributions made by air observers.

The controversy over the possible creation of a new armed forces branch produced immediate political results. Members of the sixty-sixth congress introduced legislation in the House and the Senate and the broader public began to debate the merits of both independence for military aeronautics and the future of aviation generally. The New (S. 2693), Curry (H.R. 7925) and Morin (H.R. 11206) bills proposed creation of a permanent structure for American aviation at the presidential cabinet level, a move that would not only separate aeronautics from the Army and Navy but confer upon it a status equal to the two older institutions and add a variety of civilian functions to its portfolio.[7]

The peacetime civil aspects of the proposed aeronautical department convinced some that separation did not represent a good idea and that military aviation would have a better chance of survival if the Army kept the reins. As the debate over aviation's prospects quickly spread from the Army's command center in Washington, DC to military and naval outposts throughout the country, more junior officers began to weigh in. On May 8, 1919, from his California billet future Air Force chief of Staff Henry H. Arnold wrote, "After several months out here and meeting the different Congressmen, Senators and other influential people, I am convinced that unless the War Department advocates an Air Service of suitable size, Congress will pass a law separating all aviation from the Army." Arnold's letter to Col. Milton Davis, went on to explain that although many Army officers favored a separate Air Service, "no one believed that the War Department itself was in favor of a sufficiently large Air Service ... and further, that unless this attitude was changed, Congress was liable to pass a bill for a separate Air Service." Arnold concluded that if the War Department could be convinced to recommend a properly sized aerial program legislation separating aviation from the Army might be "entirely killed."[8]

In July, Assistant Secretary of War Benedict Crowell, just back from heading an aeronautical mission to Europe, waded into the debate by recommending organization of an equal and independent air force.[9] As expected, autonomy schemes enjoyed broad support within the Air Service and vehement opposition within the Army and Naval officer corps. Crowell's advice ran contrary to an April lessons-learned report requested by Gen. John J. Pershing and prepared by a "Board of Officers to Consider Tactics and Organization" headed by Maj. Gen. Joseph T. Dickman. The Dickman Board had recommended the Army and Navy retain control of aviation.[10] Crowell's report forced Secretary of War Newton D. Baker into the risky position of choosing between his assistant secretary and his senior field commander.

The public also began expressing its concern over the issue just after the war ended. Before the end of November 1918, the Oklahoma City Chamber of Commerce queried the director of Military Aeronautics about the peacetime status of the Air Service.[11] On March 21, 1919, Davis responded to a letter from the managing editor of the *Albany Evening Journal* who worried that the Air Service might be reduced in size to prewar levels.[12] On June 7, 1919, the Richmond, Virginia, *News Leader* ran an editorial headlined "Must Not Cripple Aviation" arguing that regardless of "league of nations or no league, armament or disarmament. America must have adequate air service. To reduce it is to take chances: to cripple it is to invite disaster."[13] By the following year the national conversation had trickled all the way down to the level of high school debate competitions. Apparently anxious to keep any and all avenues of possible support open, the chief of the Air Service's Information Group, Lt. Col. Horace M. Hickam, responded to a March 21, 1920, letter from A. F. Breazeale, Jr., of Meridian High School in Mississippi, who wrote requesting information on the debate proposition: "Resolved that Congress should appropriate a sum sufficient to place the Air Service of the United States upon a par with that of Great Britain."[14] The entire nation appeared caught up in the struggle over aviation's future.

The British had decided the autonomy issue during the war.[15] Its War Cabinet had divorced its two aviation branches from Army and

Navy control to create the Royal Air Force in April 1918 largely in response to wartime organizational and supply problems. During 1917 and 1918, American aviation leaders had depended on both the British and French for technical and doctrinal advice, as well as for most of their aeronautical equipment, and after the war continued to look at their European counterparts for examples of how military aviation should be modeled. Following the armistice, the young RAF found itself immersed in the same kind of survival battles that plagued military aeronautics in the United States.

After the war both the British Army and the Royal Navy sought to undo the merger that gave birth to the Royal Air Force. Arguments in favor of returning to the status quo ante included charges that following the amalgamation, morale in the Royal Air Force "fell to pieces" and that the new service accomplished less than its two smaller predecessors.[16] Money, however, became the primary factor in the political debate over the RAF's future. At a time when military budgets were shrinking, aviation leaders throughout the world sought to argue that air forces offered effective national defense at less expense than maintaining large standing armies and navies.[17] In Britain's case, policing a still-extensive British empire at a reasonable cost figured prominently in the discussion.[18] In 1920 the British successfully tested the RAF's ability to substitute for more expensive regular Army forces in Somaliland during their pursuit of the "Mad Mullah," Sayyid Muhammad Ibn Abdulla Hassan, and subsequently put the air force to good use in the Middle East.[19] Cost of the Mad Mullah expedition, which had combined reconnaissance and bombing, had not exceeded £77,000 versus the estimated £5 million the Army would have spent had ground forces been sent instead.[20] In the interwar years British military aviation remained alive because it offered effective defense at bargain prices.

At a time when money was tight an offensive aerial capability offered the promise of economy. An aerial fleet that could defend its country from attack or deliver a nation's punch to its enemies was much less expensive to build and maintain than a comparably sized fleet of warships or a large standing army. In Great Britain, Air Marshal Hugh

Trenchard offered the Royal Air Force as a cost-effective way to police the British Empire. Trenchard's biographer, Andrew Boyle, devoted considerable attention to Trenchard's campaign against the odds to keep the RAF alive during the 1920s, a decade of lean military spending.[21] The British had given their air force independence and parity with the Army and Navy late in the war to solve supply and command problems. The air force's new independence had not come with an endorsement of air power or with any postwar guarantees. Trenchard eventually saved the RAF using a combination of early demonstrations displaying its cost effectiveness and arguments about the horror that might come England's way from a rearmed Germany.

By the end of the First World War, the French had built the largest air force in the world with a front-line strength of more than three thousand aircraft.[22] Furthermore, French manufacturers finished the war only slightly behind the British in aircraft built, while leading the world in aviation engine production.[23] Between the armistice and 1920, the French *Aviation Militaire* significantly downsized its inventory without changing its primary focus on reconnaissance. Of the 120 *escadrilles* remaining in service after the 1920 reorganization, more than half performed reconnaissance and observation as their principal duty, the remainder being divided between fighter and bombing responsibilities.[24] To maintain its aerial capability, French commanders proposed continuing the French government's interest in aviation under a civilian director who would approve designs and coordinate material and flight crew supply in order to balance military, naval, and civilian needs. The suggested reorganization scheme, which took form as the *organe de coordination générale de l'aéronautique* (General Aeronautical Coordinating Body), put the government in partnership with its civilian aviation industry in an effort to maintain technological progress in the event of another war.[25] Though the new agency did not prevent the eventual diminution of French military aviation in the postwar era, it did have some success easing the transition of the nation's manufacturers into the civil aviation market or other endeavors.[26]

Postwar developments in French politics worked to separate the air force from army and naval control without the specific debate over aerial policy that absorbed air, naval, and army leaders in the United States and Great Britain. After regaining control of their government in the 1924 election, members of the French political left pulled aviation out of the army and navy as part of a broader power play to weaken the influence of military and naval commanders. Toward that end they set up an independent air ministry by 1928. Administrative governance notwithstanding, the move did not materially affect operational control over individual units, nor did it change the basic reconnaissance and battlefield-support orientation of French military aviation. Of the 134 French *escadrilles* involved in the 1928 reorganization, 118 remained under Army control, with only sixteen devoted to strategic bombing.[27]

The armistice agreement, and later the Treaty of Versailles, ensured that in the postwar period German aviation followed a different path from that taken by its American, British, and French counterparts. Restrictions and surrender terms imposed by both documents came close to shutting down indigenous aircraft manufacture and forced German military aviation leaders to hide their efforts to resuscitate the air force.[28] The *Luftstreitkräfte* officially ceased to exist in May 1920.[29] Within three years of the armistice the German aviation industry had followed it into oblivion.[30] The obstacles imposed on German aviation compelled the Luftstreitkräfte's former leadership to seek creative methods to keep flying alive, camouflaging recruiting and training programs in youth gliding clubs and hiding manufacturing facilities in Russia.[31] Historian Walter Boyne argues that the divorce of civil and military aviation in Germany brought about by Allied efforts to prevent a revival of German aggressive capabilities ultimately worked to the German military's advantage, forcing civilian manufacturers and military leaders into a partnership that might otherwise not have developed.[32] Though titular compliance with the armistice and treaty provisions did not prevent Germany from eventual rearmament, the necessity to conceal its efforts did keep German air leaders from active public participation in the postwar debate over the future role of air power.

American aviation leaders found themselves as handcuffed by political and financial considerations in the postwar era as their British, French, and German counterparts. As possible congressional action on the question of independence loomed, the Air Service and the Army both geared up to press their cases. Acting on behalf of Secretary of War Newton Baker, the US Army's adjutant general requested Maj. Gen. Charles T. Menoher, who had become director of the Air Service on December 23, 1918, to convene a board to comment on the Curry and New bills.[33] Embarking on its mission to gather data on the potential creation of an aeronautics department, the Menoher Board requested opinions from officers in the various armed forces on the question of control of aviation.[34] Menoher went into the hearings convinced that Crowell had misled Baker about the weight of support for a separate air force and his survey of the military aimed at discovering the truth. Given his view of what Crowell had told the secretary of war, and anticipating overwhelming opposition from Army and Navy officers, Menoher went to extraordinary lengths to ensure the testimony his board members heard accurately reflected the opinions held by both sides of the dispute. He even requested that Brig. Gen. William Mitchell send members of his staff to testify, "in order to obtain as many reasons as could be obtained in favor of creating a Department of Aeronautics."[35]

As anticipated, Army officers who offered their advice to the board almost unanimously expressed hostility to the idea of an independent Air Service. Underlying those negative votes was a clear belief that the Air Service had enhanced Army and Navy performance during the war. It had made the artillery more effective, augmented battlefield communication and map-making, improved strategic and tactical planning, and rendered significant assistance in defeating the U-boat.[36] Descriptions of aviation as an "auxiliary" service figured prominently in several of the affidavits submitted to the Menoher Board.[37] These arguments even convinced some Air Service officers, for instance, Col. Frank P. Lahm, who had served in 1916 as commander of the Army's balloon school in Nebraska and later in France as chief of staff of the

First and Second Army Air Services. Lahm argued Air Service leaders should aspire to become an even more indispensible part of the Army, not a separate branch of the military.[38]

The former AEF Commander Gen. John J. Pershing, threw the considerable weight of his influence against the idea of an unattached aeronautics department, making it clear the Army and aviation had to work hand-in-hand.[39] Pershing remained convinced of aviation's value as an auxiliary service as the debate raged through the 1920s.[40] Pershing had likely compared the modest results produced by aerial bombing during the war to the abundant worth observation and reconnaissance crews had demonstrated in their work on the Western Front.[41] General Mason Patrick, who served under Pershing as commander of the US Air Service in France from May 1918 through the armistice, supported and amplified Pershing's 1925 comments.[42]

In its final report, the Menoher Board settled the issue—at least temporarily—by siding with the Army and Navy and dismissing independence proponents' fundamental argument. Reasoning that an air force could not prevail in war on its own, board members held that aeronautics constitutes an "essential combat branch" that "forms an integral part" of the Army. They applied the same logic to naval aviation.[43] Control of war-related aviation, therefore, should remain in the hands of Army and Navy commanders even if the Congress elected to organize a separate government aeronautical department to administer peace-related aviation matters.[44]

In support of its stand, the board declared military authorities the world over "practically unanimous" in their opposition to military aeronautics leaving Army control. Former British Expeditionary Force commander, Sir Douglas Haig, said the idea airplanes could take the place of infantry and artillery robbed aviation supporters "of the power to use them in their best effect."[45] A cable from the American military attaché in Great Britain further reported that, while RAF officers endorsed independence for aviation, Army and Navy leaders, were opposed, as were their French and Italian military and naval counterparts.[46] With the overwhelming majority of the world's military and naval officers opposed to forfeiting their command over aviation, Menoher and his colleagues declared advocates of Air Service independence a decided minority within the armed forces.[47]

But the Menoher Board's verdict did not kill the debate. In fact, the fight over the future of air power was just about to heat up. Postwar America's most famous independent air power advocate, Brig. Gen. William Mitchell, willingly conceded reconnaissance and observation, aviation's "auxiliary" functions, to the Army and Navy, but coveted control of the rest of aviation for the proposed independent air force.[48] Political gain clearly motivated Mitchell. Dividing military aviation into different categories allowed Mitchell and other air power advocates to write reconnaissance, photography, and observation out of the definition of "air power." This became a key tactic in the early stages of negotiation to create the US Air Force.

The Italian aviation prophet, Giulio Douhet, made perhaps the most outlandish argument in his air power manifesto, *Il domino dell'aria* (*The Command of the Air*).[49] Douhet began preaching wars would be won or lost in the air in 1913 and, when his book appeared in 1921, he became one of the leaders of the debate over the destructive potential of military aviation. Douhet went further than either Mitchell or the RAF's Hugh Trenchard in his advocacy for a stand-alone strategic force, demanding the complete abolition of auxiliary air services rather than their simple surrender to the other branches. Mitchell understood that the Navy and Army considered aerial observation and reconnaissance indispensible to their success in combat, and acknowledged as much by making administration of those functions the key part of a political bargain that would give him control over offensive air power. Conversely, Douhet constructed the convoluted argument that "auxiliary aviation is useless, superfluous, and harmful," because it diverted important aerial resources that might otherwise be devoted to achieving aerial superiority over the enemy.[50] Douhet reduced aerial reconnaissance, photography, and observation to dangerous distractions that, if maintained, would pull a nation into almost certain defeat in the next war.[51]

Building on this vision of the future, Douhet argued aviation's real contribution lay in its ability to "compel the enemy to bow to one's will."[52] Aviators flying aerial reconnaissance, photography, and observation missions had demonstrated their ability to do exactly that during the war just concluded. With the reports they made, the photos they took, and the artillery batteries they regulated, they altered their enemy's behavior on a daily basis. But considering the meager results they achieved the war's bombing crews could hardly make the same claim. The editors who prepared his work for a more recent generation of US Air Force officers appeared to recognize Douhet's overreach when they opined: "In [his] thinking, aircraft altered the fundamental character of warfare, and he argued the case at a level of abstraction and generalization that elevated argument to principle and the body of thought as a whole to theory."[53] Ignoring the value of reconnaissance in favor of bombing, Douhet constructed a thesis that set the tone for the interwar debate over the future of air power.

Douhet's broad argument in support of bombing caught on quickly with aviation leaders. Though translations of *The Command of the Air* were not published for the general reader until after the Italian general's death in 1930, the US Air Service translated the work in 1923 and used it as a training aid at the Air Service Tactical School suggesting the early regard it achieved in professional command circles. Ten years later, chief of the Air Service, Gen. Benjamin Foulois, demonstrated the work's continued influence by sending several copies of an article summarizing Douhet's air power theories to the Chairman of the House Military Affairs Committee.[54]

Though American aviation commanders did not entirely embrace Douhet's elimination of reconnaissance in favor of bombing, any degree of distinction between the low value Mitchell assigned to aerial intelligence gathering in 1919 and the absolute lack of merit Douhet saw in it two years later is ultimately irrelevant. The principal players in the interwar debate had quickly moved the conversation away from the worth of aerial reconnaissance and observation to the Army and Navy to the value of the strategic bomber and the fighter plane as weapons of attack. Douhet and Mitchell, the two most famous air power disciples of the period, both wrote forward-looking arguments that hinged on what airmen *might do* in the next war, not what they had in fact done in the last.[55]

Mitchell spent the first years after the war attempting to convince his military superiors, Congress, and the public at large of the military and commercial value of air power. Through a series of magazine articles in the *Saturday Evening Post, National Geographic, Colliers, Popular Mechanics, Atlantic Monthly*, and in two books, Mitchell conducted a public relations campaign that pitted him against senior Army and Navy commanders and political leaders.[56] From December 1924 through the first half of 1925, Mitchell pressed his argument further in more magazine pieces, concluding the campaign with an expanded version of the articles that appeared in book form as, *Winged Defense: The Development and Possibilities of Modern Air Power—Economic and Military*. In taking his case to the public, Mitchell purposely set out to generate widespread fear that the next war would subject American cities to frequent and devastating attacks from the air. He hoped the public would respond by pressuring Congress to create an independent American air force. Mitchell envisioned an air force equal in rank with the Army and Navy, all three branches of the armed services reporting to a Department of Defense that would coordinate administration. Mitchell declared himself an agent of positive change and branded Army and Navy leaders inept holdovers from the past.[57] An air force could not be developed to its full potential using the "methods and means" of the past. Reconnaissance, observation, and photography, had to be left behind in the name of progress for American air power to mature into an effective weapon.

Throughout his writings, Mitchell utilized fear to misrepresent the contemporary character of air power by exaggerating its present capabilities. In one article Mitchell explicitly described the horrific possibility of an aerial attack on New York City, detailing extensive immediate physical damage, the inability of the ground transportation system to deal with large-scale flight from Manhattan, and the inevitable public panic.[58]

Mitchell vigorously pressed his case for a strong air arm. Knowing the general public to be fascinated by air power, yet ignorant of its potential, Mitchell set out to educate the national audience about aviation's component parts. Neglecting to include any of the various forms of reconnaissance, he maintained an aerial program consisted of three "principal branches": "pursuit," "bombardment," and "attack aviation."[59] The general mentioned observation, almost as an afterthought, correctly explaining the various roles it had fulfilled during the war, but omitting it from his list of military aeronautics' "principal branches." In doing so, the Air Service's most prominent and most outspoken leader minimized nearly out of existence the war's primary aviation function.[60] By elevating the place of bombing and attack aircraft while demoting observation aviation to also-ran status, Mitchell argued contrary to the overwhelming mass of evidence produced by the First World War and to the conclusions drawn by the Menoher Board. The air commander did this to secure autonomy for aviation and guarantee a place for fliers in the American military community equal to that of soldiers and sailors. In the short term, the independence campaign revolved around a contest for money, the severely limited resources Congress might be willing to allocate to national defense in a country weary of war. In the longer term the stakes involved the future of military policy, doctrine, and the nature of war. To win the peacetime contest for political control of military aviation, Mitchell and his colleagues built a more aggressive model of air power than they had manufactured to win the war.

During the interwar years, theorists intending to sell air power put their emphasis on the "power" half of the combination to achieve immediate political goals. To achieve independence, a seat at the defense establishment table, and equality with their nation's armies and navies, airmen needed to stress aviation's ability to devastate their country's enemies. Reconnaissance and observation offered only indirect, passive methods of dealing with an opponent: pictures, maps, and an elevated vantage point for land-based artillery or a ship's guns. These capabilities, while of unquestioned value, came without the drama of bombs dropping out of the sky onto an enemy target or the glory and glamour of an enemy bomber falling victim to a friendly fighter plane. Had the disciples of air power pressed the value of reconnaissance and observation they would have irrevocably tied military aviation to the army and navy, fatally damaging rather than enhancing the argument for an independent air force. In making their case they erased the "eyes of the army and navy" status aviation had enjoyed during the first global war from public discussions of an air force's primary functions and from historical memory. Henceforth, the worth of military aviation would be judged by its ability to deliver bombs and bullets, not by its pictures, maps, and observations.

The crusade for an independent air force reached its peacetime crescendo in the United States on September 2, 1925 following the crash of the Navy's airship USS *Shenandoah*.[61] William Mitchell reacted angrily to the disaster, venting his ire to the press in a statement blasting Navy and War Department incompetence in aerial matters.[62] His statements earned Mitchell a court martial. His trial provided him an opening to showcase his positions on the proper uses of military aviation.[63] The opportunity went unfulfilled. Though the proceedings seemingly covered the broad spectrum of national defense issues, ranging from submarines to antiaircraft installations, the court-martial ultimately failed to settle the essential issue. Determining whether air power had morphed from a mere auxiliary of the army and navy into a full-fledged member of the defense establishment capable of standing side-by-side with its sister services remained for another day and another war.

CONCLUSION

The Memory and Impact of Aerial Reconnaissance in the First World War

> *Whatever the futur[e] development of aviation may be, up to the end of the war in 1918, its most important function had proved to be securing and transmitting information concerning the developments in and beyond the line of battle.*
>
> —Director US Air Service to Gen. Charlton, British air attaché, Washington, DC, June 24, 1919

> *If we maintain our faith in God, love of freedom, and superior global air power, the future looks good.*
>
> —Gen. Curtis LeMay, "60th Anniversary of the United States Air Force," *Cong. Rec.*, 110th Cong., 1st sess., 2007

Although the decade following the 1918 armistice offered little more than opportunities for debate and conjecture over the role aviation would play in modern warfare, the Second World War provided the laboratory for practical tests. The German air attacks on Poland and Great Britain, the Japanese strike on Pearl Harbor, the day-and-night bombing campaigns carried on against Germany by US Army Air Forces and RAF Bomber Command, and the use of atomic bombs in 1945, convincingly demonstrated air power's destructive potential. By the conclusion of the Second World War the model of an effective military aviation program had clearly changed. Events had even convinced the US Congress. The campaign Brig. Gen. William Mitchell initiated in the aftermath of the First World War achieved ultimate success with passage of the National Security Act of 1947 and creation of the new Department of Defense.[1] Aviation at last stood on equal footing with the Army and Navy. But victory came with a price in terms of aerial reconnaissance's place in the history of the Great War.

Amid the aerial carnage of the Second World War, the impressive record that First World War aviators achieved in reconnaissance, photography, and observation largely disappeared from discussions of air power. Moreover, interest in the first air war generally nearly ground to a halt until the guns again silenced and the bombs stopped falling.[2]

After 1945, the First World War assumed a more distant status, one that could no longer serve as the experiential foundation that framed discussions of air power doctrine for the next war. The military situation in Europe until the second half of June 1944 allowed American and British forces to rely on their ally, the Soviets, to press the ground war against Germany while the US Army Air Forces and Royal Air Force Bomber Command bombed Nazi targets from the air.[3] In front of the world the two air arms had tested theories that Douhet, Mitchell, and Trenchard had preached during the interwar decades and made at least part of the case for strategic bombing. Civilian populations had not demanded that their government cease hostilities as strategic air power advocates had predicted, but the substitution of air forces for ground troops had served to keep American and British casualties low in comparison to the losses suffered by the Soviet armies.[4] The Japanese capitulation after the American atomic bomb attacks offered some vindication to air power theorists. Military analysts and historians argued that aviation's Second World War success provided the model for future wars, allowing the United States to inflict maximum damage on an enemy while suffering minimal casualties. Aerial bombing had taken over the lead in the American vision of war so convincingly it became possible to argue for the total "elimination of ground forces as major combatants in war" and that henceforth war might "be won entirely from the air."[5] The vital auxiliary role reconnaissance and observation crews had played during the earlier war vanished in the dust of Europe's collapsed buildings and the atomic flashes that destroyed Hiroshima and Nagasaki. Professional military analysts moved on to studies of the Second World War largely taking professional historians with them. The heavy emphasis on bombing inherent in the model of air power set during the Second World War prompted historians to reexamine aviation's role in the Great War. Judged against the great success bombing had enjoyed in the later war, the modest bombing programs of the First World War appeared miniscule, even quaint. With bombing cast as the new *raison d'être* of military aviation—and few memorable bombing achievements to study from the years 1914–1918—historians began to minimize and even ignore aviation's real contribution to the Great War. They erred in doing so.

From the outbreak of war to the armistice the world's air arms dedicated the majority of their resources to watching the enemy. In the opening weeks reconnaissance fliers proved their worth at the Marne and Tannenberg, stopping the Russian advance in the east and setting up the race to the sea and the descent of the war into the trenches in the west. As stalemate developed, the threat of discovery posed by airplanes and balloons forced both sides to conduct large movements exclusively at night and to devote considerable time, effort, and resources to measures aimed at deceiving the enemy. In the war at sea, zeppelins provided a valuable reconnaissance asset to the German High Seas Fleet and balloon-equipped Allied convoy vessels helped defeat the U-boat threat in the war's final years, while seaplanes proved their worth as patrol craft to both sides. Over the course of the four years the war lasted, although all the belligerent powers developed extensive fighter and bomber programs, the amount of resources expended on reconnaissance, artillery observation, and aerial photography grew as well, never dropping out of the dominant position aerial intelligence gathering occupied when the guns first began firing. And, while reconnaissance aircraft were present from the start, it is unlikely that fighters would have appeared at all had it not been necessary to eliminate the enemy's reconnaissance planes and bombers. In the two decades that separated the two world wars the same air commanders who presided over large reconnaissance forces from 1914 to 1918 turned their attention to bombing to keep those forces from being taken over by Army and Navy leaders who coveted control of the observation, reconnaissance, and photography programs the war had proven so valuable.

The success of fascism in Italy, the seizure of power by Nazis in Germany, and Francisco Franco's victory in the Spanish Civil War—a victory significantly assisted by a newly reactivated German *Luftwaffe*—shifted attention away from academic pursuit of the air power debate of the 1920s to more serious concerns. In 1930 the British military historian Basil Liddell Hart entered the fray offering his own dramatic contribution to the air power discussion and to the loss of the aerial reconnaissance story in his war chronicle, *The Real War, 1914–1918*.[6] Liddell Hart's analysis twisted logic in a manner similar to Giulio Douhet in his interpretation of air power's earliest years. The military analyst conceded the value of aerial intelligence collection, even going so far as to write that "to relate the action of aircraft in the military sphere is not possible, for it formed a thread running through and vitally influencing the whole course of operations, rather than a separate strategic feature."[7] Liddell Hart then condemned the effect aerial reconnaissance had on the war by maintaining its early maturation prevented senior commanders from adequately developing aviation's more belligerent aspects in ways that would have brought the war to an early close. The British historian wrote:

> The very eagerness with which the armies had eventually embraced aircraft as immediate auxiliaries—for reconnaissance, artillery observation, and the protection of these duties—limited the supply of aircraft for roles of indirect cooperation and curtailed their exploitation of the bombing weapon.[8]

Liddell Hart's argument assumed as fact an idea about bombing for which no proof has yet been offered, either by himself or by any other historian. He speculated the damage that might have been done had the Great War's belligerent powers developed more powerful bombers would have exceeded the damage actually done by artillery fire regulated by aerial observation and planned with the aid of aerial reconnaissance and photography. Liddell Hart damned the war's senior commanders for lacking vision. They had failed to appreciate what a larger investment in bombers might have done to the enemy's industrial capacity to wage war. What Liddell Hart failed to acknowledge was the tremendous impact the wartime leadership had made by developing operational doctrine that properly utilized available equipment to the fullest extent then technologically possible.

Liddell Hart came late to an appreciation of air power theory. When the first edition of *The Real War, 1914–1918* appeared in 1930 it did not include the air war chapter he later entitled "Panaroma." Liddell Hart added the aviation section when reissuing the book in 1935 as *A History of the World War*, and the chapter remained in the 1970 edition, *Liddell Hart's History of the World War*. In the five years separating the first two editions the British military historian apparently developed sufficient regard for the value of military aviation to realize he needed to correct his earlier text. His enhanced opinion of the potential of air power, as well as his misunderstanding of reconnaissance within the broader topic, were likely influenced by several interwar developments, including the debate over the future of military aviation sparked by Douhet, Mitchell, and Trenchard; aviation technological advances demonstrated most dramatically by Charles Lindbergh's Atlantic crossing; the rebirth of the *Luftwaffe* in Germany; and the associated buildup of European military aviation in anticipation of the Spanish Civil War. Liddell Hart's assessment of military aviation appeared at the beginning of a revival of the debate over the future of air power, an argument that had seemed to settle down in the wake of Billy Mitchell's court-martial.[9]

Bombing's subsequent prominence in the Second World War seemed to prove what Liddell Hart had said about First World War commanders' failure to properly utilize aviation. Armed with the theory that aviation could only seriously affect the course and outcome of war when it was dropping bombs on military, naval, or civilian targets, historians writing since the end of the Second

World War have marched in the footsteps of Douhet and Liddell Hart, ignoring aviation's vital worth as an intelligence arm during the First World War.

Over the last several decades, aviation's diminution has seriously impacted the larger story of the war. First World War aviation specialists' appetite for minutiae has compartmentalized aerial operations separating aerial operations from the broader history of the First World War. Edward Jablonski opines such bifurcation has managed to "produce a history of the war in the air and make it appear that it was the only one being fought during 1914–18."[10] Peter M. Grosz, widely regarded as the leading authority on German Great War military aviation, echoed these comments in a conversation with the author, saying that he thought it possible to become very expert on the air war without knowing much at all about the war's larger history.[11] In short, the air war can be studied in total isolation, without reference to what happened on the ground or at sea. Many historians take the opposite approach as well, studying the ground or naval wars without any reference to aviation.

Yet, if military analysts and historians did a complete turnaround and acknowledged aviation's major role in the First World War they would still find their studies hampered by the improper categorization of reconnaissance and observation within the overall concept of air power. Rather than view aerial intelligence gathering as a division of military aviation, both amateur and professional historians have frequently written about reconnaissance and observation as nothing more than an early stage in the evolution of air power. Edward Jablonski wrote in 1964 that in the war's early months "the major function of planes remained scouting and reconnaissance."[12] By the end of 1914, however, Jablonski added:

> Some airmen—and some, but fewer, ground men—were awakening to the airplane's possibilities as an instrument of destruction. The offhand, almost hit-or-miss operations in which the airplane had engaged began to intimate a future role in the war. The fledglings, having sprouted more powerful wings, were growing talons.[13]

Few subsequent mentions of reconnaissance and observation appeared in Jablonski's account. His air story turned almost exclusively to fighter pilots and zeppelin raids, arguing "during World War I, air power was not conclusive," at least not in the way aviation contributed to the successful conclusion of the Second World War.[14] Considering some of the other functions aviation fulfilled between 1914 and 1918, he characterized "observation" and "photography" as "limitedly effective in a military sense."[15] Jablonski gave the reconnaissance crews a brief opportunity to counter this argument by quoting American pilot, Lt. Walter V. Barneby, who wrote to his mother "it is the observation planes that do most of the hard work and get the least credit for it. They are the eyes of the modern army, and their work is by far the most important."[16] While Barneby's claim might have impressed his mother, it failed to convince Jablonski, who concluded that, "the first war in the air was, in the main, a fighter pilot's war."[17]

Just as Jablonski's popular history wrote off the immediate value of reconnaissance and observation in favor of the more lethal potential seen in bombers and fighters, so did other more scholarly works. Irwin B. Holley took this same path in his 1971 study of US Air Service doctrine and technology. Holley argued that Brig. Gen. George Scriven's December 1914 appearance before the House Military Affairs Committee, during which the chief signal officer told Congress he did not believe airplanes had proven their worth as weapons, "exposed his failure to distinguish between the concept of the aerial weapon and its contemporary application." Holley went on to speculate that the "probable span between existing technological development and ultimate development escaped him."[18] In sum, aerial reconnaissance constituted only the beginning and the true value of aviation lies in its ability to evolve beyond its use as an elevated observation platform.

This failure of air power disciples and historians to properly characterize the status of aerial intelligence gathering during the First World War is an important key to understanding why the airplane's role has been written out of the war's larger history. Appreciating aviation's value is impossible without a thorough understanding of the worth of aerial reconnaissance and observation to ground and naval operations. Furthermore, historians, like military strategists, cannot adequately appreciate or communicate the true nature of the war without incorporating the role played by aviation into their narratives. Nor can air power students reach a complete understanding of their own discipline if they continue to minimize observation and reconnaissance; a branch that still constitutes one third of the field and which clearly dominated its early years.

The Smithsonian's National Air and Space Museum on the Washington, DC mall has lent its considerable institutional authority to the diminution of the role aerial reconnaissance played in the first air war in its "Legend, Memory and the Great War in the Air" Gallery. The aircraft on display—mostly fighters—point the visitor's attention toward the romantic image of the fighter pilot rather than the utility of aerial reconnaissance and the story told in the accompanying explanatory material depicts aviation as a failure.[19] Courtland Bryan, author of the "authorized book" on the museum's collection summed up the part aviation played in the fighting by contending:

> Most historians agree that the role played by air power during this struggle was more romantic than decisive. The most important missions the airplane carried out were reconnaissance and artillery fire control. And when the war bogged down into static frontline trench warfare and increasingly effective camouflage techniques evolved, aerial reconnaissance became less and less significant.[20]

Bryan's interpretation of aviation's diminishing importance over the course of the war does not make sense against overwhelming evidence that all the belligerent powers continually expanded their air services between 1914 and 1918. More than twenty million visitors passed through the National Air and Space Museum in the two years following its 1976 opening and more recent attendance figures still exceed six million annual visitors, making it the second most popular museum in the United States.[21] Numbers this large suggest the museum's misleading presentation must contribute significantly to the public's perception of First World War aviation history.

The mischaracterization of the aviator's role in the Great War extends beyond the museum world to the work of the conflict's leading historians. Descriptions of the airplane in its intelligence-gathering role are typically found in the first few pages of aviation histories or in the "air war" chapter of the war's general histories. John Toland's Pulitzer Prize-winning *No Man's Land: 1918—the Last Year of the Great War* discussed aviation sporadically, only occasionally mentioning reconnaissance and observation.[22] Toland noted, for example, that in the run-up to Germany's March 1918 "Operation Michael" offensive, Hindenberg hoped bad weather would keep enemy reconnaissance flights on the ground.[23] He also mentioned that during the battle of Chateau Thierry, William Mitchell, then a US Air Service colonel, flew over the front drinking in the details of the ground fighting.[24] As Toland built to the final American offensive at the Meuse-Argonne, he admitted "the safety of thousands of our attacking soldiers" rode on the success of the US Air Service's attacks on German observation balloons.[25] But, like many other historians, Toland did not discuss the role of those balloons in any depth, the role of airplanes engaged in reconnaissance or in operational planning, or the value of aerial observation to artillery operations or infantry liaison. Instead Toland concentrated on fighter pilots Eddie Rickenbacker, Manfred von Richthofen, and Quentin Roosevelt, and American air commander Billy Mitchell.[26]

Lyn MacDonald's *1915: the Death of Innocence* devoted the equivalent of just a couple pages out of more than six hundred to the RFC's early photography and artillery registration efforts. MacDonald wrote that "the mapmakers were working overtime and for the first time since the stalemate had set in the Army would have eyes, would be able to see beyond ridges and round corners, and the troops preparing for the coming battle would know precisely where they were going and what they would be up against."[27] Hopeful as they appear, these few words hardly qualify as a thorough and sifting discussion of the revolution brought to battle planning by the addition of the third dimension. Further, MacDonald's otherwise lengthy bibliography does not contain a single aviation title.

In their account of the American war effort, *The Last Days of Innocence: America at War, 1917–1918*, Meirion and Susie Harries acknowledge a variety of possible uses of air power, including reconnaissance, observation, and photography, before focusing heavily on aerial combat. The authors begin by writing that aircraft played "an important part in the battle, observing, photographing, directing artillery, strafing ground troops, bombing rear areas, bombing civilian targets … dropping propaganda leaflets, and fighting to deny the same opportunities to the enemy."[28] Forced to observe the war from a distance until 1917, Americans apparently came to regard aerial warfare as an attractive alternative to more traditional forms of battle. The Harries argue "this could be America's kind of combat with dogfights between aces offering far more scope for rugged individualism than the dirty, bloody, depersonalized struggle on the ground."[29] Focusing on romance rather than the substance of the air war, the Harries followed the development of the US Air Service on the Western Front through its climax in the Meuse-Argonne campaign, during which they maintain, "Billy Mitchell's aircraft at last began to fulfill some of the soaring hopes of the apostles of air power." At the "very last moment the air forces were putting the 'Yankee Punch' into the war and pointing the way to the air combat of the future."[30] The Harries acknowledge the importance of reconnaissance to a greater degree than others, but like their contemporaries, they relegate aviation's "eyes of the army" function to the lesser status of an early development. By implication they minimized reconnaissance, characterizing it as a stepping-stone along the path to the more aggressive, supposedly more important work that followed.

Similarly, John Keegan wrote only a few lines about the role aircraft and airmen played in the war. His *The First World War* (1998), a wide-ranging and influential account of the conflict, offered an opinion on the state of air power in the penultimate year of the fighting. Keegan concluded, "The war in the air, which by 1918 would take a dramatic leap forward into the fields of ground-attack and long-range strategic bombing, remained during 1917 largely stuck at the level of artillery observation, 'balloon busting,' and dogfighting to gain or retain air superiority."[31] In short, aviation only began to matter when it progressed beyond its reconnaissance functions.

Richard Holmes' biography of Sir John French, *The Little Field Marshal*, reserved most of its aviation discussion for French's stint as commander of British home defense efforts. As part of this assignment French had charge of protecting Great Britain from aerial attack. Attempting to coordinate Army and Navy programs for protection of the homeland made French a believer in, and an advocate of, a unified air command and an independent air force. The British Field Marshal also became an early champion of the idea that a modern air force could substitute for a larger, traditional ground army. As Lord Lieutenant of Ireland, the post he took on following his period as chief home defender, French encouraged the liberal use of force against Sinn Fein. As Holmes wrote, "French was well aware that the lack of trained troops in Ireland made the sort of action he envisaged somewhat difficult to achieve. He had his own ideas as to how this shortage could best be offset. On 14 April 1918 he had decided that aircraft could be used with good effect in Ireland."[32] Making this argument while the war was still in progress placed French ahead of Trenchard and Mitchell as an air power advocate, as neither of the more famous military aviation leaders took up this cause until after the armistice. Holmes's emphasis on home defense and imperial policing might imply that French thought little of the RFC's observation work in France. Yet no less an authority than the aerial photography pioneer, Lt. Col. John Moore-Brabazon, put French at the forefront of reliance on aerial reconnaissance, noting that, "at the end of 1914, General French asked General [David] Henderson [first commanding general of the Royal Flying Corps in the field] to start taking photographs from the air."[33]

These general histories of the war portray air power as an evolutionary process in which the importance of aerial reconnaissance diminished in direct relation to the growth of an air force's more combative arms. In their view the airplane's more aggressive and more glamorous functions simply overshadowed the mundane duty of gathering intelligence until reconnaissance and observation simply stepped out of the story altogether. Their suggestions that the limited performance, overall unreliability, lack of impressive weight-carrying capability, and total lack of armament of early military aircraft restricted their usefulness to the performance of reconnaissance carry with them the implication reconnaissance itself was of little or no military value.

Disconnecting the air war from the rest of the fighting, the failure of historians to properly characterize reconnaissance as a division of air power, and the reorganization of military aviation following the Second World War to emphasize strategic bombing have all combined to belittle the reputation of the Great War's reconnaissance fliers. And in the absence of a thorough discussion of the worth of aerial reconnaissance historians analyzing the conflict from a broader perspective have minimized aviation's importance to the point that the whole field has been practically written out of the war's overall story. The real significance of aviation in the First World War, now routinely ignored, lies in how quickly and how thoroughly aerial observation, photography, and reconnaissance became integral parts of combat on the ground through their connections to artillery spotting, map-making and intelligence gathering. From the very beginning aviation dictated the direction taken by the fighting in ways that lengthened the conflict while simultaneously adding to the casualty count in some ways, yet saving lives in others. Aviators created the conditions that led to positional warfare on the Western Front and destroyed the initial Russian effort against Germany's eastern frontier. Later their observation missions extended the possible range of artillery well beyond early efforts at indirect fire, which had previously depended on imprecise maps and ground-based observers. During the war's last two years the development of naval convoys equipped with balloons and covered by seaplane and flying boat patrols defeated the U-boat threat. And in the final phase of the Middle East campaign, aircrews proved their worth by returning quickly with vital information from terrain impervious to cavalry patrols.[34] Aviators had become absolutely vital to the war.

The development of three-dimensional warfare magnified the battlefield bringing greater numbers of troops and entire civilian populations into the fighting and turning what most had expected to be a short war of maneuver into a grueling endurance contest of attrition the Germans called *Materialschlacht*. By putting eyes all over the sky aviators not only altered the character of the First World War, they changed the nature and scope of organized warfare forever.[35]

Bibliography

Archival Primary Sources

France

Service Historique de la Maritime. SSGA Box 144. Military Archive 2005-05-19. Château Vincennes. Paris.

United Kingdom

Air Ministry World War I Files (Air 1). The National Archives: Public Record Office. London.
Frederick Laws Papers. RAF Museum. London.
J. T. C. Moore-Brabazon Papers. RAF Museum. London.
War Office Files (WO). The National Archives: Public Record Office. London.

United States

Cong. Rec., 110th Cong. 1st Sess. 2007. 143. Pt. 138: 11650.
Gorrell's History of the Air Service. Record Group 120. Records of the American Expeditionary Forces (World War I). National Archives Records Administration.
Separate Air Force. File 321.9. Box 487. Record Group 18. Air Corps Central File 1917–1938. National Archives Records Administration.
US Air Service Balloon Section Papers. Maxwell AFB, USAF: Historical Research Agency.

Secondary Published Sources

Army War College. *General Notes on the Use of Artillery*, November 1917. Washington: Government Printing Office, 1917.
Army War College. *Notes on Employment of Artillery in Trench Fighting: From Latest Sources: War Department Document No. 594: Office of the Adjutant General.* Washington: Government Printing Office, 1917.
Ashworth, Tony. *Trench Warfare 1914–1918: The Live and Let Live System.* London: Pan, 2000.
Babbitt, George. *Norman Prince: A Volunteer Who Died for a Cause He Loved.* New York: Houghton Mifflin, 1917.
Bailey, Jonathan B. A. *Field Artillery and Firepower.* Annapolis: Naval Institute Press, 2004.

Balloon Observations and Instructions on the Subject of Work in the Basket: A Free Translation of the French Booklet "Instructions au sujet du Travail en Nacelle" and an Added Discourse on Balloon Observation. Washington: Government Printing Office, 1918.

Beach, Charles. *Air Service Boys Flying for France: or the Young Heroes of the Lafayette Escadrille.* Cleveland: World Syndicate, 1919.

Beaver, Daniel R. *Modernizing the American War Department: Change and Continuity in a Turbulent Era, 1885–1920.* Kent: Kent State University Press, 2006.

Beylot, Agnès. "Military Aerial Photographs from 1914 to the Present: A Survey of the Sources," in *Images of Conflict: Military Aerial Photography and Archaeology,* edited by Birger Stichelbaut, Jean Bourgeois, Nicholas Saunders and Piet Chielens, 135–50. Cambridge: Cambridge Scholars Publishing, 2009.

Bishop, Austin. *Bob Thorpe: Sky Fighters of the Lafayette Flying Corps.* New York: Harcourt, Brace, 1919.

Bishop, William A., *Winged Warfare.* Garden City: Doubleday, 1967.

Bordeaux, Henry. *Georges Guynemer, Knight of the Air.* New Haven: Yale University Press, 1918.

Bourke, Joanna. *An Intimate History of Killing: Face-to-Face Killing in 20th Century Warfare.* New York: Basic Books, 1999.

Bowen, Ezra. *Knights of the Air.* Alexandria: Time-Life Books, 1980.

Boyle, Andrew. *Trenchard: Man of Vision.* New York: W. W. Norton Co., 1962.

Boyne, Walter J. *The Influence of Air Power upon History.* Gretna: Pelican, 2003.

British Air Ministry. *Handbook of German Military and Naval Aviation (War) 1914–1918.* 1918. Reprint, London: Imperial War Museum in association with Battery Press, 1995.

Bryan, Courtland. *The National Air and Space Museum.* New York: Abrams, 1979.

Bronnenkant, Lance J. *The Imperial German Eagles in World War I: Their Postcards and Pictures.* Atglen: Schiffer Military History, 2006.

Brown, Walt, Jr. *An American for Lafayette: The Diaries of E. C. C. Genét, Lafayette Escadrille.* Charlottesville: University Press of Virginia, 1981.

Bruce, John M. *British Aeroplanes 1914–1918.* London: Putnam, 1957.

Budiansky, Stephen. *Air Power: The Men, Machines, and Ideas that Revolutionized War, from Kitty Hawk to Gulf War II.* New York: Viking, 2004.

Campbell, Douglas. *Let's Go Where the Action Is!* Knightstown: JaaRE, 1984.

Carr, Michael. "United States Air Service," in *The United States in the First World War: An Encyclopedia,* edited by Anne Cipriano Venzon, 603–07. New York: Garland, 1995.

Chamberlain, Cyrus F. *Letters of Cyrus Foss Chamberlain.* Minneapolis: Publisher Unknown, 1918.

Chapman, Victor. *Victor Chapman's Letters from France.* New York: MacMillan, 1917.

Chandler, Charles D. *Balloon Section Report.* Tours: US Air Service Headquarters, 1918.

Chasseaud, Peter. *Artillery's Astrologers: A History of British Survey and Mapping on the Western Front 1914–1918.* Lewes: Mapbooks, 1999.

Cheeseman, E. Frank. *Reconnaissance and Bomber Aircraft of the 1914–1918 War.* Letchworth: Harleyford, 1962.

Cole, Christopher. ed. *Royal Flying Corps 1915–1916.* London: William Kimber, 1969.

Cole, Christopher, and E. Frank Cheesman. *The Air Defence of Britain 1914–1918*. London: Putnam, 1984.

Church, Frances C. *Diary of a WWI Pilot: Ambulances, Planes, Friends: Harvey Conover's Adventures in France 1917–1918*. Spokane: Conover-Patterson Publishers, 2004.

Coates, Tim. ed. *The World War I Collection: Gallipoli and the Early Battles, 1914–15: The Dardanelles Commission, 1914–16; British Battles of World War I, 1914–15*. London: The Stationery Office, 2001.

Cooke, James J. *Billy Mitchell*. Boulder: Lynne Rienner, 2002.

Cooke, James J. *The US Air Service in the Great War, 1917–1919*. Westport: Praeger, 1996.

Coulthard-Clark, Chris. *McNamara, VC: A Hero's Dilemma*. Fairbairn: Air Power Studies Centre, 1997.

Crowell, Benedict. *America's Munitions 1917–1918: Report of Benedict Crowell, the Assistant Secretary of War, Director of Munitions*. Washington: Government Printing Office, 1919.

Davilla, James. J., and Arthur M. Soltan. *French Aircraft of the First World War*. Stratford: Flying Machines Press, 1997.

Degelow, Carl. *Germany's Last Knight of the Air: The Memoirs of Carl Degelow*. Translated and edited by Peter J. Kilduff. London: William Kimber, 1979.

Division of Military Aeronautics, US Army. *Balloon Observation and Instructions on the subject of Work in the Basket: Supplement*. Washington: Government Printing Office, 1918.

Douhet, Giulio. *The Command of the Air*. 1942. Reprint, Washington: Office of Air Force History, 1983.

Driggs, Laurence L. *The Adventures of Arnold Adair, American Ace*. Boston: Little Brown, 1918.

Duiven, Rick, and Dan-San Abbott. *Schlachtflieger! Germany and the Origins of Air/Ground Support 1916–1918*. Atglen: Schiffer Military Publishing, 2006.

Dunbar, Ruth. *The Swallow: a Novel Based Upon the Actual Experiences of One of the Survivors of the Famous Lafayette Escadrille*. New York: Boni and Liveright, 1919.

Dunn, James C. *The War the Infantry Knew 1914–1919: A Chronicle of Service in France and Belgium with the Second Battalion His Majesty's Twenty-Third Foot, the Royal Welch Fusiliers*. London: Jane's, 1987.

Ellis, John. *The Social History of the Machine Gun*. New York: Pantheon, 1975.

Finnegan, Terrence J. *Shooting the Front: Allied Aerial Reconnaissance and Photographic Interpretation on the Western Front—World War I*. Washington: National Defense Intelligence College Press, 2006.

Fischer, Suzanne H. *Mother of Eagles: The War Diary of Baroness von Richthofen*. Atglen: Schiffer Military History, 2001.

Flammer, Philip. *The Vivid Air: The Lafayette Escadrille*. Athens: University of Georgia Press, 1981.

Flying Officers of the United States Navy 1917–1919. Atglen: Schiffer Military History, 1997.

Franks, Norman L. R., Frank W. Bailey, and Russell Guest. *Above the Lines: A Complete Record of the Fighter Aces of the German Air Service, Naval Air Service and Flanders Marine Corps 1914–1918*. London: Grub Street, 1993.

Franks, Norman L. R., and Frank W. Bailey. *Over the Front: A Complete Record of the Fighter Aces and Units of the United States and French Air Services, 1914–1918*. London: Grub Street, 1992.

Fuller, J. F. C. *The Conduct of War 1789–1961*. New York: Da Capo Press, 1992.

Gibbons, Floyd. *The Red Knight of Germany*. Garden City: Sun Dial Press, 1927.

Genét, Edmond. *War Letters of Edmond Genét: The First American Aviator Killed Flying the Stars and Stripes*. New York: Charles Scribner's Sons, 1918.

Girouard, Mark. *The Return to Camelot: Chivalry and the English Gentleman*. New Haven: Yale University Press, 1981.

Gordon, Dennis. *Lafayette Escadrille Pilot Biographies*. Missoula: Doughboy Historical Society, 1991.

Grinnell-Milne, Duncan. *Wind in the Wires*. Garden City: Doubleday, 1968.

Guttman, Jon. *Spa 124 Lafayette Escadrille: American Volunteers in World War I*. Oxford: Osprey, 2004.

Hahn, J. E. *The Intelligence Service within the Canadian Corps 1914–1918*. Toronto: MacMillan, 1930.

Hall, Bert. *En l'Air*. New York: New Library, 1918.

Hall, Bert. *One Man's War*. New York: Holt, 1929.

Hall, James N. *Kitchener's Mob*. Boston: Houghton Mifflin, 1916.

Hall, James N. *High Adventure: A Narrative of Air Fighting in France*. Boston: Houghton Mifflin, 1918.

Hall, James N., and Charles B. Nordhoff. *The Lafayette Flying Corps*. Boston: Houghton Mifflin, 1920.

Hall, James N., and Charles B. Nordhoff, Jr. *The Lafayette Flying Corps*. 1920. Reprint, Port Washington: Kennikat Press, 1964.

Hallion, Richard P. *The Rise of the Fighter Aircraft, 1914–1918*. Baltimore: Nautical and Aviation Press, 1984.

Halpern, Paul G. *A Naval History of World War I*. Annapolis: Naval Institute Press, 1994.

Hamady, Theodore. *The Nieuport 28: America's First Fighter*. Atglen: Schiffer Military Publishing, 2007.

Hanson, Neil. *First Blitz: The Secret German Plan to Raze London to the Ground in 1918*. London: Doubleday, 2008.

Harries, Merrion, and Susie Harries. *The Last Days of Innocence: America at War, 1917–1918*. New York: Random House, 1997.

Harris, John. *Knights of the Air: Canadian Aces of World War I*. New York: St. Martin's Press, 1958.

Haupt, Peter. "Great War Aerial Photographs in German Archives: a Guide to the Sources," in *Images of Conflict: Military Aerial Photography and Archaeology*, edited by Birger Stichelbaut, Jean Bourgeois, Nicholas Saunders and Piet Chielens, 151–64. Cambridge: Cambridge Scholars Press, 2009.

Haydon, F. Stansbury. *Military Ballooning during the Early Civil War*. Baltimore: Johns Hopkins University Press, 2000.

Headquarters American Expeditionary Force. *Aerial Observation for Artillery*. Paris: Imprimerie Nationale, 1918.

Headquarters American Expeditionary Force. *Instruction on Liaison for Troops of All Arms.* Paris: Imprimerie Nationale, 1917.

Headquarters American Expeditionary Force. *Instructions for the Employment of Aerial Observation in Liaison with the Artillery.* Paris: Imprimerie Nationale, 1917.

Herbert, Craig S. *Eyes of the Army: A Story about the Observation Balloon Service of World War I.* Lafayette Hill: Privately Published, 1986.

Higham, Robin, and Dennis E. Showalter, eds., *Researching World War I: a Handbook.* Westport: Greenwood Press, 2003.

Hilliard, Jack B. *Capronis, Farmans and SIAs: U.S. Army Aviation Training and Combat in Italy with Fiorello LaGuardia 1917–1918.* Trento: LoGisma, 2006.

Hoeppner, Ernst von. *Germany's War in the Air: The Development and Operations of German Military Aviation in the World War.* Translated by J. Hawley Larned. 1921. Reprint, Nashville: Battery Press, 1994.

Holley, Irwin B., Jr. *Ideas and Weapons: Exploitation of the Aerial Weapon by the United States during World War I; a Study in the Relationship of Technological Advance, Military Doctrine, and the Development of Weapons.* Hamden: Archon Books, 1971.

Holmes, Richard. *The Little Field Marshal: A Life of Sir John French.* 1981. Reprint, London: Cassel, 2005.

Hudson, James J. *Hostile Skies: A Combat History of the American Air Service in World War I.* Syracuse: Syracuse University Press, 1968.

Imrie, Alex, *Pictorial History of the German Army Air Service, 1914–1918.* 1971. Reprint, Chicago: Henry Regnery, 1973.

Jean, David, Bernard Palmieri, and Georges-Didier Rohrbacher. *Les Escadrilles de l'Aéronatique Militaire Française: Symbolique et Histoire 1912–1920.* Paris: Service Historique de l'Armée de l'Air, 2004.

Jablonski, Edward. *The Knighted Skies: A Pictorial History of World War I in the Air.* New York: Putnam, 1964.

Jablonski, Edward. *Man with Wings: A Pictorial History of Aviation.* Garden City: Doubleday, 1980.

Jablonski, Edward. *Warriors with Wings: The Story of the Lafayette Escadrille.* Indianapolis: Bobbs-Merrill, 1966.

Johnson, Herbert A. *Wingless Eagle: US Army Aviation through World War I.* Chapel Hill: University of North Carolina Press, 2001.

Johnson, Robert. *The American Heritage of James Norman Hall.* Philadelphia: Dorrance, 1969.

Johnson, Terry L. *Valiant Volunteers: A Novel Based on the Passion and the Glory of the Lafayette Escadrille.* Bloomington: Authorhouse, 2005.

Keegan, John. *The First World War.* New York: Knopf, 1998.

Kennett, Lee. *The First Air War 1914–1918.* New York, Free Press, 1991.

Kiernan, R. H. *Captain Albert Ball, V. C., D. S. O.* (two bars), *M. C., Croix de Chevalier, Légion d'Honneur, Russian Order of St. George.* London: John Hamilton Limited, 1933.

Kilduff, Peter. *Richthofen: Beyond the Legend of the Red Baron.* New York: John Wiley and Sons, 1993.

Knight, Clayton. *We Were There with the Lafayette Escadrille.* New York: Grosset and Dunlap, 1961.

Kommandeur der Flieger 6, *Wöchentlicher Tätigkeitsbericht, Nr. 22400,* January 14–21, 1917.

Kommandierender General der Luftstreitkräfte. *Bildmeldung der Luftschiffer.* Charleville: Kogenluft, 1917.

Kommandierender General der Luftstreitkräfte. *Bildmeldung der Flieger.* Charleville: Kogenluft, 1917.

Lahm, Frank P. *The World War I Diary of Col. Frank P. Lahm, Air Service, A.E.F.* Maxwell AFB: Historical Research Division, Aerospace Studies Institute, Air University, 1970.

Laplander, Robert J. *Finding the Lost Battalion: Beyond the Rumors, Myths and Legends of America's Famous WWI Epic.* Waterford: American Expeditionary Foundation and Lulu Press, 2006.

Layman, Richard D. *Naval Aviation in the First World War: Its Impact and Influence.* Annapolis: Naval Institute Press, 1996.

Lebow, Eileen F. *A Grandstand Seat: The American Balloon Service in World War I.* Westport: Praeger, 1998.

Lewis, Adrian R. *The American Culture of War: The History of US Military Force from World War II to Operation Iraqi Freedom.* New York: Routledge, 2007.

Liddell Hart, Basil. *The Real War, 1914–1918.* Boston: Little, Brown, 1930.

Liddell Hart, Basil. *Liddell Hart's History of the First World War.* 1930 as *The Real War 1914–1918.* Reprint, London: Papermac, 1997.

Luvaas, Jay. trans. *Frederick the Great on the Art of War.* New York: Free Press, 1966.

Lynn, Escott. *Knights of the Air.* London: N. and R. Chambers, 1918.

MacDonald, Lyn. *1915: The Death of Innocence.* London: Headline Book Publishing, 1993.

MacIsaac, David. "Voices from the Central Blue: The Air Power Theorists," in *Makers of Modern Strategy: From Machiavelli to the Nuclear Age,* edited by Peter Paret, 624–47. Princeton: Princeton University Press, 1986.

Maitland, Lester, *Knights of the Air.* Garden City: Doubleday, Doran, 1929.

Mason, Herbert Molloy, Jr. *Lafayette Escadrille: The First American Flyers to Face the German Air Force 1914–1917.* New York: Konecky and Konecky, 1964.

Maurer, Maurer, ed. *The US Air Service in World War I.* 4 vols. Washington: Office of Air Force History, 1978.

Maurer, Maurer, ed. *Aviation in the U. S. Army, 1919–1939.* Washington: Office of Air Force History, 1987.

McConnell, James. *Flying for France.* Garden City: Doubleday, 1917.

McFarland, R. M. *History of the Bureau of Aircraft Production.* Maxwell Air Force Base: US Air Force Historical Research Agency, 1951.

McPherson, James. *Battle Cry of Freedom: The Civil War Era.* Oxford: Oxford University Press, 1988.

Meeker, William H. *William Henry Meeker, his Book.* N.p.: Privately printed, 1917.

Messimer, Dwight R. *Find and Destroy: Antisubmarine Warfare in World War I.* Annapolis: Naval Institute Press, 2001.

Messimer, Dwight R. *Verscholen: World War I U-Boat Losses.* Annapolis: Naval Institute Press, 2002.

Methods of Obtaining and Transmitting Information by Balloon Service: Information from French and American Sources to Army Balloon School, American Expeditionary Forces. Washington: Government Printing Office, 1918.

Mitchell, William. *Memoirs of World War I: From Start to Finish of Our Greatest War.* New York: Random House, 1960.

Mitchell, William. *Our Air Force: The Keystone of National Defense.* New York: E. P. Dutton, 1921.

Mitchell, William. *Winged Defense: The Development and Possibilities of Modern Air Power Economic and Military.* 1925. Reprint, Mineola: Dover Publications,1998.

Molter, Bennett. *Knights of the Air.* New York: D. Appleton, 1918.

Moore, John, ed. *Jane's Fighting Ships of World War I.* New York: Military Press, 1990.

Morris, Alan. *The Balloonatics.* London: Jarrolds, 1970.

Morrow, John H., Jr. *The Great War in the Air: Military Aviation from 1909 to 1921.* Washington: Smithsonian Institution Press, 1993.

Morse, Daniel P., Jr., *The History of the 50th Aero Squadron: The "Dutch Girl" Observation Squadron in World War I.* 1920. Reprint, Nashville: Battery Press, 1990.

Mortane, Jacques. *Guynemer, the Ace of Aces.* New York: Moffat, Yard, 1918.

Nowarra, Heinz J. *50 Jahre Deutsche Luftwaffe.* Genoa: Intyprint, 1964.

Nash, Lee. "Aircraft," in *The United States in the First World War: An Encyclopedia*, edited by Anne Cipriano Venzon, 7–8. New York: Garland, 1995.

Neumann, George. *Die Deutschen Luftstreitkräfte im Weltkrieg.* Berlin: E. S. Mittler and Son, 1920.

Noffsinger, James. *World War I Aviation Books in English: An Annotated Bibliography.* Metuchen: Scarecrow, 1987.

Novick, Peter. *That Noble Dream: The "Objectivity Question" and the American Historical Profession.* Cambridge: Cambridge University Press, 1988.

O'Connor, Mike. *Airfields and Airmen of the Channel Coast.* Barnsley: Pen and Sword, 2005.

O'Connor, Martin. *Air Aces of the Austro-Hungarian Empire 1914–1918.* Mesa: Champlin Fighter Museum Press. 1986.

O'Connor, Neal W. *Aviation Awards of Imperial Germany in World War I and the Men Who Earned Them.* 7 vols. Princeton: Foundation for Aviation World War I, 1988–2007.

Office of Military Aeronautics, US Army. *Principles Underlying the Use of Balloons.* Washington: Government Printing Office, 1918.

Opdycke, Leonard. *French Aeroplanes Before the Great War.* Atglen: Schiffer, 1999.

Ovitt S. W. and Bowers, L. G., eds. *The Balloon Section of the American Expeditionary Forces.* New Haven: Privately Published, 1919.

Parsons, Edwin C. *The Great Adventure: The Story of the Lafayette Escadrille.* Garden City: Doubleday, 1937.

Parsons, Edwin C. *Flight into Hell: The Story of the Lafayette Escadrille.* London: Long, 1938.

Parsons, Edwin C. *I Flew with the Lafayette Escadrille.* Indianapolis: E. C. Seale and Company, 1963.

Paegelow, John A. *Operation of Allied Balloons in the Saint Mihiel Offensive*. Tours: US Air Service Headquarters, 1918.

Penrose, Harald. *British Aviation: The Pioneer Years 1903–1914*. London: Putnam, 1967.

Pershing, John J. *My Experiences in the World War*. New York: Frederick Stokes, 1931.

Pfleger, Arthur. *Franz im Feuer—vier Jahre Flugzeugbeobachter*. Regensburg: Manz, 1930.

Pisano, Dominick, ed. *Flight: 100 Years of Aviation*. New York: DK Publishing, 2002.

Raleigh, Walter and H. A. Jones. *The War in the Air: Being the Story of the Part Played in the Great War by the Royal Air Force*. 6 vols. Oxford: Clarendon Press, 1922–1937.

Revell, Alex. *Victoria Cross: WWI Airmen and Their Aircraft*. Stratford: Flying Machines Press, 1997.

Richthofen, Manfred von. *The Red Air Fighter*. London: Aeroplane, 1918.

Rickenbaker, Edward V. *Fighting the Flying Circus*. Garden City: Doubleday, 1965.

Rickenbaker, Edward V. *Rickenbacker: An Autobiography*. Englewood Cliffs: Prentice Hall, 1967.

Robertson, Bruce, ed. *Air Aces of the 1914–1918 War*. Letchworth: Harleyford, 1959.

Robertson, Linda R. *The Dream of Civilized Warfare: World War I Flying Aces and the American Imagination*. Minneapolis: University of Minnesota Press, 2003.

Robinson, Douglas H. *The Zeppelin in Combat: A History of the German Naval Airship Division, 1912–1918*, 3rd ed. Sun Valley: John W. Caler, 1971.

Rockwell, Kiffin. *War Letters of Kiffin Yates Rockwell, Foreign Legionaire and Aviator, France 1914–1916*. Garden City: Country Life Press, 1925.

Rogers, Les. *British Aviation Squadron Markings of World War I, RFC, RAF, RNAS*. Atglen: Schiffer Military History, 2001.

Roskill, Stephen W. *Documents Relating to the Naval Air Service 1908–1918*. London: Naval Records Society, 1969.

Samson, Charles R. *Fights and Flights: A Memoir of the Royal Naval Air Service in World War I*. 1930. Reprint, Nashville: Battery Press, 1990.

Saunders, Hilary S. *Per Ardua: The Rise of British Air Power, 1911–1939*. London: Oxford University Press, 1945.

Shirley, Noel C. *United States Naval Aviation 1910–1918*. Atglen: Schiffer Military Publishing, 2000.

Shores, Christopher, Norman Franks, and Russell Guest. *Above the Trenches: A Complete Record of the Fighter Aces and Units of the British Empire Air Forces 1915–1920*. London: Grub Street, 1990.

Springs, Elliot W. *War Birds: Diary of an Unknown Aviator*. London: John Hamilton, Limited, 1927.

Stallings, Laurence. *The Doughboys: The Story of the AEF, 1917–1918*. New York: Harper and Row, 1963.

Strachan, Hew. *The First World War*. New York: Viking, 2003.

Streckfuss, James. "Bolling Mission," in *The United States in the First World War: An Encyclopedia*, edited by Anne Cipriano Venzon, 97–98. New York: Garland, 1995.

Sturtivant, Ray, and Gordon Page. *The Camel File*. London: Air Britain, 1993.

Sturtivant, Ray, and Gordon Page. *The D.H. 4/D.H. 9 File*. London: Air Britain, 1999.

Sturtivant, Ray, and Gordon Page. *The S.E. 5 File*. London: Air Britain, 1997.

Sueter, Murray F. "Extracts from Paper by Capt. Murray F. Sueter, Director of Air Department, Admiralty," quoted in Stephen W. Roskill, *Documents Relating to the Naval Air Service 1908–1918*. London: Naval Records Society, 1969.

Supplement to the Pamphlet entitled General Notions of Organization and Tactical Suggestions Indispensable to the Balloon Observer: Division of Military Aeronautics, US Army: This Supplement Supersedes Part I of the Pamphlet. Washington: Government Printing Office, 1918.

Sykes, Frederick. *Aviation in Peace and War.* London: Edward Arnold, 1922.

Sykes, Frederick. *From Many Angles: An Autobiography.* London: George Harrap, 1942.

Thayer, Lucien H. *America's First Eagles: The Official History of the US Air Service, AEF, 1917–1918.* San Jose: R. James Bender Publishing and Champlin Fighter Museum Press, 1983.

Thenault, Georges. *The Story of the Lafayette Escadrille.* Boston: Small, Maynard, 1921.

Ticknor, Caroline, ed. *New England Aviators 1914–1918.* Boston: Houghton Mifflin, 1919.

Toland, John. *No Man's Land: 1918—the Last Year of the Great War.* New York: Smithmark, 1980.

Toulmin, Harry A., Jr. *Air Service, American Expeditionary Force, 1918.* New York: D. Van Nostrand, 1927.

Tripcony, Ralph H. *The Captive or "Kite" Balloon.* Dayton: US Air Service Engineering Division, 1922.

US Air Service. *Operations Between the Meuse and the Argonne Forest from September 26, to November 11, 1918.* Tours: US Air Service Headquarters, 1918.

Valencia, Jerry. *Knights of the Sky.* San Diego: Reed Enterprises, 1980.

"Vigilant." *Richthofen: The Red Knight of the Air.* London: John Hamilton, 1934.

Waller, Douglas. *A Question of Loyalty: Gen. Billy Mitchell and the Court-martial that Gripped the Nation.* New York: Harper Collins, 2004.

Walker, Dale. *Only the Clouds Remain: Ted Parsons of the Lafayette Escadrille.* Amsterdam: Alandale Press, 1980.

Watkis, Nicolas C. *The Western Front from the Air.* Phoenix Mill: Sutton, 1999.

Weber, Eugen. *France Fin de Siècle.* Cambridge: Belknap Press, 1986.

Wellman, William. *Go Get 'Em!: the True Adventures of an Aviator of the Lafayette Flying Corps who was the only Yankee Flyer Fighting over General Pershing's Boys of the Rainbow Division in Lorraine when they first went "Over the Top".* Boston: Page, 1918.

Werner, Johannes. *Knight of Germany: Oswald Boelcke, German Ace.* New York: Arno Press, 1972.

Westover, Oscar, "A Lecture at Army War College by Maj. Gen. Oscar Westover," quoted in Robert F. Futrell, *USAF Historical Studies No. 24: Command of Observation Aviation: A Study in Control of Tactical Airpower.* Maxwell AFB: Air University USAF Historical Division Research Studies Institute, 1956.

Westrop, Mike. *A History of No. 6 Squadron Royal Naval Air Service in World War I.* Atglen: Schiffer Military History, 2006.

Whitehouse, Arthur. *Legion of the Lafayette.* Garden City: Doubleday, 1962.

Whitehouse, Arthur. *The Laughing Falcon.* New York: Putnam, 1969.

Widmer, Emil J. *Military Observation Balloons (Captive and Free): A Complete Treatise on their Manufacture, Equipment, and Handling with Special Instructions for the Training of a Field Balloon Company.* New York: D. Van Nostrand, 1918.
Winslow, Carroll. *With the French Flying Corps.* London: Constable, 1917.
Woodhouse, Henry. *Woodhouse's Textbook of Naval Aeronautics.* Annapolis: Naval Institute Press, 1991.

Online Sources

"About." http://www.ww1aeroinc.org/about.html (accessed June 24, 2011).
"Air of Authority—A History of RAF Organization: Air Chief Marshal Sir Robert Brooke-Popham." http://www.rafweb.org/Biographies/Brooke-Popham.htm (accessed December 13, 2007).
"American Aviators Show their Bravery." New York Times, May 10, 1916. http:query.nytimes.com/mem/archive-free/pdf?res=9E05E3D91331E733A05753C1A93639C946796D6CF (accessed September 11, 2008).
American Battle Monuments Commission. "World War II Listing." http://www.abmc.gov/search/wwii.php (accessed June 25, 2011).
"American Unit Out in French Air Raids." New York Times, May 18, 1916. http:query.nytimes.com/mem/archive-free/pdf?res=9E02E3DE1031E733A0575BC1A9639C946796D6CF (accessed September 11, 2008).
"The Australian Society of World War One Aero Historians. The '14–18 Journal Index: 1964–2004." http://asww1ah.0catch.com/Journal%20Index.pdf (accessed November 11, 2008).
Baedeker, Rob. "America's 25 Most Visited Museums." www.usatoday.com/travel/destinations/2007-09-28-most-visited-museums-forber_N.htm (accessed June 27, 2011).
Bush, George W. "Public Papers of the Presidents of the United States, George W. Bush, 2004." National Office of the Federal Register. http://books.google.com/books (accessed August 19, 2004).
"Chapman Funeral Delayed: American Aviator Believed to Have Fallen in German Lines." New York Times, June 27, 1916. http://query.nytimes.com/mem/archive-free/pdf?res=F30F15F73A5B17738DDDAE0A94DE405B868DF1D3 (accessed March 4, 2011).
"Chapman is Killed in Aeroplane Fight; First American Aviator to Lose Life in War was Noted for Bravery." New York Times, June 25, 1916. http://query.nytimes.com/mem/archive-free/pdf?res=F00A14FA3F5D17738DDDAC0A94DE405B868DF1D3 (accessed March 4, 2011).
"Chapman's Opponent: Boelcke Noted for His Way of Setting Trap for Enemies." New York Times, June 30, 1916. http://query.nytimes.com/mem/archive-free/

pdf?res=F10F15FA3A5512738FDDA90B94DE405B868DF1D3 (accessed March 4, 2011).

"France Army August 1914." www.orbat.com/site/history/historical/france/army1914. html (accessed May 6, 2009).

"The Gatling Gun." www.civilwarhome.com/gatlinggun.htm (accessed May 15, 2008).

Greig, I. T. "The Convoy System and the Two Battles of the Atlantic (1914–18 and 1939–45)." Military History Journal [The South African Military History Society] 6 (December 1984). http://samilitaryhistory.org/vol064ig.html (accessed February 16, 2010).

Kirkland, Faris R. "The French Air Force in 1940: Was It Defeated by the Luftwaffe or by Politics." www.airpower.maxwell.af.mil/airchronicles/aureview/1985/sep-oct/ kirkland.html (accessed June 5, 2011).

"Income Tax (Earnings and Pensions) Act 2003. c. 1, Part 9, Chapter 17, Section 638." www.legislation.gov.uk (accessed August 3, 2008).

"Legend, Memory and the Great War in the Air." www.nasm.si.edu/exhibitions/gal206/ index.cfm (accessed June 27, 2011).

"Les Armées Francaises dans la Grande Guerre." http://toaw.free.fr/afgg/ (accessed February 11, 2011).

Manchester, William. "The Bloodiest Battle of All." New York Times, June 14, 1987. http://query.nytimes.com/gst/fullpage.html?res= 9B0DE1DE153DF937A25755C0A961948260&sec=&spon=&pagewanted=3 (accessed July 29, 2008).

National Maritime Museum. "Admiral Sir Sydney Robert Fremantle." http://www.nmm. ac.uk/collections/archive/catalogue/record.cfm (accessed March 15, 2010).

National Maritime Museum. "Rear-Admiral Sir Murray Sueter." http://www.nmm.ac.uk/ collections/explore/object.cfm (accessed May 13, 2010).

National Security Act of 1947 (Chapter 343; 61 Stat. 496; approved July 26, 1947) [As Amended Through P.L. 110-53, Enacted August 3, 2007]. http://intelligence. senate.gov/nsaact1947.pdf (accessed June 8, 2011).

Price, R. G. "Casualties of War—Putting American Casualties in Perspective." http:// rationalrevolution.net/articles/casualties_of_war.htm (accessed June 25, 2011).

"The Royal Flying Corps." http://www.flightglobal.com/pdfarchive/view/1913/1913%20-% 201119.html (accessed May 13, 2009).

"Second World War: Fatalities." www.secondworldwar.co.uk/index.php/fatalities (accessed June 25, 2011).

Sengupta, Narayan. American Aviators of WWI: US Naval Aviation. www.usaww1.com/ united-states-naval-aviation.php4 (accessed April 22, 2010).

SGA/Mémoire des hommes, www.memoiredeshommes.sga.defense.gouv.fr (accessed February 11, 2011).

Survey Associates. "The Survey for August 5, 1916." http://books.google.com/ books?id=6qEqAAAAMAAJ&pg=PA467&lpg (accessed January 18, 2009).

"That Liberty Shall Not Perish from the Earth." http://library.marshallfoundation.org/ posters/library/posters/poster_full.php?poster=209 (accessed September 25, 2010).

US Centennial of Flight Commission. "Balloons in the American Civil War." http://www.centennialofflight.gov/essay/Lighter_than_air/Civil_War_balloons/LTA (accessed February 15, 2011).

"The Victoria Cross Registers." www.nationalarchives.gov.uk/documentsonline/victoriacross.asp (accessed July 31, 2008).

Wells, H. G. *The War in the Air*. London: MacMillan, 1908. http://etext.library.adelaide.edu.au/w/wells/hg/w45wa/chapter4.html (accessed December 5, 2007).

Articles

"Attack by Air: The Lessons of the Sheerness Incident." *Flight*, December 14, 1912: 1174.

"The Australian Society of World War I Aero Historians." *Cross and Cockade (Great Britain)* 1, no. 4, Winter 1970: 84.

"Aviation in the Services." *Flight*, January 13, 1912: 26.

Capper, John E. "Military Aspect of Dirigible Balloons and Aeroplanes." *Flight*, January 22, 1910: 60–61, and January 29, 1910: 78–79.

Driggs, Laurence LaTourette. "Aces Among Aces." *National Geographic*, June 1918: 568–80.

Fisher, Howard G. "What's Left to be Done: The First Thirty Years." *Over the Front* 6, no. 2, Summer 1991: 129–38.

Gavish, Dov and Dieter H. M. Gröschel. "Leutnant der Reserve Friedrich Rüdenberg, Pilot of Artillerie-Flieger-Abteilung 209, Feldflieger-Abteilung 26/Flieger-Abteilung (A) 259, Jagdstaffel 10, and Jagdstaffel 75." *Over the Front* 16, no. 2, Summer 2001: 99–132.

Gorrell, Edgar S. "What, No Airplanes?" *Over the Front* 5, no. 3, Autumn 1990: 196–212.

Gröschel, Dieter H. M. Letter to the editor. *Over the Front* 17, no. 4, Winter 2002: 369–70.

Hayzlett, Janice, trans. "Nachrichtenblat der Luftstreitkräfte, No. 14." *Over the Front*, 16, no. 2, Summer 2001: 178–82.

Hayzlett, Janice, and Peter Kilduff, trans. "Nachrichtenblat der Luftstreitkräfte No. 15." *Over the Front* 16, no. 3, Autumn 2001: 270–77.

Henderson, David. "The Design of a Scouting Aeroplane." *Flight*, May 18, 1912: 450, 466–67.

Hearne, R. P. "Airships in Peace and War." *Flight*, March 5, 1910: 157.

Ingersoll, Harold R. "Our Insular Position." *Flight*, June 11, 1910: 453–54.

Kastner, Reinhard R. Translated by Dieter Gröschel. "Fatal Accidents in Bavarian Military Training Centers." *Over the Front* 16, no. 4, Winter 2000: 299–325.

"Let's Go 'Over the Front.'" *Over the Front* 1, no. 1, Spring 1986: 2.

"Military Authorities on Aeronautics." *Flight*, March 20, 1909: 164.

Mitchell, William. "America in the Air: The Future of Airplane and Airship, Economically and as Factors in National Defense." *National Geographic*, March 1921: 330–52.

Mitchell, William. "Aeronautical Era." *Saturday Evening Post*, December 20, 1924: 3–4, 99–100, 103.

"The Navy and Aviation." *Flight*, April 5, 1913: 380–81.

"Navy Estimates." *Flight*, March 21, 1914: 292–93.

Nelsen, Stephen F. "French Naval Aircraft." *Cross and Cockade Journal* 7, no. 3, Autumn 1966: 274–83.

O'Connor, Neal W. "Orders, Decorations and Medals Awarded to Leading German Airmen." *Cross and Cockade Journal* 11, no. 3, Autumn 1970: 252–66.

Parks, James J. "Award of the Naval Victory Trophy to Leutnant zur See Wolfram Eisenlohr." *Cross and Cockade Journal* 18, no. 2, Summer 1977: 125–27.

Phillips, Gervase. "Scapegoat Arm: Twentieth-Century Cavalry in Anglophone Historiography." *Journal of Military History* 71, no. 1, January 2007: 37–74.

Rabe, Hanns-Gerd. "Comments and Reminiscences, Flying as an Observer in Flieger-Abteilung (A) 253." Translated by Peter Kilduff. *Over the Front* 17, no. 4, Winter 2002: 292–301.

Radloff, Bill, and Robert Niemann. "The Ehrenbechers–Where Are They Now?" *Cross and Cockade Journal* 10, no. 4, Winter 1969: 366–67.

"Repatriation Report of Lt. Gordon Hunter, No. 60 Squadron, RFC." Quoted in Stewart Taylor. "Letter to the Editor." *Over the Front* 17, no. 4, Winter 2002: 370–73.

"The Royal Flying Corps: RFC Military Wing." *Flight*, October 18, 1913: 1145.

Ruffin, Steve. "'Dutch Girl' Over the Argonne: The 50th Aero Squadron in WWI. *Over the Front* 25, no. 2, Summer 2010: 110–135.

Ruffin, Steve. "Mortal-Immortal: Goettler and Bleckley: 50th Aero Squadron Medal of Honor Airmen." *Over the Front* 25, no. 2, Spring 2010: 136–56.

Sheldon, Bob. "Infantry Contact Patrols In WWI." *Cross and Cockade Journal* 16, no. 3, Autumn 1975: 231–43.

Sieyes, Jacques De. "Aces of the Air." *National Geographic*, January 1918: 5–9.

Stone, F. G. "Defence of Harbours Against Naval Airships." *Flight*, March 13, 1909: 150–51.

Wolff, Guenther, as told to Noel C. Shirley. "Observations from a Beobachter: Ltn. Guenther Wolff, Fl. Abt. (A) 209." *Cross and Cockade Journal* 14, no. 4, Winter 1973: 309–43.

Wynne, H. Hugh. "Origins of the Organization." *Cross and Cockade Journal* 1, no. 1, Spring 1960: 1–2.

Electronic Media and Non-Published Sources

Chasseaud, Peter, ed. *The Imperial War Museum Trench Map Archive on CD-ROM*. London: Naval and Military Press in association with the Imperial War Museum, 2000.

Doerflinger, Joseph. *Side Lights from History: Joseph Doerflinger Talks About his Experiences in Aviation from World War I to World War II*. Thompson Productions, Recording 4075, 33 rpm, undated.

"Enlist Your Lens in the Air Service." Advertisement, *National Geographic* (January 1918), 118.

Fisher, Howard G., "The Men Who Brought You the History" [paper presented at the biennial conference of the League of World War I Aviation Historians, Dayton, OH, September 10, 2003].

Pollock, Granville. "He was Lost Far Up in the Air." *Muskogee Times-Democrat*, April 16, 1918. Quoted in Victoria Pardoe. 2009. *Granville Pollock's Long Lost Letters*. Paper submitted to League of World War I Aviation Historians Mike Carr Essay Contest.

Notes

Introduction

1 H. G. Wells, *The War in the Air* (London: MacMillan, 1908).

2 Frederic Krome, *Fighting the Future War: An Anthology of Science Fiction War Stories, 1914–1945* (New York: Routledge, 2011), 42–46. Krome's anthology examines several futuristic visions of warfare that appeared during the First World War, including Hugo Gernsback's warning of an aerial attack on New York City.

3 F. Stansbury Haydon, *Military Ballooning during the Early Civil War* (1941; repr., Baltimore: Johns Hopkins University Press, 2000), passim.

4 John H. Morrow, Jr., *The Great War in the Air: Military Aviation from 1909 to 1921* (Washington: Smithsonian Institution Press, 1993), 35; Edward Jablonski, *The Knighted Skies: A Pictorial History of World War I in the Air* (New York: G. P. Putnam's Sons, 1964), 11, Jablonski translates Foch's comment as "useless."

5 Morrow, *Great War in the Air*, 45; R. D. Layman, *Naval Aviation in the First World War: Its Impact and Influence* (Annapolis: Naval Institute Press, 1996), 76. Layman offers a February 1917 comment attributed to Haig that he did not think British aerial bombing had "seriously affected" steel production in Germany.

6 August G. Blume, *The Russian Military Air Fleet in World War I: Volume 1: A Chronology 1910–1917* (Atglen: Schiffer, 2010), 177.

7 Walter Raleigh, *The War in the Air: Being the Story of the Part Played in the Great War by the Royal Air Force* (London: Oxford University Press, 1922), 1: 450.

8 ? to the director of Military Aeronautics, December 11, 1918, "A Few Selling Points for a Separate Air Service," File 321.9, box 487, Separate Air Force, RG 18, Air Corps Central File 1917–1938, NARA; William Mitchell, *Winged Defense: The Development and Possibilities of Modern Air Power Economic and Military* (1925; repr., Mineola: Dover Publications, 1998), xii.

Chapter 1

1 George W. Bush, "Public Papers of the Presidents of the United States, George W. Bush, 2004," National Office of the Federal Register, http://books.google.com/books (accessed August 19, 2004).

2   Linda R. Robertson, *The Dream of Civilized Warfare: World War I Flying Aces and the American Imagination* (Minneapolis: University of Minnesota Press, 2003), xii. Robertson concludes that "the dream of dominance through air power, of exerting American will throughout the world without having to risk the lives of ground soldiers, and of relying on bombing to achieve that end," is now firmly established in the psyche of the American people, having begun to take hold "at the time of America's entry into World War I."

3   The Gatling Gun in the Civil War, www.civilwarhome.com/gatlinggun.htm (accessed May 15, 2008); James M. McPherson, *Battle Cry of Freedom* (Oxford: Oxford University Press, 1988), 474, 854.

4   John Ellis, *The Social History of the Machine Gun* (New York: Pantheon, 1975), 42–45.

5   Mark Girouard, *The Return to Camelot: Chivalry and the English Gentleman* (New Haven: Yale University Press, 1981), 14, argued their behavior "suggests an attitude in which heroism [became] more important than the intelligent forethought which would make heroism unnecessary."

6   Ibid., 4–6.

7   Ibid., 14.

8   Ellis, *Social History*, 47–54.

9   Girouard, *Return to Camelot*, v. Arthurian legend figures prominently in Girouard's analysis of factors that led to a nineteenth-century British resurgence in living life according to chivalric principles. In support, he cites examples from architecture, art, fashion, literature, pedagogical principles applied in British public schools, and sport. He might also have cited the American boys' movement "the Knights of King Arthur," the Mark Twain novel *A Connecticut Yankee in King Arthur's Court*, romantic visions of the demise of George Custer and the Seventh Cavalry at the Battle of Little Bighorn and the charge up San Juan Hill led by then-Col. Theodore Roosevelt.

10   Richard Holmes, *The Little Field Marshal: A Life of Sir John French* (London: Cassell, 1981), 58. Holmes praised under-armed and outnumbered Boers facing the British Army at the turn of the twentieth century writing that despite "their idiosyncracies in terms of dress or discipline, the Boers were, quite simply, the best mounted riflemen in the world."

11   The Gatling Gun in the Civil War, www.civilwarhome.com/gatlinggun.htm (accessed May 15, 2008).

12   Dominick Pisano, ed., *Flight: 100 Years of Aviation* (New York: DK Publishing, 2002), 14.

13   Walter J. Boyne, *The Influence of Air Power upon History* (Gretna: Pelican, 2003), 33.

14   Edward Jabonski, *Man with Wings: a Pictorial History of Aviation* (Garden City: Doubleday, 1980), 58.

15   Ibid. Also see Pisano, *Flight: 100 Years*, 20.

16   Jablonski, *Man with Wings*, 63–65. Alberto Santos-Dumont first flew a distance of seven meters in France on September 13, 1906. Longer subsequent flights in October and November of the same year earned the Brazilian-born Parisian the Archdeacon Cup and the French Aero Club prize for flights of twenty-five and one hundred meters respectively.

17   Leonard Opdycke, *French Aeroplanes Before the Great War* (Atglen: Schiffer, 1999), 5.

18   Pisano, *Flight: 100 Years*, 40, 50, 55; Jablonski, *Man with Wings*, 73; Eugen Weber, *France Fin de Siècle* (Cambridge: Belknap Press, 1986), 206–07, connects the development of bicycles, automobiles, and airplanes in France and the United States both through the inventiveness and the competitiveness of those involved in their inception, characterizing their "inspiration" as growing out of "love of danger and novelty, of speed and adventure."

19   Pizano *Flight: 100 Years*, 43.

20   Harald Penrose, *British Aviation: the Pioneer Years* (London: Putnam, 1967), 239.

21   Ibid., 240.

22   Ibid.

23   Walter Raleigh, *The War in the Air: Being the Story of the Part Played in the Great War by the Royal Air Force* (London: Oxford University Press, 1922), 1:138.

24   Penrose, *British Aviation*, 240.

25   Douglas Robinson, *The Zeppelin in Combat: a History of the German Naval Airship Division, 1912–1918* (Sun Valley: Caler, third edition, 1971), 12.

26   Ibid., 14.

27   Ibid., 15.

28   H. G. Wells, *The War in the Air* (London: MacMillan, 1908), http://etext.library. adelaide.edu.au/w/wells/hg/w45wa/chapter4.html (accessed December 5, 2007).

29   F. G. Stone, "Defence of Harbours Against Naval Airships," *Flight* (March 13, 1909), 150–51. Stone's article was an abstract of a speech he delivered on March 10, 1909 to the United Service Institution, a London-based defense studies organization.

30   "Military Authorities on Aeronautics," *Flight* (March 20, 1909), 164.

31   John E. Capper, "Military Aspect of Dirigible Balloons and Aeroplanes," *Flight* (January 22, 1910), 60–61 and *Flight* (January 29, 1910), 78–79.

32   Ibid. (January 29, 1910), 79.

33   *Flight* (March 5, 1910), 157.

34   Ibid.

35   Harold R. Ingersoll, "Our Insular Position," *Flight* (June 11, 1910), 454.

36   Air Chief Marshal Sir Robert Brooke-Popham, http://www.rafweb.org/ Biographies/Brooke-Popham.htm (accessed December 13, 2007). This biographical site documents Henry Robert Moore Brooke-Popham's assignment to the

Oxford Light Infantry at the time his comments appeared in *Flight*. Within a few months he was seconded to duty with the Royal Flying Corps where he served throughout the First World War reaching the temporary rank of brigadier general by the time of the armistice. Brooke-Popham remained with the Royal Air Force following the First World War and retired as an air chief marshal.

37 "Aviation in the Services," *Flight* (January 13, 1912), 26.

38 Ibid.

39 David Henderson, "The Design of a Scouting Aeroplane," *Flight* (May 18, 1912), 450, 466–67.

40 Ibid., 450.

41 Ibid.

42 Ibid.

43 "From the Four Winds: Attack by Air; Lessons of the Sheerness Incident," *Flight* (December 14, 1912), 1174.

44 Ibid.

45 Ibid. Hptm. von Stockhausen's allusion to the lesser capacities of non-rigid and semi-rigid airships effectively pointed the finger at Great Britain and France. Both nations had developed non-rigid and semi-rigid lighter-than-aircraft in preference to rigid airships contrary to German pre-Great War practice.

46 "The Navy and Aviation," *Flight* (April 5, 1913), 380.

47 Ibid.

48 Ibid., 381. Annie Pinder, of the United Kingdom Parliamentary Archives, www.parliament.uk/archives provided Mr. Long's full name.

49 *Flight* (March 21, 1914), 292.

50 Irwin B. Holley, Jr., *Ideas and Weapons: Exploitation of the Aerial Weapon by the United States During World War I; A Study in the Relationship of Technological Advance, Military Doctrine, and the Development of Weapons* (Hamden: Archon, 1971), 146, makes a similar argument analyzing the US Air Service asserting that American commanders based their July 1918 plan to organize 202 squadrons on "calculations of probable rates of production," rather than on doctrine.

51 *Flight* (March 21, 1914), 293.

52 Ibid.

Chapter 2

1 Edwin C. Parsons, *I Flew with the Lafayette Escadrille* (Indianapolis: E. C. Seale and Company, 1963), 61.

2 Jack B. Hilliard, *Capronis, Farmans and SIAs: US Army Aviation Training and Combat in Italy with Fiorello LaGuardia 1917–1918* (Trento: LoGisma, 2006), passim.

3 Elliot White Springs, *War Birds: Diary of an Unknown Aviator* (London: John Hamilton, Limited, 1927), 26–27.

4   Frances Conover Church, *Diary of a WWI Pilot: Ambulances, Planes, Friends: Harvey Conover's Adventures in France 1917–1918* (Spokane: Conover-Patterson Publishers, 2004), 127–28.

5   Peter Kilduff, *Richthofen: Beyond the Legend of the Red Baron* (New York: John Wiley and Sons, 1993), facing 96.

6   Neil Hanson, *First Blitz: the Secret German Plan to Raze London to the Ground in 1918* (London: Doubleday, 2008), 167.

7   Hilliard, *Capronis, Farmans and SIAs*, 535.

8   R. H. Kiernan, *Captain Albert Ball, V. C., D. S. O.* (two bars), *M. C.*, Croix de Chevalier, Légion d'Honneur, *Russian Order of St. George* (London: John Hamilton Limited, 1933), 37, 43.

9   Douglas Campbell, *Let's Go Where the Action Is!* (Knightstown: JaaRE, 1984), 18–19, documents an exception made for Campbell due to a need for officers to oversee organization of the US Air Service's Third Aviation Instruction Center at Issoudun, France.

10   Joseph Doerflinger, *Side Lights from History: Joseph Doerflinger Talks About his Experiences in Aviation from World War I to World War II*, Thompson Productions, Recording 4075, 33 rpm, undated.

11   Dr. Martin O'Connor, *Air Aces of the Austro-Hungarian Empire 1914–1918* (Mesa: Champlin Fighter Museum Press. 1986), 31.

12   Ibid.

13   James J. Hudson, *Hostile Skies: A Combat History of the American Air Service in World War I* (Syracuse: Syracuse University Press, 1968), 26.

14   Ibid., 31; Edward V. Rickenbacker, *Rickenbacker: An Autobiography* (Englewood Cliffs: Prentice Hall, 1967), 92.

15   Hilliard, *Capronis, Farmans, and SIAs*, 256.

16   Ibid., 258.

17   Ibid.

18   Martin Francis, *The Flyer: British Culture and the Royal Air Force 1939–1945* (Oxford, Oxford University Press, 2008), 128.

19   William Manchester "The Bloodiest Battle of All," *New York Times* (June 14, 1987), http://query.nytimes.com/gst/fullpage.html?res=9B0DE1DE153DF937A25755C0A961948260&sec=&spon=&pagewanted=3 (accessed July 29, 2008); Neal W. O'Connor, *Aviation Awards of Imperial Germany in World War I and the Men Who Earned Them—Volume I: The Aviation Awards of the Kingdom of Prussia* (Princeton: Foundation for Aviation World War I, 1990), iii.

20   Jay Luvaas, trans., *Frederick the Great on the Art of War* (New York: Free Press, 1966), 150, 92.

21   Emory M. Thomas, *Bold Dragon: The Life of J. E. B. Stuart* (New York: Harper and Row, 1986), 74.

22   Gervase Phillips, "Scapegoat Arm: Twentieth-Century Cavalry in Anglophone Historiography," *Journal of Military History* 71, no. 1 (January 2007): 52.

23 Joanna Bourke, *An Intimate History of Killing: Face-to-Face Killing in Twentieth-Century Warfare* (New York: Basic Books, 1999), 47.

24 William Avery Bishop, *Winged Warfare* (Garden City: Doubleday, 1967), 21.

25 Ibid.

26 Ibid.

27 J. M. Bruce, *British Aeroplanes 1914–1918* (London: Putnam, 1957), 358, 361; Peter Gray and Owen Thetford, *German Aircraft of the First World War* (London: Putnam, 1962), x; James J. Davilla and Arthur M. Soltan, *French Aircraft of the First World War* (Stratford: Flying Machines Press, 1997), 3–4.

28 Manfred von Richthofen, *The Red Air Fighter* (London: Aeroplane, 1918), 42. Richthofen had originally published *The Red Air Fighter* in 1917 in Germany as *Der Rote Kampflieger*. The appearance of an English translation of the book issued by a British publisher during the war provides strong evidence of the wide popularity tales of fighter pilots commanded with the reading public.

29 Ibid., 44.

30 Edmond Genét, *War Letters of Edmond Genét: The First American Aviator Killed Flying the Stars and Stripes* (New York: Charles Scribner's Sons, 1918), 177.

31 "American Aviators Show their Bravery," *New York Times* (May 10, 1916), http:query.nytimes.com/mem/archive-free/pdf?res=9E05E3D91331E733A05753C1A93639C946796D6CF (accessed September 11, 2008).

32 "American Unit Out in French Air Raids," *New York Times*, May 18, 1916, http:query.nytimes.com/mem/archive-free/pdf?res=9E02E3DE1031E733A0575BC1A9639C946796D6CF (accessed September 11, 2008). In referring to the new American squadron the *New York Times* article used the word "flotilla" rather than the more appropriate "squadron." This translation of the French word "escadrille" reflects both the term's traditional naval usage and the level of ignorance on military aviation matters that prevailed in the United States in the year before the country's entry into the war.

33 James N. Hall and Charles B. Nordhoff, Jr., *The Lafayette Flying Corps* (1920; repr., Port Washington: Kennikat Press, 1964), 1:i; David Jean, Bernard Palmieri, and Georges-Didier Rohrbacher, *Les Escadrilles de l'Aéronatique Militaire Française: Symbolique et Histoire 1912–1920* (Paris: Service Historique de l'Armée de l'Air, 2004), 288; Herbert Molloy Mason, Jr., *Lafayette Escadrille: The First American Flyers to Face the German Air Force 1914–1917* (New York: Konecky and Konecky, 1964), 154.

34 "Chapman is Killed in Aeroplane Fight; First American Aviator to Lose Life in War was Noted for Bravery," *New York Times* (June 25, 1916), http://query.nytimes.com/mem/archive-free/pdf?res=F00A14FA3F-5D17738DDDAC0A94DE405B868DF1D3 (accessed March 4, 2011); "Chapman Funeral Delayed: American Aviator Believed to Have Fallen in German Lines," *New York Times* (June 27, 1916), http://query.nytimes.com/mem/archive-free/pdf?res=F30F15F73A5B17738DDDA-

E0A94DE405B868DF1D3 (accessed March 4, 2011); "Chapman's Opponent: Boelcke Noted for His Way of Setting Trap for Enemies," *New York Times* (June 30, 1916), http://query.nytimes.com/mem/archive-free/pdf?res=F10F15FA3A5512738FDDA90B94DE405B868DF1D3 (accessed March 4, 2011).

35   Mason, *Lafayette Escadrille*, 105.

36   Ibid.

37   Dennis Gordon, *Lafayette Escadrille Pilot Biographies* (Missoula: Doughboy Historical Society, 1991), 43, 55.

38   Ibid., 253.

39   Hall and Nordhoff, *The Lafayette Flying Corps*, 1:68.

40   Gordon, *Lafayette Escadrille Pilot Biographies*, 255–56; Mason, *Lafayette Escadrille*, 40.

41   James N. Hall, *Kitchener's Mob* (Boston: Houghton Mifflin, 1916).

42   James N. Hall, *High Adventure: a Narrative of Air Fighting in France* (Boston: Houghton Mifflin, 1918).

43   James N. Hall and Charles Bernard Nordhoff, *The Lafayette Flying Corps* (Boston: Houghton Mifflin, 1920). Collaboration on *The Lafayette Flying Corps* marked the beginning of a long-running successful writing partnership between Hall and Nordhoff. Their careers peaked with release of the classic trilogy, *Mutiny on the Bounty, Men Against the Sea*, and *Pitcairn's Island*.

44   Wartime titles include: Victor Chapman, *Victor Chapman's Letters from France* (New York: MacMillan, 1917); James McConnell, *Flying for France* (Garden City: Doubleday, 1917); William Henry Meeker, *William Henry Meeker, his Book* (Location unlisted: Privately printed, 1917); George Babbitt, *Norman Prince: a Volunteer Who Died for a Cause He Loved* (New York: Houghton Mifflin, 1917); Carroll Winslow, *With the French Flying Corps* (London: Constable, 1917); Bert Hall, *En l'Air* (New York: The New Library, 1918); Cyrus Foss Chamberlain, *Letters of Cyrus Foss Chamberlain* (Minneapolis: No publisher listed, 1918); Edmond Genét, *War Letters of Edmond Genét* (New York: Scribner's, 1918); James Norman Hall, *High Adventure: a Narrative of Air Fighting in France* (Boston: Houghton Mifflin, 1918); and William Wellman, *Go Get 'Em!: the True Adventures of an Aviator of the Lafayette Flying Corps who was the only Yankee Flyer Fighting over General Pershing's Boys of the Rainbow Division in Lorraine when they first went "Over the Top"!* (Boston: Page, 1918).

45   Edwin C. Parsons, *The Great Adventure: The Story of the Lafayette Escadrille* (Garden City: Doubleday, 1937); Edwin C. Parsons, *Flight into Hell: The Story of the Lafayette Escadrille* (London: Long, 1938); Edwin C. Parsons, *I Flew with the Lafayette Escadrille* (Indianapolis: Seale, 1963).

46   Walt Brown, Jr., *An American for Lafayette: the Diaries of E. C. C. Genet, Lafayette Escadrille* (Charlottesville: University Press of Virginia, 1981).

47 Charles Beach, *Air Service Boys Flying for France: or the Young Heroes of the Lafayette Escadrille* (Cleveland: World Syndicate, 1919); Austin Bishop, *Bob Thorpe: Sky Fighters of the Lafayette Flying Corps* (New York: Harcourt, Brace, 1919; Ruth Dunbar, *The Swallow: a Novel Based Upon the Actual Experiences of One of the Survivors of the Famous Lafayette Escadrille* (New York: Boni and Liveright, 1919); Georges Thenault, *The Story of the Lafayette Escadrille* (Boston: Small, Maynard, 1921); Kiffin Rockwell, *War Letters of Kiffin Yates Rockwell, Foreign Legionnaire and Aviator, France 1914–1916* (Garden City: The Country Life Press, 1925); Bert Hall, *One Man's War* (New York: Holt, 1929); Clayton Knight, *We Were There with the Lafayette Escadrille* (New York: Grosset and Dunlap, 1961); Arthur G. Whitehouse, *Legion of the Lafayette* (Garden City: Doubleday, 1962); Herbert M. Mason, Jr., *The Lafayette Escadrille* (New York: Random House, 1964); Edward Jablonski, *Warriors with Wings: the Story of the Lafayette Escadrille* (Indianapolis: Bobbs-Merrill, 1966); Robert Johnson, *The American Heritage of James Norman Hall* (Philadelphia: Dorrance, 1969); Arthur Whitehouse, *The Laughing Falcon* (New York: Putnam, 1969); Dale Walker, *Only the Clouds Remain: Ted Parsons of the Lafayette Escadrille* (Amsterdam: Alandale Press, 1980); Philip Flammer, *The Vivid Air: the Lafayette Escadrille* (Athens: University of Georgia Press, 1981); Terry L. Johnson, *Valiant Volunteers: A Novel Based on the Passion and the Glory of the Lafayette Escadrille* (Bloomington: Authorhouse, 2005); Jon Guttman, *Spa 124 Lafayette Escadrille: American Volunteers in World War I* (Oxford: Osprey, 2004); and, as this book goes to press, Steven A. Ruffin, *The Lafayette Escadrille: A Photo History of the First American First Fighter Squadron* (London: Casemate, 2016); *Lafayette Escadrille*, directed by William A. Wellman, Warner Brothers, 1958, and *Flyboys*, directed by Tony Bill, Electric Entertainment, 2006.

48 Edward V. Rickenbaker, *Fighting the Flying Circus* (Garden City: Doubleday, 1965), 145.

49 Ibid.

50 Mark Girouard, *The Return of Camelot: Chivalry and the English Gentlemen* (New Haven: Yale University Press, 1981), preface. Though Girouard's study concentrates on Great Britain, he cites examples indicating the revival of interest in chivalry also occurred in the United States and Germany.

51 Neal O'Connor, *Aviation Awards of Imperial Germany in World War I and the Men Who Earned Them* (Princeton: Foundation for Aviation World War I, 1988–2007), 1:9. This seven-volume series is the best source on the topic of German aviation awards during the First World War.

52 Victor Chapman, *Victor Chapman's Letters from France* (New York: MacMillan, 1917), 17.

53 Ibid., 36.

54 Ibid., 25.

55 Henry Bordeaux, *Georges Guynemer, Knight of the Air* (New Haven: Yale University Press, 1918); Escott Lynn, *Knights of the Air* (London: N. and R. Chambers, 1918); Bennett Molter, *Knights of the Air* (New York: D. Appleton, 1918); Floyd Gibbons, *The Red Knight of Germany* (Garden City: Sun Dial Press, 1927); Lester Maitland, *Knights of the Air* (Garden City: Doubleday, Doran, 1929); "Vigilant," *Richthofen: The Red Knight of the Air* (London: John Hamilton, 1934); John Harris, *Knights of the Air: Canadian Aces of World War I* (New York: St. Martin's Press, 1958); Edwin Jablonski, *The Knighted Skies: A Pictorial History of World War I in the Air* (New York: Putnam, 1964); Johannes Werner, *Knight of Germany: Oswald Boelcke, German Ace* (New York: Arno Press, 1972); Carl Degelow, *Germany's Last Knight of the Air: The Memoirs of Carl Degelow* (London: William Kimber, 1979); Ezra Bowen, *Knights of the Air* (Alexandria: Time-Life Books, 1980); Jerry Valencia, *Knights of the Sky* (San Diego: Reed Enterprises, 1980). These titles illustrate the early and continuing popularity of the term "knight" in First World War aviation literature.

56 Caroline Ticknor, ed., *New England Aviators 1914–1918* (Boston: Houghton Mifflin, 1919), xvi.

57 John Morrow, *The Great War in the Air: Military Aviation from 1909 to 1921* (Washington: Smithsonian Institution Press, 1993), 91–92.

58 See Jacques Mortane, *Guynemer, the Ace of Aces* (New York: Moffat, Yard, 1918); Laurence LaTourette Driggs, *The Adventures of Arnold Adair, American Ace* (Boston: Little Brown, 1918); Laurence LaTourette Driggs, "Aces Among Aces," *National Geographic* (June 1918), 568–80. Driggs' article contains one of the first published lists of aces in what has become the accepted format of descending numerical order. Driggs also collaborated with Edward V. Rickenbacker on the American leading ace's wartime autobiography, *Fighting the Flying Circus* (New York: Frederick A. Stokes, 1919).

59 Jacques De Sieyes, "Aces of the Air," *National Geographic* (January 1918), 5.

60 Bill Radloff and Robert Niemann, "The Ehrenbechers—Where Are They Now?," *Cross & Cockade Journal* 10, no. 4 (Winter 1969), 366; James J. Parks, "Award of the Naval Victory Trophy to Leutnant zur See Wolfram Eisenlohr," *Cross & Cockade Journal* 18, no. 2 (Summer 1977), 125.

61 Neal W. O'Connor, "Orders, Decorations and Medals Awarded to Leading German Airmen," *Cross & Cockade Journal* 11, no. 3 (Autumn 1970): 252.

62 O'Connor, *Aviation Awards,* 2:61–63.

63 Kommandeur der Flieger 6, *Wöchentlicher Tätigkeitsbericht,* No. 22400, January 14–21, 1917, 2.

64 O'Connor, *Aviation Awards,* 2:63.

65 Ibid., Appendix III, 218. Within that overall total, seventy-six (43.6 percent) won their Blue Max for service in aviation. Of the remainder awarded, twenty-seven were earned by members of the submarine service, while seventy-one had to do to cover bestowals to members of all other branches of the German military.

66 Ibid., Appendix IV, 219–20; Appendix VI, 225; 122; Appendix X, 245–46. The high command parsed out the fourteen aviation awards not made to fighter pilots along the following lines: five bomb squadron commanders, eight observers, and one reconnaissance pilot. As if this distribution was not sufficiently lopsided in favor of fighters over reconnaissance crew, surviving records indicate at least an additional twenty-two fighter pilots were proposed for the *Pour le Mérite*, but were denied the order due to their untimely deaths or to the proposal not having made it through channels before the war ended. No reconnaissance pilot was denied the *Pour le Mérite* for similar reasons. O'Connor cites only one known example of a posthumous recipient of the Blue Max, *Ltn.* Wilhelm Schreiber, a ground-attack pilot. The German high command might have made an exception in Schreiber's case, in O'Connor's opinion, to encourage other pilots to engage in ground attacks during the 1918 spring offensive, a time when close support with the Army was vital.

67 Ibid., 124.

68 Ibid., 167.

69 Ibid., Appendix XVII, 269–70. Of the sixty-nine aviation Golden Military Merit Cross recipients, only thirty-one (44.9 percent) were awarded to men in reconnaissance units, and while this clearly represents an improvement over the stingy award of the Blue Max, twenty-one of the remaining awards went to fighter pilots. Seven Golden Military Merit Crosses were awarded to bomber pilots, one went to a man working at an Army Aviation Park (probably for work as a flight instructor), and the last went to a member of a seaplane station.

70 Ibid., 147, 161. Fritz Kosmahl received the first Member's Cross awarded to an airman while a member of a photo-reconnaissance unit, *Flieger-Abteilung (A) 261 LB,* though his success in shooting down enemy aircraft (Koshmal had scored three of an eventual nine victories at the time of the award) might have occasioned the honor. The other award of a Member's Cross possibly made for reconnaissance work went to Albert Jünger, a member of *Flieger-Abteilung 300,* an all-purpose unit stationed in Palestine that performed bombing missions in addition to its reconnaissance duties.

71 Ibid., 124; *Nachrichtenblatt der Luftsteitkräfte* 2:35:551.

72 O'Connor, *Aviation Awards,* 2:110–26. The five officer observers include: Hermann Fricke (160 or more front flights); Erich Homburg (239 missions); Hans-Jürgen Horn (300 missions); Friedrich Nielebock (280 missions); and Paul *Freiherr* von Pechmann (400–700 successful reconnaissance sorties).

73 Franks, Bailey, and Guest, *Above the Lines,* 186.

74 Alex Revell, *Victoria Cross: WWI Airmen and Their Aircraft* (Stratford: Flying Machines Press, 1997), 1; The Victoria Cross Registers, www.nationalarchives. gov.uk/documentsonline/victoriacross.asp (accessed July 31, 2008).

75 Revell, *Victoria Cross,* 84; The Victoria Cross Registers, www.nationalarchives. gov.uk/documentsonline/victoriacross.asp (accessed July 31, 2008).

76 Revell, *Victoria Cross*, 20–21; The Victoria Cross Registers, www.nationalarchives. gov.uk/documentsonline/victoriacross.asp (accessed July 31, 2008).

77 Chris Coulthard-Clark, *McNamara, VC: a Hero's Dilemma* (Fairbairn: Air Power Studies Centre, 1997), 116; Revell, *Victoria Cross*, 67; The Victoria Cross Registers, www.nationalarchives.gov.uk/documentsonline/victoriacross. asp (accessed July 31, 2008).

78 Revell, *Victoria Cross*, 1; Bruce Robertson, ed., *Air Aces of the 1914–1918 War* (Letchworth: Harleyford, 1959), 41–42; Also see Walter Raleigh and H. A. Jones, *The War in the Air: Being the Story of the Part Played in the Great War by the Royal Air Force* (London: Oxford University Press, 1922–1937), vol. 1–6, passim.

79 Revell, *Victoria Cross*, 39–40; The Victoria Cross Registers, www.nationalarchives. gov.uk/documentsonline/victoriacross.asp (accessed July 31, 2008).

80 Norman L. R. Franks and Frank W. Bailey, *Over the Front: A Complete Record of the Fighter Aces and Units of the United States and French Air Services, 1914–1918* (London: Grub Street, 1992), 112–227.

81 "Income Tax (Earnings and Pensions) Act 2003. c. 1, Part 9, Chapter 17, Section 638," www.legislation.gov.uk (accessed August 3, 2008). This part of the Income Tax Act documents a pension benefit for recipients of Britain's Victoria Cross.

Chapter 3

1 F. Stansbury Haydon, *Military Ballooning during the Early Civil War* (Baltimore: Johns Hopkins University Press, 2000), 1.

2 Ibid., 10.

3 Ibid., 8.

4 Ibid., 14n66; Jonathan B. A. Bailey, *Field Artillery and Firepower* (Annapolis: Naval Institute Press, 2004), 178n155.

5 Haydon, *Military Ballooning*, 15–33.

6 Ibid., 187–88.

7 US Centennial of Flight Commission, "Balloons in the American Civil War," http://www.centennialofflight.gov/essay/Lighter_than_air/Civil_War_balloons/LTA (accessed February 15, 2011).

8 Ibid.

9 Harald Penrose, *British Aviation: The Pioneer Years 1903–1914* (London: Putnam, 1967), 56.

10 Ibid., 57.

11 Ibid., 278; Robert Brooke-Popham, 1919, "Early History of RFC: Notes by General Brooke-Popham," Air 1/1/4/1, TNA: PRO, 19. Brooke-Popham for example, mentions Maj. John Frederick Andrews Higgins, formerly of the Royal Field Artillery, and a Sgt. Ridd, who had worked as a bricklayer before enlisting.

12   E. W. Griffin, 1917, "Some Rough Notes on the Early Development of the RNAS 1912–1917," Air 1/625/17/1, TNA: PRO, 5 [hereafter "Notes on the RNAS"]; see also Hilary St. George Saunders, *Per Ardua: The Rise of British Air Power, 1911–1939* (London: Oxford University Press, 1945), 87; Eileen F. Lebow, *A Grandstand Seat: The American Balloon Service in World War I* (Westport: Praeger, 1998), 50.

13   Ralph H. Tripcony, *The Captive or "Kite" Balloon* (Dayton: US Air Service Engineering Division, 1922), 8.

14   Ibid., 9.

15   Ernst von Hoeppner, *Germany's War in the Air: The Development and Operations of German Military Aviation in the World War* (Nashville: Battery Press, 1994), 27, 43.

16   Ian Burns, "The Balloon at Sea," *Cross & Cockade International* 46, no. 1 (Autumn 2015), 23 also documents Parseval-Sigisfeld balloons of 600 and 830 cubic meter capacities.

17   Tripcony, *Captive or "Kite" Balloon*, 11. Tripcony opined, the Caquot was "a great improvement on the *drachen* balloon," and he praised its ability to continue observing over land "in winds considerably greater than 20 meters" and at sea in "a relative wind velocity of 35 meters per second."

18   Royal Flying Corps War Diary, October 29, 1915, Air 1/1176/204/2895, TNA:PRO.

19   "Brief History of 5th Balloon Company, RAF," Air 1/163/15/127/1, TNA: PRO, 6 [hereafter "History of 5th Balloon Company"]; "Brief History of No. 22 Balloon Section, RAF," Air 1/163/15/133/1, TNA: PRO, 1 [hereafter "No. 22 Balloon Section"]; "Brief History of No. 19 Balloon Section, RAF, August 1916–November, 1918," Air 1/163/15/132/1, TNA: PRO, 2; "History of the 6th Balloon Company, RAF (No. 9 Balloon Section, No. 32 Balloon Section) 1919," Air 1/163/15/129/1, TNA: PRO, 2. All these unit records document early service on *Drachen* types with conversion to Caquots late in 1916 or early in 1917; See also R. M. McFarland, *History of the Bureau of Aircraft Production* (Maxwell AFB: USAF HRA, 1951), 8:2342.

20   Hoeppner, *Germany's War in the Air*, 89–90.

21   "History of No. 6 Balloon Section, Royal Air Force," Air 1/163/15/128/1, TNA: PRO, 1.

22   "Royal Flying Corps Summary of Aeronautical Information, General Headquarters, Royal Flying Corps, No. 22, November 1, 1917," Air 1/7/4/56/11, TNA: PRO, 4.

23   "Royal Naval Air Service Kite Balloon Development 1914–1916," Air 1/674/21/6/75, TNA: PRO, 9.

24   Royal Flying Corps War Diary, January 9, 1916, Air 1/1184.

25   Hanns-Gerd Rabe (Peter Kilduff, trans.), "My Last Combat Flight, A Personal Memoir of Hanns-Gerd Rabe, Flieger Abteilung (A) 253," *Cross & Cockade Journal* 18, no. 3 (Autumn 1977), 235.

26   Hoeppner, *Germany's War in the Air*, 157, alludes to eighteen-hour missions by some German crews.

27   "History of No. 13 Balloon Section, Royal Air Force, 1919," Air 1/163/15/130/1, TNA: PRO, 1; Hal Giblin and Norman Franks, *The Military Cross to Flying Personnel of Great Britain and the Empire 1914–1919: With Service and Biographical Details of Recipients* (London: Savannah Publications, 2008), 208–09.

28   John H. Morrow, Jr., *The Great War in the Air: Military Aviation from 1909 to 1921* (Washington: Smithsonian Institution Press, 1993), 4.

29   Bailey, *Field Artillery and Firepower*, 178n155. Bailey reports that "observation balloons remain in service around the world, for example on the Israeli border with Lebanon following the IDF's withdrawal from Lebanon in May 2000." NBC Nightly News, January, 2, 2009, confirmed Israel's even more recent use of observation balloons in its battle against Hamas in the Gaza Strip.

30   Emil J. Widmer, *Military Observation Balloons (Captive and Free): A Complete Treatise on their Manufacture, Equipment, and Handling with Special Instructions for the Training of a Field Balloon Company* (New York: D. Van Nostrand, 1918), 44.

31   John F. C. Fuller, *The Conduct of War 1789–1961* (New York: Da Capo Press, 1992), 160.

32   "Balloon Notes: AEF, No. 1," December 3, 1917, Maxwell AFB, USAF: HRA, 4; "Balloon Notes: AEF, No. 12," January 6, 1918, Maxwell AFB, USAF: HRA, 6–12 [hereafter "Balloon Notes: No. 12"]; See also Maurer Maurer, ed., *The US Air Service in World War I* (Washington: Office of Air Force History, 1978), 1:206.

33   Basil Liddell Hart, *History of the First World War* (London: MacMillan, 1997), 234–35. Liddell Hart, for example, illustrates topographical challenges faced by attacking British forces during the Somme offensive in 1916.

34   "No. 6 Kite Balloon Section, Royal Naval Air Service Summary of Work, August 17, 1915–March 28, 1916," Air 1/163/15/128/2, TNA: PRO, 1. This summary references targets ranged at distances up to 12,000 yards; Also see, James C. Dunn, *The War the Infantry Knew 1914–1919: A Chronicle of Service in France and Belgium with the Second Battalion His Majesty's Twenty-Third Foot, the Royal Welch Fusiliers* (London: Jane's, 1987), 224, 339; Bailey, *Field Artillery and Firepower*, 240–41. Bailey establishes the dominance of artillery by citing British casualty statistics that give the artillery first place among causative factors with 58.51 percent of all British casualties.

35   "Balloon Notes: No. 12;" See also Dunn, *War the Infantry Knew*, 150; Fuller, *Conduct of War*, 160.

36   SGA/Mémoire des hommes, www.memoiredeshommes.sga.defense.gouv.fr (accessed February 11, 2011). This source documents *Compagnies d' Aérostiers* 21, 23, 24, and 30–39 formed between August and December 1914; Lebow,

A Grandstand Seat, 50. Lebow puts the number of French companies at ten in October 1914.

37   Mike O'Connor, *Airfields and Airmen of the Channel Coast* (Barnsley: Pen and Sword, 2005), 17.

38   "Development of the Air Department Admiralty 1912–1916," Air 1/674/21/6/59, TNA: PRO, 10; Saunders, *Per Ardua,* 87; Royal Flying Corps War Diary, May 8, 1915, Air 1/1176/204/2895, TNA:PRO; H. A. Jones, *The War in the Air: Being the Story of the part played in the Great War by the Royal Air Force* (Oxford: Clarendon Press, 1928–1937) 2:115–16.

39   "History of the 2nd Balloon Wing HQ, March 5, 1916–November 30, 1918," Air 1/163/15/126/1, TNA: PRO, 1 [hereafter "History 2nd Balloon Wing"].

40   Saunders, *Per Ardua,* 143. Saunders claims that forty of the Royal Flying Corps' ninety units on the Western Front during the battle of Messines (June 1917) were kite balloon sections.

41   "History 2nd Balloon Wing," 2.

42   Dunn, *The War the Infantry Knew,* 224.

43   "Royal Flying Corps Periodical Summary of Aeronautical Information, No. 24, November 30, 1917," Air 1/7/4/56/11, TNA: PRO, 3–4.

44   Ray Sturtivant and Gordon Page, *The Camel File* (London: Air Britain, 1993); Ray Sturtivant and Gordon Page, *The S.E. 5 File* (London: Air Britain, 1997); Ray Sturtivant and Gordon Page, *The D.H. 4/D.H. 9 File* (London: Air Britain, 1999); Theodore Hamady, *The Nieuport 28: America's First Fighter* (Atglen: Schiffer Military Publishing, 2007). These works reflect the current trend in First World War aviation books devoted to a single aircraft type; John M. Bruce, *British Aeroplanes 1914–1918* (London: Putnam, 1957); E. F. Cheeseman, *Reconnaissance and Bomber Aircraft of the 1914–1918 War* (Letchworth: Harleyford, 1962); and James J. Davilla and Arthur M. Soltan, *French Aircraft of the First World War* (Mountain View: Flying Machines Press, 2002); Robert B. Casari, *American Military Aircraft 1908–1919* (San Jose: Aeronaut Books, 2014). These works, by contrast, represent impressive attempts at a comprehensive approach. None of these titles includes a dedicated chapter on observation balloons.

45   Griffin, "Notes on the RNAS," 5–9; Saunders, *Per Ardua,* 96.

46   "Brief History of No. 29 Balloon Section, Royal Air Force November 29, 1916–March 1919," Air 1/163/15/134/1, TNA: PRO, 3–4, notes the worth of the section's observations during the infantry's July 1918 capture of the village of Hamel; See also Saunders, *Per Ardua,* 144, which documents the services of a British balloon observer who, during the battle of Messines, relayed news of a German buildup opposite the II Anzac Corps in time for British artillery fire to totally destroy the intended enemy counterattack.

47   Maurer, *US Air Service,* 1:18, 117; Lee Kennett, *The First Air War 1914–1918* (New York, Free Press, 1991), 215; James J. Hudson, *Hostile Skies: A Combat*

History of the American Air Service in World War I (Syracuse: Syracuse University Press 1968), 300; Morrow, *Great War in the Air*, 338. Lee Kennett puts the total number of US Air Service squadrons on the Western Front on November 11, 1918, at forty-five, a total that includes only heavier-than-air squadrons. James Hudson segregates heavier- and lighter-than-air units reporting forty-five of the former and twenty-three of the latter. John Morrow lists the strength of the US Air Service at the armistice at forty-five squadrons without mention of balloon companies.

48   S. W. Ovitt and L. G. Bowers, eds., *The Balloon Section of the American Expeditionary Forces* (New Haven: Privately Published, 1919), passim; Morris, *The Balloonatics,* passim; Craig S. Herbert, *Eyes of the Army: A Story about the Observation Balloon Service of World War I* (Lafayette Hill: Privately Published, 1986), passim; and Lebow, *A Grandstand Seat,* passim, for accounts of USAS balloon operations.

49   Shirley, *United States Naval Aviation*, 36–58, 158 and 189–90; www.usaww1. com/united-states-naval-aviation.php4 (accessed April 22, 2010) (US stations).

50   SGA/Mémoire des hommes, www.memoriedeshommes.sga.gouv.fr. (accessed February 11, 2001).

51   Jones, *War in the Air,* Appendices: XVI, XXVI and XXX. Seven RAF balloon companies served in the Middle East, the remainder working on the Western Front.

52   Ibid.

53   George Neumann, *Die Deutschen Luftstreitkräfte im Weltkrieg* (Berlin: E. S. Mittler and Son, 1920), 14; Heinz J. Nowarra, *Eisernes Kreuz und Balken Kreuz* (Mainz: Verlag Dieter Hoffmann, 1968), 44–45.

54   William Mitchell, *Memoirs of World War I: From Start to Finish of Our Greatest War* (New York: Random House, 1960), 11.

55   Survey Associates, "The Survey for August 5, 1916," http://books.google.com/ books?id=6qEqAAAAMAAJ&pg=PA467&lpg (accessed January 18, 2009).

56   Ovitt and Bowers, *Balloon Section*, 10; James J. Cooke, *The US Air Service in the Great War, 1917–1919* (Westport: Praeger, 1996), 6–7; Lebow, *A Grandstand Seat*, 17.

57   Ibid., 19–21.

58   Mitchell, *Memoirs*, 16–18; Hoeppner, *Germany's War in the Air*, 133; Benedict Crowell, *America's Munitions 1917–1918: Report of Benedict Crowell, the Assistant Secretary of War, Director of Munitions* (Washington: GPO, 1919), 239; Maurer, *US Air Service*, 1:51; Lucien H. Thayer, *America's First Eagles: The Official History of the US Air Service, AEF (1917–1918)* (San Jose: Bender Publishing, 1983), 9; Cooke, *Air Service*, 1–2; Morrow, *Great War in the Air*, 265. All these sources document American aeronautical deficiencies.

59   Lee Nash, "Aircraft," *The United States in the First World War: an Encyclopedia,* ed. Anne Cipriano Venzon (New York: Garland, 1995), 7; Michael Carr, "United States Air Service," ibid., 603.

60   Charles D. Chandler, *Balloon Section Report* (Tours: USAS HQ, 1918), 1.

61   Crowell, *America's Munitions*, 335.

62   Ibid. The single balloon, a gift from the Goodyear Company, equipped one of the National Guard units that deployed to Mexico.

63   Maurer, *US Air Service*, 2:105; Morrow, *Great War in the Air*, 268; Linda Robertson, *The Dream of Civilized Warfare: World War I Flying Aces and the American Imagination* (Minneapolis: University of Minnesota Press, 2003), 27–51.

64   Noel C. Shirley, *United States Naval Aviation 1910–1918* (Atglen: Schiffer Military Publishing, 2000), 104.

65   Edgar S. Gorrell, "What, No Airplanes?," *Over the Front* 5:3 (Autumn 1990): 201: James Streckfuss, "Bolling Mission," *The United States in the First World War: An Encyclopedia*, ed. Anne Cipriano Venzon (New York: Garland, 1995), 97.

66   Chandler, *Balloon Section Report*, 1.

67   Ibid.

68   Ibid.

69   Ibid.

70   Ibid., 13.

71   Ibid.

72   Ibid.

73   Ibid., 14; Maurer, *US Air Service*, 1:51.

74   "Royal Flying Corps Periodical Summary of Aeronautical Information, No. 24," November 30, 1917, Air 1/7/4/56/11, TNA: PRO, 5.

75   Chandler, *Balloon Section Report*, 16.

76   "The Battle of Arras, Preparatory Period, with Summary of Contents, November 1916–April 1917," Air 1/676/21/13/1777, TNA: PRO, 13.

77   "Les Armées Francais dans la Grande Guerre," http://toaw.free.fr/afgg/ (accessed February 11, 2011); SGA/Mémoire des hommes, www.memoriedeshommes (accessed February 11, 2011).

78   Office of Military Aeronautics, US Army, *Principles Underlying the Use of Balloons* (Washington: GPO, 1918), 17–20; "USAS, Balloon Notes, AEF," No. 58, October 4, 1918, Maxwell AFB, USAF: HRA, 1; "USAS, Balloon Notes, AEF," No. 13, January 7, 1918, Maxwell AFB, USAF: HRA, 10.

79   Mitchell, *Memoirs*, 16; Frank P. Lahm, *The World War I Diary of Col. Frank P. Lahm, Air Service, AEF* (Maxwell AFB: Historical Research Division, Aerospace Studies Institute, Air University, 1970), xiv; Maurer, *US Air Service*, 2:105. Maurer explains the details of the telegram French Premier Alexandre Ribot sent to the US government proposing a tentative American aviation program; Streckfuss, "Bolling Mission," 97–98.

80   Army War College, *Notes on Employment of Artillery in Trench Fighting: From Latest Sources: War Department Document No. 594: Office of the Adjutant General* (Washington: GPO, 1917), 6.

81   *Balloon Observations and Instructions on the Subject of Work in the Basket:*
      A Free Translation of the French Booklet "Instructions au sujet du Travail en
      Nacelle" and an Added Discourse on Balloon Observation (Washington: GPO,
      1918); *Methods of Obtaining and Transmitting Information by Balloon Service:*
      Information from French and American Sources to Army Balloon School, American
      Expeditionary Forces (Washington: GPO, 1918). Like most American military
      aviation manuals these were little more than translations of comparable French
      manuals or were heavily influenced by what US forces learned from the French,
      a practice made necessary by the lack of aviation expertise in the US Army.

82   John A. Paegelow, *Operation of Allied Balloons in the Saint Mihiel Offensive*
      (Tours: USAS HQ, September 28, 1918), 1. US Air Service balloons taking
      part included those of the following companies: 1, 2, 3, 5, 6, 7, 8, 9, 10, 11,
      12, 16, 42, 43, and 69. Also participating were the following French companies:
      20, 39, 41, 52, 53, and 93.

83   William Mitchell, *Memoirs*, 237–38.

84   Paegelow, *Operation of Allied Balloons*, 2, reports that on September 16, 1918
      the 2nd Company registered 157 rounds, the 3rd Company 118 shots, and
      the 11th Company 118.

85   Ibid., 3.

86   Ibid; Maurer, *US Air Service*, 3:11. Maurer notes that the single heavier-than-
      air night reconnaissance unit, the 9th Aero Squadron, had only just come into
      service and had no operational experience prior to the St. Mihiel battle.

87   US Air Service, *Operations Between the Meuse and the Argonne Forest from*
      September 26, to November 11, 1918 (Tours: USAS HQ, 1918), 138. The thirteen
      companies included: 1, 2, and 5 (all with the First Corps); 3, 4, 9, and 42 (all
      with the Third Corps); 6, 7, 8, and 12 (all with the Fifth Corps); and 11 and
      43, along with French companies 39 and 93 (all assisting the Army Artillery).

88   Ovitt and Bowers, *Balloon Section,* 56.

89   Bailey, *Field Artillery and Firepower*, 268; "History of 5th Balloon Company,"
      8, reports twenty-nine moves for the Royal Air Force's Fifth Balloon Company
      in two months during the war's final summer; "History of No. 14 Balloon
      Section," Air 1/163/15/131/1, TNA: PRO, 1. This unit moved more than
      50 miles between August 8, 1918 and the armistice.

90   Paegelow, *Operation of Allied Balloons*, 3.

91   Maurer, *US Air Service*, 1:383.

92   USAS, *Operations Meuse and Argonne*, 141.

93   Maurer, *US Air Service*, 4:205.

94   "No. 22 Balloon Section," 2.

95   "Enlist Your Lens in the Air Service," advertisement, *National Geographic*,
      January 1918, following 114.

96   Chandler, *Balloon Section Report*, 36; Terrence J. Finnegan, *Shooting the Front:*
      Allied Aerial Reconnaissance and Photographic Interpretation on the Western

Front-World War I (Washington: National Defense Intelligence College Press, 2006), 335.

97 Maurer, *US Air Service*, 2:407, 4:203.

98 Division of Military Aeronautics, *US Army, Balloon Observation and Instructions on the subject of Work In The Basket: Supplement* (Washington: GPO, 1918), 5–6.

99 Chandler, *Balloon Section Report*, 16.

100 "Memorandum for Gen. Menoher, March 21, 1921," File 321.9, box 487, Separate Air Force, RG 18, Air Corps Central File, 1917–38, box 487, NARA. Included in a synopsis of the Curry Bill, H.R. 16151, prepared by staff in the Office of the chief of Air Service for Gen. Charles Menoher, is a recommendation that "all kite balloons should be turned over entirely to the Army and Navy, as they are in no sense combat units. Their use is entirely for observation purposes."

101 Chandler, *Balloon Section Report*, 74–109.

102 "History 2nd Balloon Wing," 2.

103 Hoeppner, *Germany's War in the Air*, 118.

104 Crowell, *America's Munitions*, 336.

105 Ibid., 335–36.

106 Ibid.

107 Chandler, *Balloon Section Report*, 75.

108 "A Lecture at Army War College by Maj. Gen. O. Westover," quoted in Robert F. Futrell, *USAF Historical Studies No. 24: Command of Observation Aviation: A Study in Control of Tactical Airpower* (Maxwell AFB: Air University USAF Historical Division Research Studies Institute, 1956), 5.

109 Crowell, *America's Munitions*, 332.

110 Ibid.

111 Chandler, *Balloon Section Report*, 74–109.

Chapter 4

1 Tim Coates, ed., *The World War I Collection: Gallipoli and the Early Battles, 1914–15: The Dardanelles Commission, 1914–16; British Battles of World War I, 1914–15* (London: The Stationery Office, 2001), 32–34.

2 J. C. Nerney, "The Campaign on the Western Front Ypres to the Somme: 'Neuve Chapelle,' 10th March 1915, Series No. 1," Air 1/674/21/6/95, TNA: PRO, 2 [hereafter "Neuve Chapelle"].

3 "Aerial Activity of the German 1st Army During the Operations Directly Before and During the Battle of the Marne 2nd to 9th September 1914," Air 1/2132/207/127/1, TNA: PRO, 8.

4 "Intelligence Summaries by GHQ (Int.) 8th September–2nd November 1914," Air 1/751, TNA: PRO, 9.

5 Ibid., 7.

6   Nerney, "Neuve Chapelle," 1:5–7.

7   "Co-operation of Aeroplanes with Artillery," WO 158/681, TNA: PRO, 1 [hereafter "Co-operation of Aeroplanes"].

8   Ibid.; Virginia S. Thatcher and Alexander McQueen, *The New Webster Encyclopedic Dictionary of the English Language* (Chicago: Consolidated Book Publishers, 1971), 154, 770, 868, describes these instruments as used to measure angles for surveying or nautical navigation purposes.

9   Nerney, "Neuve Chapelle," 1:5–7.

10   Ibid., 8. Adoption of wireless equipment did not proceed uniformly across the Western Front. German artillery observation units, for example, did not all receive wireless radio equipment until mid-1916. See Dov Gavish and Dieter H. M. Gröschel, "Leutnant der Reserve Friedrich Rüdenberg, Pilot of Artillerie-Flieger-Abteilung 209, Feldflieger-Abteilung 26/Flieger-Abteilung (A) 259, Jagdstaffel 10, and Jagdstaffel 75," *Over the Front* 16, no. 2 (Summer 2001), 104–5.

11   Dieter H. M. Gröschel, letter to the editor, *Over the Front* 17, no. 4 (Winter 2002), 369–70; "Gallipoli 1915: Mapping from Aeroplane Photographs in the Gallipoli Peninsula," WO 317/13, TNA: PRO, 1. Acting on his own initiative, Royal Field Artillery Maj. W. V. Nugent, while serving at Gallipoli, made use of aerial photographs to construct his own map of the area replacing the less accurate map he had been issued.

12   Nicolas C. Watkis, *The Western Front from the Air* (Phoenix Mill: Sutton, 1999), 2. Aerial photography is discussed at greater length in the next chapter.

13   Ibid., 26.

14   Nerney, "Neuve Chapelle," 1:9.

15   "Co-operation of Aeroplanes," 2.

16   "No. 4 Squadron RFC Draft Confidential Order 20/4/1915 Co-operation of Aeroplanes with other Arms," Air 1/746/204/3/17, TNA: PRO, passim.

17   Ibid., 7.

18   Ibid.

19   Ibid.

20   Ibid., 10.

21   Final Report of the Committee on Monitor Spotting, February 21, 1918, "W/T Spotting September 1916–September 1918," Air 1/71/15/9/126, TNA: PRO, 1 [hereafter "W/T Spotting"]. To adapt the system for naval use, the Royal Navy urged the letters "G" through "P" be added to the code to provide for the greater ranges at which naval actions took place and that the placement of the north-south line be made in relation to the firing ship.

22   Headquarters AEF, *Aerial Observation for Artillery* based on the French edition of December 29, 1917 (Paris: Imprimerie Nationale, 1918), passim; British Air Ministry, *Handbook of German Military and Naval Aviation (War) 1914–1918* (1918; repr., London: Imperial War Museum in association with Battery Press,

1995), 59; Report of Committee on Spotting Procedure, "W/T Spotting," 31. Misinformation provided to members of the Monitoring Spotting Committee on use of the clock code as they deliberated its adoption suggests they believed the system had been adopted not only by the RFC, but by French and German forces as well.

23 Harold Wilder, "History of Aerial Observation in the American EF: Section II: The Development of Observation Work During the War," M990, p. 72, R34, F652, Gorrell's History of the Air Service, Ser. J, vol. 2, RG 120, Records of the American Expeditionary Forces (World War I), NARA.

24 Royal Flying Corps War Diary, September 28, 1915, Air 1/1176/204/2895, TNA: PRO.

25 "Military Aviation," Prepared by the War College Division, General Staff Corps, as a supplement to "Statement of a Proper Military Policy for the United States" [1915]. Washington: GPO, 1916, discussed in Herbert A. Johnson, *Wingless Eagle: US Army Aviation through World War I* (Chapel Hill: University of North Carolina Press, 2001), 154.

26 Nerney, "Neuve Chapelle," 1:12–13.

27 J. T. C. Hervey, "Campaign on the Western Front Ypres to the Somme Series No. III: Festubert May/June 1915," 1, Air 1/674/21/6/206, TNA:PRO.

28 Ibid., 3.

29 No. 3 Squadron RFC War Diary (Intelligence Summary) Period 1 January to 26 August 1915, Air 1/737/204/2/3.

30 Guenther Wolff, as told to Noel C. Shirley, "Observations from a Beobachter: Ltn. Guenther Wolff, Fl. Abt. (A) 209," *Cross & Cocade Journal* 14, no. 4 (Winter, 1973), 313. Wolff discusses Germany's work with aircraft wireless voice receivers, efforts that appear to have achieved only limited success.

31 Hugh M. Trenchard to deputy director of military aeronautics, June 19, 1915, "For Inclusion of a Wireless Officer in establishment of each Wing Headquarters 19 June–12 July 1915," Air 1/128/15/40/188, TNA: PRO.

32 "Summary of Information, RFC, 14 May 1915," Air 1/746/204/3/30, TNA: PRO, 4, 1–2. German commanders also used their aerial reconnaissance photos to confirm the real-time location of their front lines during attacks. Advanced units frequently outran their telephone connections to headquarters during an attack or lost them to enemy shelling. In these instances confirmation of their location on aerial photographs kept them from falling victim to friendly artillery fire. See Gavish and Gröschel, "Friedrich Rüdenberg," 107.

33 Royal Flying Corps War Diary, July 6, 1915, Air 1/1184, TNA:PRO.

34 See Richard P. Hallion, *The Rise of the Fighter Aircraft, 1914–1918* (Baltimore: Nautical and Aviation Press, 1984), passim; Irwin B. Holley, Jr., *Ideas and Weapons: Exploitation of the Aerial Weapon by the United States During World War I: A Study in the Relationship of Technological Advance, Military Doctrine, and the Development of Weapons* (Hamden: Archon, 1971), 58.

35   "W/T Spotting," 192.

36   Ibid., 212.

37   Ibid., 232.

38   Ibid., 8.

39   Hilary St. George Saunders, *Per Ardua: The Rise of British Air Power 1911–1939* (London: Oxford University Press, 1945), 88.

40   J. C. Nerney, "Campaign on the Western Front, Ypres to the Somme, Festubert, May/June 1915, Series No. 3," Air 1/674/21/6/106, TNA: PRO, 12.

41   Ibid., 25.

42   "The Battle of Arras (Preparatory Period) November 1916–April 1917," Air 1/676/21/12/1872, TNA: PRO, 9 [hereafter "Battle of Arras (Preparatory)"].

43   Saunders, *Per Ardua*, 88.

44   John A. Chamier, "Training of Observers, Royal Air Force," Air 1/161/15/123/15, TNA: PRO, 1.

45   "Battle of Arras (Preparatory)," 9.

46   No. 2 Squadron, RFC Operational Flying Daily Records, July 1–31, 1916, Air 1/734/204/1/10, TNA:PRO.

47   Ibid.

48   Ibid., 10.

49   Ibid.

50   Ibid., 11; "No. 2 Squadron RFC Operational Flying Daily Records 1–30 June 1916," Air 1/734/204/1/9, TNA: PRO, 2. Artillery officers had already occasionally flown on observation missions, including Lt. J. Wilkinson, commanding officer of the 115 Royal Field Artillery, who flew in the rear cockpit on a No. 2 Squadron, RFC mission regulating his battery on June 19, 1916.

51   "Battle of Arras (Preparatory)," 11.

52   Ibid., 12 and 8.

53   Ibid., 13.

54   Ibid., 19.

55   Ibid., 14.

56   Ibid., 20.

57   Saunders, *Per Ardua*, 89.

58   "Battle of Arras (Preparatory)," 21.

59   Royal Flying Corps War Diary, July 24, 1916, Air 1/1184, TNA:PRO.

60   Ibid.

61   Ibid.

62   "Battle of Arras (Preparatory)," 21.

63   Squadron Record Book No. 16 Sqdn. 18–20 July 1916, Air 1/1342/204/19/11, TNA:PRO.

64   Jonathan B. A. Bailey, *Field Artillery and Firepower* (Annapolis: Naval Institute Press, 2004), 266.

65 Ibid.

66 Ibid., n86.

67 James J. Hudson, *Hostile Skies: A Combat History of the American Air Service in World War I* (Syracuse: Syracuse University Press, 1968), 4–6; Maurer Maurer, ed., *The US Air Service in World War I* (Washington: Office of Air Force History, 1978), 2:105; Lucien H. Thayer, *America's First Eagles: The Official History of the US Air Service, AEF (1917–1918)*, (San Jose and Mesa: Bender Publishing and Champlin Fighter Museum Press, 1983), 9–12; James J. Cooke, *The US Air Service in the Great War, 1917–1919* (Westport: Praeger, 1996), 17–19; Linda R. Robertson, *The Dream of Civilized Warfare: World War I Flying Aces and the American Imagination* (Minneapolis: University of Minnesota Press, 2003), 27–49.

68 Benedict Crowell, *America's Munitions 1917–1918* (Washington: GPO, 1919), 243; Maurer, 1:117. Crowell puts the total number of airplanes procured from the Allies at 5,198 without breaking down the total by nation. Maurer gives the total purchased in Europe as 5,151, of which 4,874 came from the French.

69 Harold Wilder, "History of Observation Training," M990, p. 1, R34, F581, Gorrell's History of the Air Service, Ser. J, vol. 2, RG 120, Records of the American Expeditionary Forces (World War I), NARA [hereafter "Observation Training"].

70 Ibid.

71 Ibid.

72 Ibid.

73 Geoffrey J. Dwyer, "Air Service Training Section, AEF, France, Report on Air Service Training Department in England," M990, p. 4, R34, F108, Gorrell's History of the Air Service, Ser. J, vol. 1, RG 120, Records of the American Expeditionary Forces (World War I), NARA. Dwyer mentions "that no observation pilots were trained in England owing to the difference between American and British systems employed in the field."

74 See, for example: Headquarters AEF, *Instruction on Liaison for Troops of All Arms* (translated from the French edition of 1917) (Paris: Imprimerie Nationale, 1917); Headquarters AEF, *Instructions for the Employment of Aerial Observation in Liaison with the Artillery* (translated from the French edition of January 19, 1917) (Paris: Imprimerie Nationale, 1917); Army War College, *General Notes on the Use of Artillery* (translated and edited at the Army War College, November 1917) (Washington: GPO, 1917); Headquarters AEF, *Aerial Observation for Artillery*.

75 "W/T Spotting," 26.

76 Wilder, "Observation Training," 2.

77 "Chart Showing System of Training Artillery Observers as of September 1, 1918" M990, p. 1, R34, F69, Gorrell's History of the Air Service, Ser. J, vol. 1, RG 120, Records of the American Expeditionary Forces (World War I), NARA.

78   "Resume of Cables for Personnel Sent to US, Cable 1744-S Par. 3, S. Par A (Aug. 3, 1918)," M990, p. 1, R34, F371, Gorrell's History of the Air Service, Ser. J, vol. 2, RG 120, Records of the American Expeditionary Forces (World War I), NARA.

79   "Resume of Cables for Personnel Sent to US, Cable 1744-S Par. 3 (Oct. 4, 1918)." M990, p. 5, R34, F372, Gorrell's History of the Air Service, Ser. J, vol. 2, RG 120, Records of the American Expeditionary Forces (World War I), NARA.

80   "Air Service Training Section, American Expeditionary Forces, France: Time in Training Observation," M990, p. 38, R34, F412, Gorrell's History of the Air Service, Ser. J, vol. 2, RG 120, Records of the American Expeditionary Forces (World War I), NARA.

81   Wilder, "Observation Training," 2.

82   Office of Chief of Air Service, "Weekly Training Bulletin No. 3 (October 28, 1918)," M990, p. 1, R34, F149, Gorrell's History of the Air Service, Ser. J, vol. 1, RG 120, Records of the American Expeditionary Forces (World War I), NARA.

83   Ibid.

84   Ibid. Norman L. Franks and Frank W. Bailey, *Over the Front: A Complete Record of the Fighter Aces and Units of the United States and French Air Services, 1914–1918* (London: Grub Street, 1992), 161; Christopher Shores, Norman Franks and Russell Guest, *Above the Trenches: A Complete Record of the Fighter Aces and Units of the British Empire Air Forces 1915–1920* (London: Grub Street, 1990), 105–6, 114–15, 368, 389–90. Only five World War I fighter pilots achieved six aerial combat victories in one day: the French and Allied Ace of Aces, Rene Fonck, who did it twice, British Royal Naval Air Service pilot Raymond Collishaw, and John L. Trollope, Henry W. Woollett, and William G. Claxton, all three members of Great Britain's Royal Flying Corps.

85   Office of Chief of Air Service, "Weekly Training Bulletin No. 4 (November 6, 1918)," M990, p. 1, R34, F164 Gorrell's History of the Air Service, Ser. J, vol. 1, RG 120, Records of the American Expeditionary Forces (World War I), NARA.

86   Wilder, "Observation Training," 67.

87   "Report of the 1st, 2nd, 4th, 7th, and 8th AICs" in Edgar S. Gorrell, *History of the US Army Air Service*, M990, p. 14, R34, F1088, Gorrell's History of the Air Service, Ser. J, vol. 3, RG 120, Records of the American Expeditionary Forces (World War I), NARA [hereafter "Report of the AICs"]; Maurer, *US Air Service*, 1:105.

88   "Report of the AICs," 14.

89   Headquarters AEF, *Aerial Observation for Artillery*, 3.

90   Ibid., 4.

91   Office of Chief of Air Service, "Weekly Training Bulletin No. 2 (October 20, 1918)," M990, p. 3, R34, F136, Gorrell's History of the Air Service, Ser. J,

vol. 1, RG 120, Records of the American Expeditionary Forces (World War I), NARA.

92　R. M. B. Aaronson, "Instructions to Observers in the Preparation of Missions: A lecture given at the 2nd AIC," M990, p. 1, R34, F738, Gorrell's History of the Air Service, Ser. J, vol. 2, RG 120, Records of the American Expeditionary Forces (World War I), NARA.

93　*Aerial Observation for Artillery*, 13. The circumstances under which procedures permitted the aerial observer to intervene in the firing included: "If observation is poor and the observer desires time or volley fire, or salvos by 2; if the circumstances seem to warrant precision fire; If the result has clearly been obtained; if fire on a neighboring objective is urgently necessary; when adjustment on the objective itself is impossible on account of obstacles; when observation becomes impossible for any other reason."

94　Ibid., 10.

95　Ibid., 8.

96　Ibid., 17 and 21.

97　Thomas E. Hibben, "Topography: Lecture delivered at the 2nd A. I. C.," M990, p. 4, R34, F762, Gorrell's History of the Air Service, Ser. J, vol. 3, RG 120, Records of the American Expeditionary Forces (World War I), NARA; Terrence J. Finnegan, *Shooting the Front: Allied Aerial Reconnaissance and Photographic Interpretation on the Western Front—World War I* (Washington: National Defense Intelligence College, 2006), 49–50; Peter Chasseaud, ed., *The Imperial War Museum Trench Map Archive on CD-ROM* (London: Naval and Military Press in association with the Imperial War Museum, 2000), passim.

98　Office of Chief of Air Service, "Weekly Training Bulletin No. 1 (October 9, 1918)," M990, p. 4, R34, F119 Gorrell's History of the Air Service, Ser. J, vol. 1, RG 120, Records of the American Expeditionary Forces (World War I), NARA.

99　Ibid; Tony Ashworth, *Trench Warfare 1914–1918: The Live and Let Live System* (London: Pan, 2000), 18, 137. Ashworth argues that prolonged trench warfare created a culture in which each side refrained from provoking the other through what both came to regard as pointless attacks.

100　Wilder, "Observation Training," 72.

101　Ibid.

102　Ibid. American artillery batteries also fired at night, but without the benefit of real-time aerial adjustment. To assist an artillery battery to ready itself for night operations, airplane pilots were advised to fly over the objective during daylight hours and observe as the battery fired a pair of practice salvos. Using these results to fix its target the battery fired for effect later that evening.

103　Ibid; Janice Hayzlett and Peter Kilduff, trans., "Nachrichtenblat der Luftstreitkräfte No. 15," *Over the Front* 16, no. 3 (Autumn, 2001), 270–71. Milling might have drawn inspiration for a suggestion like this one from equally silly ruses perpetuated by the French and British prior to his arrival in Europe. These troops set off firecrackers meant to resemble the impact of German shells in places where no shells had actually landed.

104 "Notes on Observation Work at Chateau-Thierry Campaign, July 2nd–August 12th, 1918," M990, p. 1, R12, F24, Gorrell's History of the Air Service, Ser. C, vol. 1, RG 120, Records of the American Expeditionary Forces (World War I), NARA.

105 Ibid.

106 Ibid., 2–3.

107 L. P. Jocelyn, "US Army Infantry, Introductory Outline of Observation: Lecture given at the 2nd AIC," M990, p. 1, R34, F592, Gorrell's History of the Air Service, Ser. J, vol. 2, RG 120, Records of the American Expeditionary Forces (World War I), NARA.

108 *Aerial Observation for Artillery,* 26–27.

109 Saunders, *Per Ardua,* 275.

110 *Supplement to the Pamphlet entitled General Notions of Organization and Tactical Suggestions Indispensable to the Balloon Observer: Division of Military Aeronautics, US Army: This Supplement Supersedes Part I of the Pamphlet* (Washington: GPO, 1918), 6–9. Photographic sections did not fly. Their duties included developing photographic plates brought in by the reconnaissance squadrons and distributing the resulting prints. Air parks repaired and replaced damaged aircraft received from the front.

111 Maurer, *US Air Service,* 1:18 and 20.

112 James J. Davilla and Arthur M. Soltan, *French Aircraft of the First World War* (Stratford: Flying Machines Press, 1997), 14–15.

113 Walter Raleigh and H. A. Jones, *The War in the Air: Being the Story of the Part Played in the Great War by the Royal Air Force* (Oxford: Clarendon, 1922–1937), 1:6 and App.:129. On the comparatively aggressive doctrine of the British compared to the French or the United States, see John H. Morrow, Jr., *The Great War in the Air: Military Aviation from 1909 to 1921* (Washington: Smithsonian Institution Press, 1993), 345–48.

114 Saunders, *Per Ardua,* 274.

115 Office of Chief of Air Service, "Weekly Training Bulletin No. 5 (November 27, 1918)," M990, p. 4, R34, F174, Gorrell's History of the Air Service, Ser. J, vol. 1, RG 120, Records of the American Expeditionary Forces (World War I), NARA.

Chapter 5

1 Bob Sheldon, "Infantry Contact Patrols In WWI," *Cross & Cockade Journal* 16, no. 3 (Autumn 1975), 231.

2 "Summary of Information 26-1-15, G/112/87" in "HQRFC Summaries of Information Issued Daily G112/1-121 October 11, 1914–February 28, 1915,"

Air 1/751/204/4/13, TNA: PRO, 1. This report, for example, discusses the tendency of troops to take cover when aircraft flew over as well as the danger of ground fire.

3   Sheldon, "Infantry Contact Patrols," 234; *NBC Nightly News* (April 2, 2011), reported that this problem continues into the twenty-first century noting that Libyan rebels mistakenly fired on a NATO aircraft attempting to provide friendly aerial support.

4   "Aeronautics GHQ General File August 1915–November 1918," Air 1/2265/209/70/1, TNA: PRO, 31. This Air Ministry file contains a memo from the chief of the General Staff, GHQ dated March 30, 1916, that documents continuing problems with the improper identification of aircraft. The order changed reporting procedures so that only personnel assigned to antiaircraft batteries or Royal Flying Corps units could report the sighting of enemy aircraft to command posts. The memo also ordered aircraft recognition training for selected members of artillery batteries so that each battery had at least one person at hand capable of distinguishing between friendly and enemy aircraft.

5   Walter Raleigh, *The War in the Air: Being the Story of the Part Played in the Great War by the Royal Air Force* (Oxford: Oxford University Press, 1922), 1:348–49; "War Diary of No. 4 Squadron RFC 1–31 October 1914," Air 1/749/204/3/67, TNA: PRO, 7.

6   Les Rogers, *British Aviation Squadron Markings of World War I, RFC, RAF, RNAS* (Atglen: Schiffer Military History, 2001), 17. The British reversed the color order of the French roundel, using a red center and a blue outer ring.

7   Maurer Maurer, *The US Air Service in World War I* (Washington: GPO, 1978), 1:253; See also, Steve Ruffin, "'Dutch Girl' Over the Argonne: The 50th Aero Squadron in WWI," *Over the Front* 25, no. 2 (Summer 2010), 110, for a photo of a sign intended to educate American troops that showed the USAS insignia and instructed, "When you see this sign on an airplane he is an American. Don't shoot at him. He is trying to help you."

8   Raleigh and Jones, *War in the Air*, 2:233.

9   "Co-operation of Infantry and R.A.F.: Issue of Aerial Signaling Apparatus 23/11/16–25/1/19," Air 1/613/16/15/310, TNA: PRO, 3 [hereafter "Aerial Signaling Apparatus"].

10   Raleigh and Jones, *War in the Air*, 2:97, 109–110; Sheldon, "Contact Patrols," 231. The official history credits the first British endeavors at aerial infantry liaison to crews of No. 3 and No. 16 Squadrons, who made attempts at contact patrol flights during the Neuve Chapelle battle in March 1915. Sheldon maintains the French had begun developing aerial infantry liaison even earlier, but does not give a specific date.

11   J. C. Nerney, "Contact Patrol Liaison Between Infantry and Aircraft 1917," Air 1/674/21/6/120, TNA: PRO, 1 [hereafter "Contact Patrol Liaison"].

12 J. C. Nerney, "Ypres to the Somme: Festubert, May/June 1915," Air 1/674/21/6/106, TNA: PRO, 3.

13 Ibid., 4.

14 Ibid.

15 Ibid., 11. Nerney notes that with the exception of two hours around midday, No. 16 Squadron's crews patrolled from 5:00 A.M. until 6:25 P.M., during which time its crews sent forty-two messages. The ground stations received all but one or two of these messages.

16 Ibid., 20.

17 Ibid.

18 R. J. Kentish to G. H. Q. Home Forces, London, November 8, 1916, in "Aerial Signaling Apparatus."

19 Andrew Boyle, *Trenchard: Man of Vision* (New York: W. W. & Norton Co., 1962), 128; See also David MacIsaac, "Voices from the Central Blue: the Air Power Theorists," in Peter Paret, ed., *Makers of Modern Strategy: From Machiavelli to the Nuclear Age* (Princeton: Princeton University Press, 1986), 627–28; William Mitchell, *Memoirs of World War I: From Start to Finish of Our Greatest War* (New York: Random House, 1960), 133–41. Boyle quotes British air leader, Hugh Trenchard, who wrote of the future British Expeditionary Force's commander-in-chief, Douglas Haig, after their first meeting about the use of aircraft in battle that, "he accepted what I said, though he did not understand very much about it." Writing from a later time in the war, but during a period when the United States occupied much the same position in terms of military aviation preparedness that Britain, France or Germany held in 1914, Mitchell suggested that AEF commander, John J. Pershing, listened to and acted upon Mitchell's advice, but did so without taking the lead in anything to do with aviation.

20 Raleigh and Jones, *War in the Air*, 2:130.

21 Ibid.

22 Maurer, *US Air Service*, 1:190, 194.

23 Ibid., 212.

24 Nerney, "Contact Patrol Liaison," 8.

25 Raleigh and Jones, *War in the Air*, 2:211, documents the existence of targets so isolated behind enemy lines they could only be reported by airplanes.

26 Nerney, "Contact Patrol Liaison," 4–5; Raleigh and Jones, *War in the Air*, 2:180, 288–89. The official historians note that French success using balloons in infantry-liaison work prompted the British to open a school to teach these skills to balloon observers. Three appropriately trained British kite balloon sections deployed during the Somme battle and the official history draws attention to a significant success achieved by a balloon observer in September 1916.

27 Quoted in Nearny, "Contact Patrol Liaison," 5.

28 Ibid.

29 W. G. H. Salmond to director general military aeronautics, April 13, 1916, in "Instructions for the Guidance of Officers Commanding Detachments RFC when Co-operating with Columns of All Arms 13 April 1916," Air 1/131/15/40/220, TNA: PRO.

30 "Instructions for the Guidance of Officers Commanding Detachments RFC when Co-operating with Columns of All Arms 13 April 1916," Air 1/131/15/40/220, TNA: PRO, 1.

31 Ibid., 2.

32 Basil Liddell-Hart, *Liddell Hart's History of the First World War* (1930, as *The Real War 1914–1918*; repr., London: Papermac, 1997), 301.

33 Ernst von Hoeppner, *Germany's War in the Air: The Development and Operations of German Military Aviation in the World War*, trans. J. Hawley Larned (1921; repr., Nashville: Battery Press, 1994), 111.

34 Ibid.

35 Rick Duiven and Dan-San Abbott, *Schlachtflieger! Germany and the Origins of Air/Ground Support 1916–1918* (Atglen: Schiffer Military Publishing, 2006), 23.

36 *Nachrichtenblatt der Luftstreitkräfte* (Berlin: Deutsche Luftstreitkräfte, 1917) 1:10:4. The *Luftstreitkräfte* published the *Nachrichtenblatt*, a weekly service newspaper, between January 1917 and the end of the war to highlight important aviation contributions to the conflict, including the victory scores of German airmen.

37 Duiven and Abbott, *Schlachtflieger!*, 19.

38 W. G. Braithwaite, for Lt. Gen. commanding 23rd Army Corps, to GHQ Home Forces, May 16, 1918 in "Aerial Signaling Apparatus."

39 W. G. Braithwaite, for Lt. Gen. commanding 23rd Army Corps, to GHQ The Forces in Great Britain, July 22, 1918 in "Aerial Signaling Apparatus."

40 Maurer, *US Air Service*, 1:177.

41 "Historical Account of the Organization and Functioning of the 50th Aero Squadron," M990, p. 6, R18, F66, Gorrell's History of the Air Service, Ser. E, vol. 8, RG 120, Records of the American Expeditionary Forces (World War I), NARA [hereafter "Historical Account of the 50th"].

42 Ibid.

43 Ibid., 15.

44 Ibid., 8.

45 Maurer, *US Air Service*, 1:231.

46 Ibid., 1:252–53.

47 Ibid., 1:213.

48 "Historical Account of the 50th," 10; Daniel P. Morse, Jr., *The History of the 50th Aero Squadron: The "Dutch Girl" Observation Squadron in World War I* (1920; repr., Nashville: Battery Press, 1990), 31, 39, 65–73; Ruffin, "Dutch Girl," 117.

49 "An Account of the Argonne-Meuse Operations as Far as the 50th Aero Squadron is Concerned," M990, p. 4, R 18, F97, Gorrell's History of the Air Service, Ser. E, vol. 8, RG 120, NARA [hereafter "Account of the Argonne-Meuse"].

50 Ibid.

51 Ibid. Gorrell wrote rather cryptically about this incident. He did not make clear whether his comments about the lack of training were intended as an indictment of the Army for not properly training its infantry or a slight directed at the African-American troops. Evidence suggests the latter.

52 Ibid., 7, documents infantry contact patrols flown on October 3, 1918 and October 4, 1918.

53 Ibid., 8; Laurence Stallings, *The Doughboys: The Story of the AEF, 1917–1918* (New York: Harper and Row, 1963), 270.

54 Ibid., 272.

55 Steve Ruffin, "Mortal-Immortal: Goettler and Bleckley: 50th Aero Squadron Medal of Honor Airmen," *Over the Front* 25, no. 1 (Spring 2010), 144.

56 Robert J. Laplander, *Finding the Lost Battalion: Beyond the Rumors, Myths and Legends of America's Famous WWI Epic* (Waterford: American Expeditionary Foundation and Lulu Press, 2006), 563. Bleckley and Goettler first received posthumous Distinguished Service Crosses for their final mission, both of which were later upgraded to Medals of Honor.

57 Morse, *History of the 50th*, 49, 84; Laplander, *Finding the Lost Battalion*, 338–39, 532; "Account of the Argonne-Meuse," 18; Ruffin, "Dutch Girl," 120. Interestingly, Laplander accuses the 50th Aero Squadron's commanding officer, Daniel P. Morse, Jr., of helping to "muddy the Lost Battalion story waters" by his unwillingness to admit that the unit's supply dropping efforts had been largely in vain. Laplander's doubts about Morse's exaggerated claims on behalf of the squadron are supported by comparison of the official statistical summary of the unit's efforts on behalf of the "Lost Battalion" contained in "Account of the Argonne-Meuse," with the statistics Morse presents in his postwar book.

58 "Account of the Argonne-Meuse," 11.

59 Ibid., 13.

60 Ibid.

61 Ibid., 18.

62 Joseph E. Eaton, "Methods in Observation Practiced with Fifth Corps, First American Army, on the Fronts: St. Mihiel Sector, September 12th to 16th, Meuse-Argonne Sector, September 26th to November 11th," M990, p. 5, R47, F986, Gorrell's History of the Air Service, Ser. M, vol. 47, RG 120, Records of the American Expeditionary Forces (World War I), NARA.

63 Ibid.

64 Ibid., 6.

65   Ibid.
66   Ibid.
67   Ibid.
68   Ibid.
69   Ibid.
70   Ibid., 7.
71   Raleigh and Jones, *War in the Air,* 2:179.
72   Ibid., 2:210, 233.
73   Ibid., 2:245.
74   Ibid., 2:245–46.
75   Ibid., 2:273.
76   Ibid., 2:310.
77   Ibid., 2:228.
78   Hoeppner, *Germany's War in the Air,* 110.
79   Raleigh and Jones, *War in the Air,* 2:170, 232–33.
80   Maurer, *US Air Service,* 1:212, 81.
81   Raleigh and Jones, *War in the Air,* 2:244, 274. This volume of the *Official History* notes comments by a British commander who lauded the detail and accuracy of the information provided by the aircrews providing contact patrol support, as well as an incident in which commanders canceled an attack due to an air observer's report that showed heavier defenses than had previously been expected.
82   Maurer, *US Air Service,* 1:216, describes radio as "the form of liaison which is ideal for use in war of movement."

Chapter 6

1   Frederick Laws, interviews by Barrington J. Gray, February 1972, transcript, Frederick Laws Papers, RAF Museum, London, 6 [hereafter "Laws Interviews"]. Group Capt. Laws stated that at the time he joined the Royal Flying Corps photography consisted of "two men and a darkroom under the stairs."
2   Walter von Eberhardt, *Unsere Luftstreitkräfte 1914–1918* (Berlin: Verlag C. A. Weller, 1930), 93, quoted in Hanns-Gerd Rabe (Peter Kilduff, trans.), "Comments and Reminiscences, Flying as an Observer in Flieger-Abteilung (A) 253," *Over the Front* 17, no. 4 (Winter 2002), 297.
3   Louis Morgat, "L'Aviation en Berry avant la Grande Guerre," *Revue historique des armées,* 1980, no. 1: 196, quoted in John M. Morrow, Jr., *The Great War in the Air: Military Aviation from 1909–1921* (Washington: Smithsonian, 1993), 35.
4   G. W. Mapplebeck, Report of Reconnaissance of Gembloux, August 19, 1914, "Reconnaissance Report 19/22 August 1914 (including the first reconnaissance report by the RFC in the 1914–1918 War, by Lt. G.W. Mapplebeck, No. 4

Squadron, RFC)," Air 1/749/204/3/76, TNA: PRO, 2 [hereafter "Report 19/22 August 1914"].

5   "No. 4 Squadron Reconnaissance Reports, August 1914: Appendices to War Diary," Air 1/744/204/3/8, TNA: PRO, 42 [hereafter "No. 4 Squadron Reconnaissance Appendices"].

6   "RFC (MW) Form of Observers' Reports in Aerial Reconnaissance 1914/1915," Air 1/782/204/4/514, TNA: PRO, 11. Aircrews were ordered to mount the form to a clipboard with the central clip at top and the lower edges clipped to board with bulldog pattern paper chips, covering the form with a waterproof sheet when not writing on it. The observer's report ultimately adopted the following form:

No. of Reconnaissance	Date	Squadron	Aeroplane No. Type	Pilot	Observer	Ref. Map	Hour Started	Hour Landed

Time			Place			Observation page no. _____
						Signed _____ Observer

7   Reconnaissance No. 10 (Combined), August 22, 1914, "Report 19/22 August 1914," 10.

8   Ibid; "Composition of the Units of the German Army: Circulated 6-8-1914," Air 1/746/204/3/23, TNA: PRO, 2–3, advised RFC aircrews on the length of various German units they might observe from the air.

9   "No. 4 Squadron Reconnaissance Appendices," 7.

10   Orders for Reconnaissance October 26, 1914, "HQ RFC Orders for Reconnaissance from 24th October 1914 to 28 November 1914," Air 1/751/204/4/8, 35 [hereafter "RFC Orders for Reconnaissance"].

11   Peter Chasseaud, *Artillery's Astrologers: A History of British Survey and Mapping on the Western Front 1914–1918* (Lewes: Mapbooks, 1999), 25–26.

12   Reconnaissance Report August 19, 1914, "Report 19/22 August 1914," 7; Reconnaissance No. 10 (Combined), August 22, 1914, "Report 19/22 August 1914," 10.

13   "No. 4 Squadron Reconnaissance Reports," 48; French Army August 1914, www.orbat.com/site/history/historical/france/army1914.html (accessed May 6, 2009). This source identifies the commanding officer of the French XVIII Corps in August 1914 as *General* de Mas.

14   "No. 4 Squadron Reconnaissance Reports," 31. This report includes the statement: "1 Regiment of infantry moving South along the ridge West of

Estourmelle, this outflanked the Allied left. Behind the British line the retirement appeared to be general but orderly."

15 Orders for Reconnaissance, October 28, 1914, "RFC Orders for Reconnaissance," 2.

16 "Notes for Observer: Cards (Carried in Aeroplanes) July 1915 23/6/15–26/7/15," Air 1/128/15/40/178, TNA: PRO, 3.

17 "Aerial Reconnaissance Reports to Hejaz Operations," WO 158/645, TNA: PRO, passim. This report of the RFC/RAF experience in the Middle East made it clear that aerial reconnaissance's value was not limited to geography where cavalry operations were restricted owing to the presence of trenches and barbed wire, but proved equally valuable in areas where extreme weather conditions made cavalry operations challenging.

18 Walter Raleigh, *The War in the Air: Being the Story of the Part Played in the Great War by the Royal Air Force* (Oxford: Oxford University Press, 1922), 1:329. The *Official History* quotes Sir John French's first wartime dispatch, dated September 7, 1914, in which the British commander-in-chief praised the Royal Flying Corps for having provided him "with the most complete and accurate information, which has been of incalculable value in the conduct of operations." Richard Holmes maintains French had emerged from the Boer War as "the country's most successful cavalry leader." Richard Holmes, *The Little Field Marshal: A Life of Sir John French* (1981; repr., London: Cassel, 2005), 153.

19 "HQRFC Summaries of Information Issued Daily G112/1–121, October 11, 1914–February 28, 1915," Air 1/751/204/4/13, TNA: PRO, 65. This intelligence summary provides a good example of the desire commanders felt for verification of information brought in by aviators and for the comfort they took when photos provided confirmation. The summary for January 12, 1915, contains the statement: "A German illustrated paper contains a picture of a ruined girder bridge with the title 'Bridge at FRELINGHIEN destroyed by English Artillery fire.' This bridge was twice reported by aviators as 'apparently destroyed,' and the illustration appears to place the matter beyond a doubt."

20 E. Geoffrey Toye, "History of Photography in the Air Branches of His Majesty's Service (1914–1918), General Article," Frederick Laws Papers, RAF Museum, London, 1 [hereafter "History of Photography"].

21 Ibid.

22 Ibid.

23 Raleigh, *War in the Air*, 1:250, 343, discuss No. 3 Squadron's prewar photography experiments and Pretyman's activities on September 15, 1914; Nicholas C. Watkis, *The Western Front from the Air* (Phoenix Mill: Sutton, 1999), 8–9; "The Royal Flying Corps: R. F. C. Military Wing," *Flight* (October 18, 1913), 1145, http://www.flightglobal.com/pdfarchive/view/1913/1913%20-%201119.html (accessed May 13, 2009) confirmed Lieutenant

Pretyman's Christian name; "No. 3 Squadron War Diary (Intelligence Summary) 6 August–31 December 1914," Air 1/737/204/2/2, TNA: PRO, 53–56.

24 "Laws Interviews," 7–9. Laws contends that no one in No. 3 Squadron had any interest in photography and that during his time there he performed other duties, not resuming his work in photography until his transfer to No. 9 Squadron.

25 Toye, "History of Photography," 4.

26 Hilary St. George Saunders, *Per Ardua: The Rise of British Air Power 1911–1939* (London: Oxford University Press, 1945), 52.

27 J. C. Nerney, "The Campaign on the Western Front (1) Ypres to the Somme–"Neuve Chapelle" 10 March 1915, Series No. 1," Air 1/674/21/6/95), 6. Other than Laws, supporters of photography in the unit included Lts. John Moore-Brabazon and Charles Campbell, and Second Air-Mechanic W. D. Corse.

28 Ibid., 8.

29 Ibid.

30 Saunders, *Per Ardua*, 54.

31 J. C. Nerney, "The Campaign on the Western Front: Ypres to the Somme: Festubert, May and June 1915," Air 1/674/21/6/106, 1. This source documents the postponement of the Festubert attack for twenty-four hours because of bad weather, which in turn nearly impeded artillery registration and other aerial reconnaissance activities.

32 ? at First Army Headquarters to J. T. C. Moore-Brabazon, June 1, 1915, "J. T. C. Moore-Brabazon Papers," RAF Museum, London [hereafter "? to Moore-Brabazon"].

33 Terrence J. Finnegan, *Shooting the Front: Allied Aerial Reconnaissance and Photographic Interpretation on the Western Front—World War I* (Washington: National Defense Intelligence College Press, 2006), 5.

34 Tim Coates, ed., *The World War I Collection: Gallipoli and the Early Battles, 1914–15: The Dardanelles Commission, 1914–16; British Battles of World War I, 1914–15* (London: The Stationery Office, 2001), 64.

35 Peter Chasseaud, *Official History of the Great War: Military Operations Other Theatres 1914–18: Maps*, CD-ROM (London: Military and Naval Press in Association with the Imperial War Museum, 2002).

36 Ernest M. Dowson, "Gallipoli 1915: Mapping from Aeroplane Photographs," WO 317/13, TNA: PRO, 3 [hereafter "Gallipoli: Mapping"]. A *flèche* was a small aerial anti-personnel bomb about the length of a pencil, the shaft of which was cut in cross form to provide stability during its fall, and pointed on the end that struck the target.

37 Chasseaud, *Military Operations Other Theatres*; Jones, *War in the Air*, 2:28.

38 Ibid.; Charles R. Samson, *Fights and Flights: A Memoir of the Royal Naval Air Service in World War I* (1930; repr., Nashville: Battery Press, 1990), 228;

Chasseaud, *Artillery's Astrologers*, 12. He notes that the 2nd Ranging and Survey Section, RE, assigned to mapping duties in Gallipoli, did not embark from England until June 8, 1915.

39 Charles R. Samson to Murray K. Sueter, June 27, 1915, "Semi-official Letter from Commander C. R. Samson on Experiences at Gallipoli June 1915," Air 1/7/6/98/20, TNA: PRO, 3.

40 Dowson, "Gallipoli: Mapping," 2, 22. Aerial photos of Gallipoli generally taken at around 6,000 feet (1,829 m) provided a photo on a scale of 1:6,000 with a 17 × 12 cm plate, covering an area of 1,000 × 700 m.

41 Ibid., 4.

42 Ibid., 153; Finnegan, *Shooting the Front*, 144–46.

43 Dowson, "Gallipoli: Mapping," 4, 7.

44 Ibid., 6.

45 Ibid., 2–3. "? to Moore-Brabazon" also documents the growing preference for intelligence obtained from aerial photographs.

46 Frederick H. Sykes, "Report from Col. F. H. Sykes, RFC, on the Subject of the RNAS Units and Aerial Requirements of the Naval and Military Forces at Dardanelles, 9-7-1915," Air 1/625/17/12, TNA: PRO, 2.

47 Robert Brooke-Popham, "Notes on a Visit to Headquarters of the French Northern Group of Armies" in "Aeronautics General File," 1. Brooke-Popham visited the French Headquarters on November 27, 1915.

48 Ibid.

49 Heinz J. Nowarra, *50 Jahre Deutsche Luftwaffe* (Genoa: Intyprint, 1964), 2:12. At the outset of the First World War, German military aviators served as the "*Luftfahrtruppen*" (aerial troops). When the German Army reorganized on October 8, 1916, the Luftfahrtruppen achieved a greater degree of independence within the Army and changed names to the *Luftstreitkräfte* (Air Force).

50 Chasseaud, *Artillery's Astrologers*, 42; Peter Haupt, "Great War Aerial Photographs in German Archives: a Guide to the Sources," in Birger Stichelbaut, Jean Bourgeois, Nicholas Saunders and Piet Chielens, *Images of Conflict: Military Aerial Photography and Archaeology* (Cambridge: Cambridge Scholars Press, 2009), 151–64.

51 Alex Imrie, *Pictorial History of the German Army Air Service, 1914–1918* (1971; repr. Chicago: Henry Regnery, 1973), 87 and 103. The aircraft depicted is an Albatros B. I, an unarmed type that served at the front only until Germany introduced armed aircraft in early 1915.

52 *Kommandierender General der Luftstreitkräfte, Bildmeldung der Luftschiffer* (Charleville: *Kogenluft*, 1917), 2.

53 Ibid.; See also *Kommandierender General der Luftstreitkräfte, Bildmeldung der Flieger* (Charleville: *Kogenluft*, 1917), passim.

54 Finnegan, *Shooting the Front*, covers the development of aerial photographic equipment.

55 Toye, "History of Photography," 3.

56 Saunders, *Per Ardua*, 52.

57 J. E. Hahn, *The Intelligence Service within the Canadian Corps 1914–1918* (Toronto: MacMillan, 1930), xvii.

58 Ibid., 14.

59 Charles Campbell, "Report on Progress of Photography in the RFC 31 December 1915–27 April 1916," Air 1/123/15/40/14/1, TNA: PRO, 1 [hereafter "Progress of Photography"].

60 Reinhard R. Kastner (Dieter Gröschel trans.), "Fatal Accidents in Bavarian Military Training Centers," *Over the Front* 16, no. 4 (Winter 2000), 300.

61 Saunders, *Per Ardua*, 89.

62 Lionel Charlton to general officer commanding Training Brigade, November 24, 1916, "Formation of a Pool of Photographers at Recruits Depot, RFC, 26-9-1916–16-6-1917," Air 1/127/15/40/146, TNA: PRO, 1.

63 Chasseaud, *Artillery's Astrologers*, 90, notes the French origin of the British aerial photography manual.

64 Royal Flying Corps, *Notes on the Interpretation of Aeroplane Photographs*, Rev. ed., March 1917, Frederick Laws Papers, RAF Museum, London.

65 Chasseaud, *Artillery's Astrologers*, 40, lists fifty-eight types of "other maps" drawn and printed by British cartographers during the war ranging in purpose from railway maps to artillery practice maps to water supply maps.

66 Ibid., 41.

67 Thomas E. Hibben, "Topography: Lecture delivered at the Second Aviation Instruction Center," M990, p. 1, R34, F759, Gorrell's History of the Air Service, Ser. J, vol. 3, RG 120, Records of the American Expeditionary Forces (World War I), NARA [hereafter "Topography"]; Chasseaud, *Artillery's Astrologers*, provides extensive details on mapping procedures and the sort of details available on British trench maps.

68 No. 1 Wing, RNAS, December 19, 1916, Report on W/T Spotting, "W/T Spotting September 1916–September 1918," Air 1/71/15/9/126, TNA: PRO, 2.

69 GHQ, American Expeditionary Forces, Office of the Chief of Staff, *Aerial Observation for Artillery*, M990, pp. 8–9, R34, F715, Gorrell's History of the Air Service, Ser. J, vol. 2, RG 120, Records of the American Expeditionary Forces (World War I), NARA.

70 Hibben, "Topography," 3.

71 *Interpretation of Aeroplane Photographs*, plate 18, contains a view of a dummy artillery battery; Toulmin, *Air Service*, 372, discusses USAS experience with dummy batteries and other camouflage measures; Jan Hayzlett, (trans.), *"Nachrichtenblat der Luftstreitkräfte*, No. 14," *Over the Front*, 16, no. 2, 181, documents aerial photos that showed dummy aircraft located on airfields at Hareaucourt and Pullnoy.

72 *Interpretation of Aeroplane Photographs*, 7.

73 Report on Photographic Speed Tests Carried Out by the Three Squadrons in 1st Wing, 1st Brigade, Royal Flying Corps, June 10–18, 1916, "Progress of Photography," 1; Saunders, *Per Ardua*, 101, address the issue of the timely receipt of photographs within the context of the July 25, 1916 (part of the Somme battle) British attack on a German trench known as Munster Alley noting that the attack might have developed along different lines or not taken place at all had the relevant aerial photographs been received prior to its launch.

74 Charles Campbell to J. T. C. Moore-Brabazon, May 24, 1917, "J. T. C. Moore-Brabazon Papers," RAF Museum, London.

75 "Study of RNAS Photographs Nos. 949, 951–955, 946, Reconnaissance of May 5th 1917. Jacobinessen Battery, R.434," in "French and English Photographic Studies—Dunkirk Command, 12 September 1916–15 July 1917," Air 1/82/15/9/204, TNA: PRO, 1:2 [hereafter "Photographic Studies"].

76 "Preparation for Battle of Arras November 1916–April 1917," Air 1/676/21/13/1872, TNA: PRO, 22.

77 "Study of English Photographs 315 to 319 of Ostende Harbour made by the *Canevas de Tir*," "Photographic Studies," 2:2; Oostacker, Mariakerke, Rieme and Ghent Docks, RNAS Photos Nos. 1811, 1815, 1831, 1833, December 19, 1917, in ibid., 2:100.

78 Ibid., 2:82.

79 "Study of RNAS Photographs Nos. 1244, 1251, 1257, 1261, 1266, 1271 Reconnaissance of June 15, 1917, Hoboken and Cockerils Works—Antwerp, R.493," in ibid., 1:1.

80 "Breedene/Clemskerke Area, RNAS Photos 1742/3, October 21, 1917," in ibid., 2:87.

81 "Study of Ostende, RNAS Photos 1585–1594, September 5, 1917," in ibid, 2:64; "Study of Ostende, RNAS Photos 1608, 1609, 1611, 1613 and 1617, and Stereos Nos. 18, 19 and 20, September 22, 1917," in ibid, 2:67.

82 Headquarters 5th Group, RAF, Study of Photographs Taken on 17th October 1918, "Photographic Studies Dunkirk Command September 1918–November 1918," Air 1/82/15/9/207, TNA: PRO, 229.

83 Finnegan, *Shooting the Front*, 336.

84 Ibid.

85 GHQ, Aerial Observation for Artillery, 7; Thomas E. Hibben, "Interpretation of Aerial Photography: Lecture given at the 2nd Aviation Instruction Center," M990, p. 2, R34, F942, Gorrell's History of the Air Service, Ser. J., vol. 3, RG 120, Records of the American Expeditionary Forces (World War I), NARA [hereafter "Interpretation of Aerial Photography"].

86 Toye, "History of Photography," 5.

87 "Study of RNAS Photographs Nos. 785–787–9, 805, 810, 812, Reconnaissance of April 24th 1917, Region South and Southwest of Bruges, R.426," "Photographic Studies," 1:65.

88 "The Duties of Operations Officers in US Air Service Units (Observation, Pursuit, Day Bombing, Night Reconnaissance)," M990, p. 18, R34, F120, Gorrell's History of the Air Service, Ser. J, vol. 1, RG 120, Records of the American Expeditionary Forces (World War I), NARA.

89 James J. Hudson, *Hostile Skies: A Combat History of the American Air Service in World War I* (Syracuse: Syracuse University Press, 1968), 1–63; Maurer Maurer, *The US Air Service in World War I* (Washington: Office of Air Force History, 1978), 2:1–103; Lucien H. Thayer, *America's First Eagles: The Official History of the US Air Service, AEF (1917–1918)* (San Jose and Mesa: Bender Publishing and Champlin Fighter Museum Press, 1983), 9–27; James J. Cooke, *The US Air Service in the Great War, 1917–1919* (Westport: Praeger, 1996), 17–34.

90 Toye, "History of Photography," 8.

91 Christopher Cole, ed., *Royal Flying Corps 1915–1916* (London: William Kimber, 1969), 73, quotes RFC Communiqué No. 17, which includes specific mention of the capture of a German photo-reconnaissance aircraft carrying a camera equipped with a Zeiss lens.

92 Ibid., 450.

93 Ibid.

94 "Enlist Your Lens in the Air Service," advertisement, *National Geographic* (January 1918), 118.

95 J. T. C. Moore-Brabazon, "Minutes Interallied Photographic Conference, August 19, 1918," Frederick Laws Papers, RAF Museum, London, 3–5.

96 Geoffrey J. Dwyer, "Report on Air Service Flying Training Department in England," M990, p. 4, R34, F108, Gorrell's History of the Air Service, Ser. J, vol. 1, RG 120, Records of the American Expeditionary Forces (World War I), NARA.

97 Information Officer to Training Section, Air Service, "Report on Organization of Information Office," November 8, 1918, M990, p. 2, R34, F181, Gorrell's History of the Air Service, Ser. J, vol. 1, RG 120, Records of the American Expeditionary Forces (World War I), NARA; "USA. Summary of Assistance Given by British Air Service to American Air Service During the War," TNA: PRO, Air 1/109/15/26, 1, documents the dispatch of seventy-five British officers to the United States to advise their American aviation counterparts on a wide variety of aviation topics, including photography.

98 "Course in Aerial Photography for Bombing Pilots and Observers," M990, p. 6, R35, F227, Gorrell's History of the Air Service, Ser. J, vol. 4, RG 120, Records of the American Expeditionary Forces (World War I), NARA [hereafter "Photography for Bombing Pilots"].

99 Russell A. Clapp, "Notes on Aerial Photography: Lecture given at 3rd Aviation Instruction Center," M990, p. 1, R34, F1101, Gorrell's History of the Air Service, Ser. J, vol. 3, RG 120, Records of the American Expeditionary Forces (World War I), NARA; James J. Cooke, *Billy Mitchell* (Boulder: Lynne

Rienner, 2002), 57; John J. Pershing, *My Experiences in the World War* (New York: Frederick Stokes, 1931) 1:109, discusses the division of the American Expeditionary Force's French area of operations into two regions. The rear area, where supply and training functions took place, became designated the "service of supply." The front lines became variously the "zone of operations," or the "zone of advance."

100 C. C. Benedict, "Observation Training at 2nd Corps Aeronautical School," M990, p. 2, R34, F614, Gorrell's History of the Air Service, Ser. J, vol. 3, RG 120, Records of the American Expeditionary Forces (World War I), NARA.

101 "Air Service American Expeditionary Forces, France, Second Aviaton Instruction Center, Tours (Indre-et-Loire), France, Report of the 1st, 2nd, 4th, 7th, and 8th AICs," p. 22, R34, F1096, Gorrell's History of the Air Service, Ser. J, vol. 3, RG 120, Records of the American Expeditionary Forces (World War I), NARA. On September 1, 1918, for example, the Air Service estimated that by October 31, 1918 it would deliver 1,090 trained pilots (pursuit, 250; bombing, 280; observation, 560) and one thousand trained observers (pursuit, 120; bombing, 330; observation, 550).

102 Ibid., 15.

103 "History of the Aerial Photography School, 2nd Aviation Instruction Center," M990, p. 5, R35, F1122, Gorrell's History of the Air Service, Ser. J, vol. 7, RG 120, Records of the American Expeditionary Forces (World War I), NARA.

104 "Photography for Bombing Pilots," 1.

105 Hibben, "Interpretation of Aerial Photography," 26.

106 Office of Chief of Air Service, "Weekly Training Bulletin No. 2," October 20, 1918, M990, p. 2, R34, F135, Gorrell's History of the Air Service, Ser. J., vol. 1, RG 120, Records of the American Expeditionary Forces (World War I), NARA [hereafter "Training Bulletin No. 2"].

107 Office of Chief of Air Service, "Weekly Training Bulletin No. 1," October 9, 1918, M990, p. 4, R34, F119, Gorrell's History of the Air Service, Ser. J, vol. 1, RG 120, Records of the American Expeditionary Forces (World War I), NARA [hereafter "Training Bulletin No. 1"].

108 John Snyder, "Notes on Reconnaissance: Lecture given at 2nd Aviation Instruction Center," M990, p. 6, R34, F891, Gorrell's History of the Air Service, Ser. J, vol. 3, RG 120, Records of the American Expeditionary Forces (World War I), NARA [hereafter "Reconnaissance Lecture"].

109 "Photography for Bombing Pilots," 3. Line work refers to missions that took series of overlapping photos specifically intended for mapping.

110 John Snyder, "Notes on Army Observation: Lecture given at 2nd Aviation Instruction Center," M990, p. 1, R34, F831, Gorrell's History of the Air Service, Ser. J, vol. 3, RG 120, Records of the American Expeditionary Forces (World War I), NARA. The war ended before the USAS achieved this degree of specialization.

111 "Training Bulletin No. 1," 2.

112 "Training Bulletin No. 2," 10.

113 Edward M. Urband, "Three Essential Forms of Reports: Lecture given at 2nd Aviation Instruction Center," M990, p. 3, R34, F1002, Gorrell's History of the Air Service, Ser J., vol. 3, RG 120, Records of the American Expeditionary Forces (World War I), NARA, 4.

114 Harold Wilder, "Advanced Artillery Aerial Observation Schools," M990, p. 1, R34, F621, Gorrell's History of the Air Service, Ser. J, vol. 3, RG 120, Records of the American Expeditionary Forces (World War I), NARA.

115 Hibben, "Interpretation of Aerial Photography," 1.

116 Snyder, "Reconnaissance Lecture," 1.

117 Thomas A. Box, "Night Reconnaissance: Lecture given at 2nd Aviation Instruction Center," 1, M990, p. 1, R34, F1160, Gorrell's History of the Air Service, Ser. J, vol. 3, RG 120, Records of the American Expeditionary Forces (World War I), NARA [hereafter "Night Reconnaissance"].

118 "Instructions for Night Reconnaissance Units," M990, p. 18, R34, F988, Gorrell's History of the Air Service, RG 120, Records of the American Expeditionary Forces (World War I), NARA; W. W. Thomas, "Night Reconnaissance and Observation: Lecture given at 2nd Aviation Instruction Center," M990, p. 1, R34, F1151, Gorrell's History of the Air Service, Ser. J, vol. 3, RG 120, Records of the American Expeditionary Forces (World War I), NARA.

119 Box, "Night Reconnaissance," 1.

120 "The Development of Aerial Photography, Treatise by Photographic Department, HQ, AS, SOS, July 12, 1918," M990, p. 1, R34, F919, Gorrell's History of the Air Service, Ser. J, vol. 3, RG 120, Records of the American Expeditionary Forces (World War I), NARA; Box, "Night Reconnaissance," 1.

121 HQ First Army Corps, AEF, Office of the Chief of Air Service, "Operations Report for the 4th May 1918," M990, p. 3, R12, F60, Gorrell's History of the Air Service, Ser. C, vol. 2, RG 120, Records of the American Expeditionary Forces (World War I), NARA, for example, which documents a 94th Aero Squadron reconnaissance flight on May 4, 1918; "Repatriation Report of Lt. Gordon Hunter, No. 60 Squadron, RFC," quoted in Over the Front 17, no. 4 (Winter, 2002), 372, documents similar single-seat reconnaissance missions by the British.

122 "Notes on Observation Work at Chateau-Thierry Campaign July 2nd–August 12th 1918," M990, p. 1, R12, F24, Gorrell's History of the Air Service, Ser. C, vol. 1, RG 120, Records of the American Expeditionary Forces (World War I), NARA.

123 Ralph E. DeCastro, "Notes for Observation Pilots: Lecture given at 3rd Aviation Instruction Center," M990, p. 3, R34, F1107, Gorrell's History of the Air Service, Ser. J, vol. 3, RG 120, Records of the American Expeditionary Forces (World War I), NARA.

124 "Royal Flying Corps War Diary," October 10, 1916, Air 1/1184, TNA: PRO, 3.
125 Jones, *War in the Air*, 4:381.
126 "Photography Army Book 135," Frederick Laws Papers, RAF Museum, London, 10, puts the totals at 221,254 negatives and 4,934,353 prints.
127 Raleigh, *War in the Air*, 1:6.
128 Agnès Beylot, "Military Aerial Photographs from 1914 to the Present: A Survey of the Sources," in Stichelbaut, et al, *Images of Conflict*, 137; Peter Haupt, "Great War Aerial Photographs in German Archives: A Guide to the Sources," in Stichelbaut, et al, *Images of Conflict*, 153–63. Colin A. Owers, Jon S. Guttman and James J. Davilla, *Salmson Aircraft of World War I: Salmson-Moineau S.M.1, Salmson 2, Salmson 3, Salmson 4, Salmson 5, Salmson 6, Salmson 7* (Boulder: Flying Machines Press, 2001), 18, provides annual totals for French aerial photographs taken during the war at: 48,000 (1914–15); 293,000 (1916); 474,000 (1917); and 675,000 (1918).
129 Maurer, *US Air Service*, 1:17.
130 Harold Wilder, "History of Aerial Observation Training in the American Expeditionary Forces, 1917–1918," M990, p. 2, R34, F581, Gorrell's History of the Air Service, Ser. J, vol. 2, RG 120, Records of the American Expeditionary Forces (World War I), NARA.

Chapter 7

1   Paul G. Halpern, *A Naval History of World War I* (Annapolis: Naval Institute Press, 1994), 22–23; Hew Strachan, *The First World War* (New York: Viking, 2003), 214–15.
2   Ibid., 216; Suzanne Hayes Fischer, *Mother of Eagles: The War Diary of Baroness von Richthofen* (Atglen: Schiffer Military History, 2001), 23–27, 138; Lance J. Bronnenkant, *The Imperial German Eagles in World War I: Their Postcards and Pictures* (Atglen: Schiffer Military History, 2006), 24. These authors provide accounts of the difficulties the blockade presented to even privileged Germans in search of products ranging from food to leather and rubber and the creative methods they developed at home and at the front to obtain scarce items.
3   Henry Woodhouse, *Woodhouse's Textbook of Naval Aeronautics* (Annapolis: Naval Institute Press, 1991), 27.
4   "Development of the Air Department Admiralty 1912–1916," Air 1/674/21/6/59, TNA: PRO, 1; J. C. Nerney, "History of the Anti-Submarine Campaign 1914–1917," Air 1/675/21/13/1385, TNA: PRO, 1:2 [hereafter "History Anti-Submarine Campaign"].
5   E. W. Griffin, "Some Rough Notes on the Early Development of the R.N.A.S., 1912–1917," Air 1/625/17/1, TNA: PRO, 3 [hereafter "Notes on the RNAS"].
6   Ibid.; James J. Davilla and Arthur M. Soltan, *French Aircraft of the First World War* (Stratford: Flying Machines Press, 1997), 21. Though no separate verification

of prewar French development of an anti-submarine capability has been located, Davilla and Soltan note that the French began studying the use of airplanes with their Navy as early as 1910 and established anti-submarine warfare centers at Dunkerque and Boulogne in December 1914, suggesting that French naval officers had given at least some thought to the matter prior to the outbreak of hostilities.

7   "History Anti-Submarine Campaign," 1:2; "Extracts from Paper by Capt. Murray F. Sueter, director of Air Department, Admiralty," quoted in Stephen W. Roskill, *Documents Relating to the Naval Air Service 1908–1918* (London: Naval Records Society, 1969), 1:56, dates Sueter's paper August 29, 1912; National Maritime Museum, "Rear-Admiral Sir Murray Sueter," http://www. nmm.ac.uk/collections/explore/object.cfm (accessed May 13, 2010), describes Sueter as "largely instrumental in the rapid build-up to full war strength of the Royal Naval Air Service."

8   "Admiralty Letter M.01495/12 of 2 November 1912 to the Admiral Commanding Coast Guard and Reserves," Air 1/652, TNA: PRO, 1. This letter lists Sueter's recommended locations somewhat differently: Dover, Sheppey (Eastchurch Flying School), Harwich, Cromer, Cleethorpes, Filey, Newcastle, Rosyth or N. Berwick, Aberdeen, Cromarty, Portsmouth, Plymouth, Weymouth, and Pembroke.

9   "History Anti-Submarine Campaign," 1:3; "Extracts from the First Annual Report of the Air Committee on the Progress of the Royal Flying Corps, June 7, 1913," quoted in Roskill, *Documents Relating to the Naval Air Service*, 1:96. Roskill notes that by June 7, 1913 airplane facilities had been constructed at "Eastchurch, the Isle of Grain, Calshot, Harwich, Yarmouth, and Rosyth," and that negotiations were underway for additional facilities at "Dover, Cleethorpes, Newcastle, Peterhead, Cromarty, Scapa Flow, and in other localities."

10   "History Anti-Submarine Campaign," 1:5.

11   Ibid., 1:7.

12   Ibid.

13   Ibid., 1:8.

14   Ibid., 1:17; Griffin, "Notes on the RNAS," 1; "Summary of Events Connected with the Royal Flying Corps (Naval Wing) January–August 1914," Air 1/674/21/6/21, TNA: PRO, 2. Griffin dates the transfer of airship development from the Army to the Admiralty to October 1913, while the latter report claims January 1, 1914 as the date of the takeover.

15   Halpern, *Naval History of World War I*, 293.

16   "History Anti-Submarine Campaign," 1:18.

17   Ibid; National Maritime Museum, "Admiral Sir Sydney Robert Fremantle," http://www.nmm.ac.uk/collections/archive/catalogue/record.cfm (accessed March 15, 2010).

18   "History Anti-Submarine Campaign," 1:22.

19   Ibid., 1:23.

20 Ibid., 1:25. In removing the air stations from the director of the Air Department's control in favor of the senior naval officer the Navy achieved an intra-service victory the artillery failed to win in its ongoing campaign to wrest control of land-based observation balloons away from the Army's Royal Flying Corps.

21 Ibid., 1:26.

22 Christopher Cole and E. F. Cheesman, *The Air Defence of Britain 1914–1918* (London: Putnam, 1984), 34. The authors outline early changes in the measures taken for the aerial defense of the British mainland during the First World War.

23 "History Anti-Submarine Campaign," 1:27.

24 "Extracts from Report on the Performance of No. 1 Wing, RNAS, during 1915," quoted in Stephen W. Roskill, *Documents Relating to the Naval Air Service 1908–1918* (London: Naval Records Society, 1969), 1:262.

25 Ibid., 1:263.

26 "History Anti-Submarine Campaign," 1:12–13.

27 Dwight R. Messimer, *Verscholen: World War I U-Boat Losses* (Annapolis: Naval Institute Press, 2002), 13, 59, 88, 112, 208, 214, 226, 309. Messimer outlines the continuing controversy over the degree of success airplanes and airships achieved as offensive weapons against the U-boat during the First World War. Though airmen frequently thought they had sunk, or assisted in the sinking of, enemy submarines, and reported so to their superiors, the number of verified sinkings is low. He credits seven submarines lost to aircraft-involved attacks out of a total of 203 missing during the war. Doubtless aircrew sighted and reported submarines, contributing to the protection of naval and merchant fleets by forcing submarine commanders to miss potential targets while they remained submerged hiding until the aircraft overhead had passed.

28 "History Anti-Submarine Campaign," 1:20.

29 Douglas H. Robinson, *The Zeppelin in Combat: A History of the German Naval Airship Division, 1912–1918*, 3rd ed. (Sun Valley: John W. Caler, 1971), 404.

30 Ibid; *Jane's Fighting Ships of World War I* (New York: Military Press, 1990), 39, 313–16. Jane calculates British wartime naval losses at thirteen battleships, three battle cruisers, fourteen light cruisers, eight monitors, twenty sloops, twenty-six minesweepers, five torpedo gunboats, sixty-nine flotilla leaders and destroyers, two patrol boats, eleven torpedo boats, fifty-eight submarines, eighty-one auxiliaries, twenty-nine motor launches, and seventeen coastal motor boats. Just one of those ships, the battleship *Audacious*, a *King George V*-class vessel, cost £1,945,200, nearly a half million pounds more than all the damage inflicted on England by German airships.

31 "History Anti-Submarine Campaign," 1:21.

32 Frederick Sykes, *Aviation in Peace and War* (London: Edward Arnold, 1922), 35. Sykes documents the slow start noting that British aviators attacked only ten German submarines from the air in 1915. During 1918 the number of submarines sighted rose to 126 with ninety-three of those attacked.

33   Halpern, *Naval History of World War I*, 341. Halpern estimates the annual seagoing tonnage loss as "nearly 23 percent per year" prior to Germany's resumption of unrestricted submarine warfare in February 1917, a figure that would rise "to more than 50 percent per year in the last fortnight of April" 1917. In tons lost, German submarines sunk 328,391 tons in January 1917, the month before their commanders removed the restrictions on their activities. The monthly figures rose dramatically during February and March before peaking at 860,334 tons in April 1917.

34   Strachan, *The First World War*, 188, 195. Strachan puts German casualties during the battle of Verdun at 337,000 (143,000 killed) compared with 377,231 (162,440 killed) French losses. At 1916's second major Western Front engagement, the battle of the Somme, Strachan estimates German losses at between 465,000–650,000, depending on how casualties are computed, and Allied casualties at 614,000 (420,000 British). John Keegan provides a more specific breakdown of the Somme's Allied casualties, listing 419,654 British losses and 194,451 French, though he settles for a rather vague estimate (maybe "over 600,000 killed and wounded") of German casualties. Keegan does not provide a total number for losses at the battle of Verdun. John Keegan, *The First World War* (New York: Alfred A. Knopf, 1999), 298–99.

35   Dwight R. Messimer, *Find and Destroy: Antisubmarine Warfare in World War I* (Annapolis: Naval Institute Press, 2001), 130.

36   "History Anti-Submarine Campaign," 1:33.

37   Ibid., 2:2–3.

38   "Extracts from Letter No. 164/H.F. 0036 from Admiral Sir David Beatty, C-in-C, Grand Fleet to the Admiralty from H.M.S. *Iron Duke*, dated 21 January 1917, and Admiralty reply thereto M.0182 dated 14 February 1917" Stephen W. Roskill, *Documents Relating to the Naval Air Service 1908–1918* (London: Naval Records Society, 1969), 1:460–63.

39   "Extracts from Minutes of War Cabinet Meeting, December 22, 1916," quoted in Ibid., 1:450.

40   Halpern, *A Naval History*, 338.

41   John H. Morrow, Jr., *The Great War: An Imperial History* (2004, repr. London: Routledge, 2010), 225–26.

42   "History Anti-Submarine Campaign," 2:8.

43   Ibid., 2:5.

44   Ibid., 2:6.

45   Ibid., 2:14–15.

46   Ibid., 2:24–25.

47   I. T. Greig, "The Convoy System and the Two Battles of the Atlantic (1914–18 and 1939–45)," *Military History Journal* [The South African Military History Society] 6 (December 1984), http://samilitaryhistory.org/vol064ig.html (accessed February 16, 2010).

48 "History Anti-Submarine Campaign," 3:1.

49 Halpern, *Naval History of World War I*, 426. Halpern notes that the French maintained only three naval *escadrilles* at Dunkirk in 1916, units that experienced heavy losses to their German opponents in the first half of 1917.

50 *Jane's Fighting Ships*, 153.

51 Chief of Bureau to Commander de Blanpre, French Naval Attaché, Washington, DC, May 12, 1917, SSGA box 144, Military Archive 2005-05-19, *Service Historique de la Maritime*. See also Noel C. Shirley, *United States Naval Aviation 1910–1918* (Atglen: Schiffer Military Publishing, 2000), 104.

52 US secretary of the Navy to Ministre de la Marine Aviation Maritime, July 11, 1917, SSGA Box 144, Military Archive 2005-05-19, *Service Historique de la Maritime*.

53 Ibid.

54 Shirley, *United States Naval Aviation*, 158, 237. Shirley notes that the first of these US naval aviation patrols took place a full three months before US Air Service operations began on the Western Front with the first ascensions made by the US 2nd Balloon Company and the first fighter missions flown by the 103rd Aero Squadron.

55 US Naval Aviation Forces, Foreign Service, Confidential Bulletin No. 4, June 1, 1918, 1, SSGA Box 144/143, Military Archive 2005-05-19, *Service Historique de la Maritime*.

56 Ibid., 2; Messimer, *Verschollen*, 175. Messimer credits the April 24, 1918 loss of *Kapitänleutnant* Ralph Wenninger's *UB-55* to a mine in the Dover Strait, somewhat east of the position identified in the RAF report but makes no menton of the involvement of an airship.

57 US Naval Aviation Forces, Foreign Service, Confidential Bulletin No. 2, May 18, 1918, 6, SSGA Box 143, Military Archive 2005-05-19, *Service Historique de la Maritime*; *Jane's Fighting Ships*, 148. Jane identifies the *Stewart* as a *Bainbridge* class (420-ton displacement) coast torpedo vessel laid down in 1902 that achieved 29.69 knots at trial.

58 Shirley, *United States Naval Aviation*, 36–58, 158 and 189–90; www.usaww1. com/united-states-naval-aviation.php4 (accessed April 22, 2010) (US stations). Nineteen of the US Navy's European stations engaged in active anti-submarine operations. The remaining eight overseas stations included five that conducted test flights, two of which did not become completely operational by the armistice, and the Northern Bombing Group, which, as suggested by its title, performed offensive attacks.

59 Alan R. Hawley, Chairman, Advisory Committee on Aeronautics, "Aerial Defenses Needed for the Third Naval District," April 2, 1917 Memo to RAdm. Nathaniel R. Usher, Commandant, Third Naval District, quoted in Henry Woodhouse, *Textbook of Naval Aeronautics* (Annapolis: Naval Institute Press, 1991), 64–68.

60   Shirley, *United States Naval Aviation*, 158.

61   Lucien H. Thayer, *America's First Eagles: The Official History of the US Air Service, AEF, 1917–1918* (San Jose: R. James Bender Publishing and Champlin Fighter Museum Press, 1983), appendix 1; Maurer Maurer, ed., *The US Air Service in World War I* (Washington: GPO, 1978) 1: 391–92; James J. Hudson, *Hostile Skies: A Combat History of the American Air Service in World War I* (Syracuse: Syracuse University Press, 1968), 300. These popular histories of the US aviation program during World War I are typical of many that cover only the forty-five airplane squadrons the US Army placed on the Western Front prior to the armistice. Thayer mentions thirty-seven USAS airplane squadrons and seventeen balloon companies that participated in battles during 1918. By contrast Maurer Maurer counts forty-five airplane squadrons and twenty-three balloon companies, including six companies that received orders to report to the front but had not actually arrived there by the armistice and James J. Hudson includes forty-five airplane units and all twenty-three balloon companies.

62   Halpern, *A Naval History*, 426.

63   Richard D. Layman, *Naval Aviation in the First World War: Its Impact and Influence* (Annapolis: Naval Institute Press, 1996), 206–08; Stephen F. Nelsen, "French Naval Aircraft," *Cross & Cockade Journal* 7, no. 3 (Autumn 1966): 275.

64   Shirley, *United States Naval Aviation*, 59.

65   Layman, *Naval Aviation*, passim.

66   Mike Westrop, *A History of No. 6 Squadron Royal Naval Air Service in World War I* (Atglen: Schiffer Military History, 2006), 144.

Chapter 8

1   Chief of Training to Division Executive, November 29, 1918, File 321.9, box 487, Separate Air Force, RG 18, Air Corps Central File 1917–1938, NARA. Davis's reference to the Post Office likely referred to a November 16, 1918, memo from the director of military aeronautics to John D. Ryan, the assistant secretary of war, which enumerated mail carrying among possible uses of a peacetime Air Service.

2   ? to the director of military aeronautics, December 11, 1918, "A Few Selling Points for a Separate Air Service," File 321.9, box 487, Separate Air Force, RG 18, Air Corps Central File 1917–1938, NARA.

3   Ibid.

4   Ibid.

5   Brig. Gen. William Mitchell, Third Assistant Executive, to the director of the Air Service, April 16, 1919, "Air Service Program Prepared by the DAS, April 15, 1919," File 321.9, box 487, Separate Air Force, RG 18, Air Corps Central File 1917–1938, NARA.

6   James J. Cooke, *Billy Mitchell* (Boulder; Lynne Reinner, 2002), 13. See also Douglas Waller, *A Question of Loyalty: Gen. Billy Mitchell and the Court-martial*

that Gripped the Nation (New York: Harper Collins, 2004), 73, for an example of how Mitchell requested his father to exercise political influence on his behalf during the Spanish American War.

7   Harry S. New (R-IN), Charles F. Curry (R-CA), and John M. Morin (R-PA) respectively sponsored these bills proposing creation of a separate air force.

8   Henry H. Arnold to Col. Milton F. Davis, office of the DAS, May 8, 1919, File 321.9, box 487, Separate Air Force, RG 18, Air Corps Central File 1917–1938, NARA.

9   Maj. Gen. Charles T. Menoher to Army Chief of Staff, Request for Papers, August 18, 1919, File 321.9, box 487, Separate Air Force, RG 18, Air Corps Central File 1917–1938, NARA [hereafter "Request for Papers"].

10   Maurer Maurer, *Aviation in the US Army, 1919–1939* (Washington: Office of Air Force History, USAF, 1987), 40–41.

11   Director of military aeronautics to Oklahoma City, Oklahoma Chamber of Commerce on the Permanent Establishment of Air Service, November 27, 1918, File 321.9, box 487, Separate Air Force, RG 18, Air Corps Central File 1917–1938, NARA.

12   Col. Milton F. Davis to Managing Editor, *Albany Evening Journal*, March 21, 1919, File 321.9, box 487, Separate Air Force, RG 18, Air Corps Central File 1917–1938, NARA.

13   "Must Not Cripple Aviation," *The News Leader*, Richmond, VA, June 7, 1919, File 321.9, box 487, Separate Air Force, RG 18, Air Corps Central File 1917–1938, NARA.

14   Capt. J. A. Healey, Special Assistant to Chief for Lt. Col. H. M. Hickam, Chief Information Group, to A. F. Breazeale, Jr., File 321.9, box 487, Separate Air Force, RG 18, Air Corps Central File 1917–1938, NARA.

15   H. A. Jones, *The War in the Air: Being the Story of the Part Played in the Great War by the Royal Air Force* (Oxford: Clarendon Press, 1937), 6:1–27.

16   "Official Summary of British and French Viewpoint Concerning a Separate Department of Aeronautics," October 7, 1919, , 9, File 321.9, box 487, Separate Air Force, RG 18, Air Corps Central File 1917–1938, NARA [hereafter "British and French Viewpoint"].

17   Walter J. Boyne, *The Influence of Air Power upon History* (Gretna: Pelican, 2003), 89, for example, details the financial allotment dedicated to US military aviation during the war and in the years that followed.

18   Ibid., 177.

19   Ibid., 177–78; Stephen Budiansky, *Air Power: The Men, Machines, and Ideas that Revolutionized War, from Kitty Hawk to Gulf War II* (New York: Viking, 2004), 139–41.

20   Boyne, *Influence of Air Power*, 178; Budiansky, *Air Power, 141*, put the cost of the RAF operation at £70,000.

21   Andrew Boyle, *Trenchard: Man of Vision* (New York: W. W. Norton, 1962), passim, devoted six chapters to Trenchard's postwar activities in support of

continued RAF independence, the same number devoted to the Marshal of the RAF's First World War service, during which time Trenchard commanded the Royal Flying Corps in the field and then the Inter-Allied Independent Force, a strategic bombing program, a comparison that might indicate the importance of the postwar air power debate to Trenchard's career.

22 James J. Davilla and Arthur M. Soltan, *French Aircraft of the First World War* (Mountain View: Flying Machines Press, 1997), 20, puts French front-line strength at 3,222 aircraft; John H. Morrow, *The Great War in the Air: Military Aviation from 1909 to 1921* (Washington: Smithsonian, 1993), 295, 356, also puts the number of French aircraft on the Western Front at 3,222, but later increases the total "at the front" slightly to 3,437, possibly including aircraft with French units serving in other theaters.

23 Davilla and Soltan, *French Aircraft*, 36.

24 Ibid., 114–15, 443–44, and 566; Morrow, *Great War in the Air*, 356.

25 "British and French Viewpoint," 11, File 321.9, box 487, Separate Air Force, RG 18, Air Corps Central File 1917–1938, NARA.

26 Morrow, *Great War in the Air*, 357.

27 Faris R. Kirkland, "The French Air Force in 1940: Was It Defeated by the Luftwaffe or by Politics," www.airpower.maxwell.af.mil/airchronicles/aure-view/1985/sep-oct/kirkland.html (accessed June 5, 2011).

28 Morrow, *Great War in the Air*, 350–56.

29 Ibid., 354.

30 Ibid., 355.

31 Boyne, *Influence of Air Power*, 154–55.

32 Ibid.

33 Maurer, *Aviation in the US Army*, 41.

34 "Proceedings of a Board of Officers Convened at Washington, DC, Pursuant to the Following Order: 'War Department, The Adjutant General's Office Washington. From: The Adjutant General of the Army. To: Major General Charles T. Menoher, Office Director of Air Service, Washington, DC,'" August 8, 1919, 4, File 321.9, box 487, Separate Air Force, RG 18, Air Corps Central File 1917–1938, NARA [hereafter "Proceedings of a Board"].

35 "Proceedings of a Board."

36 Maj. Gen. W. M. Wright, Industry Efficiency Board to the adjutant general of the Army, September 3, 1919, File 321.9, box 487, Separate Air Force, RG 18, Air Corps Central File 1917–1938, NARA. Col. William R. Smith, a Coast Artillery officer assigned to the General Staff College in Washington, DC, succinctly bottom-lined the opposition's position. "[A] thing as vital to the Army and to the Navy as aeronautics must be a part of the Army and of the Navy and not something loaned to them and responsible to a third department."

37 "Proceedings of a Board," August 8, 1919, p. 9, File 321.9, box 487, Separate Air Force, RG 18, Air Corps Central File 1917–1938, NARA; Statement of

Brig. Gen. Malin Craig, August 25, 1919, File 321.9, box 487, Separate Air Force, RG 18, Air Corps Central File 1917–1938, NARA; Statement of Lt. Col. (formerly Brig. Gen.) Briant A. Wells, n.d., in response to adjutant general's letter of August 23, 1919, File 321.9, box 487, Separate Air Force, RG 18, Air Corps Central File 1917–1938, NARA; Maj. Dennis E. Nolan, Infantry, to director Air Service, August 27, 1919, File 321.9, box 487, Separate Air Force, RG 18, Air Corps Central File 1917–1938, NARA. Maj. George S. Simonds, a wartime infantry commander, testified that a stand-alone air force was "inadvisable," basing his opinion on "experience with our own forces and as an observer with the French and British armies in the past war. [Aviation] must be considered as one of the auxiliaries of the principal arm—the Infantry." Brig. Gen. Malin Craig, chief of Staff First Army Corps and Third American Army, categorized aviation as the equivalent of the "Signal Corps, the Field Artillery, and other auxiliaries." Brig. Gen. Briant A. Wells, suggested that aviation "is closely associated with the Infantry, Artillery and Cavalry. The Air Service is an auxiliary service … I do not believe the personnel would ever acquire proper conception of an auxiliary status if they are given, by law, an independent organization." Dennis E. Nolan, assistant chief of staff, G-2 (intelligence), AEF, labeled the Air Service an "auxiliary arm." He testified that the value of aeronautics depended "almost entirely on the degree of co-operation obtained in the reconnaissances immediately preceding the battle and the varied operations of the air forces in the battle itself."

38 Col. Frank P. Lahm to director Air Service, September 5, 1919, File 321.9, box 487, Separate Air Force, RG 18, Air Corps Central File 1917–1938, NARA.

39 Gen. John J. Pershing to Maj. Gen. Charles T. Menoher, director Air Service, January 12, 1920, File 321.9, box 487, Separate Air Force, RG 18, Air Corps Central File 1917–1938, NARA. Pershing told the board: "Military forces can never be efficiently trained nor operated without an air force. A military air force is an essential combat branch and should form an integral part of the army."

40 Lt. Col. H. J. Miller for Brig. Gen. H. A. Drum to Chief of Staff, September 19, 1925, File 321.9, box 487, Separate Air Force, RG 18, Air Corps Central File 1917–1938, NARA. A few years after the war, Pershing noted, "Enthusiasts often forget the obligations of military aviation to other troops, and sometimes credit that service with ability to achieve results in war that have not yet received practical demonstration."

41 Maurer Maurer, ed., *The US Air Service in World War I* (Washington: Office of Air Force History, 1978), 1:17, credits American bombers with dropping approximately 275,000 pounds of bombs on German targets prior to the armistice. Conversely, USAS aircrews had taken 18,000 photos during the war, from which the Air Service's Photographic Section had made and distributed 585,000 prints.

42 Request for Cost Estimates for a Separate Air Force, October 1925, File 321.9, box 487, Separate Air Force, RG 18, Air Corps Central File 1917–1938, NARA. Patrick observed that "the Army needs a certain Air Service for … reconnoitering the ground in front of it, for regulating and adjusting the fire of its missile-throwing weapons, such as cannon, howitzers, and for maintaining liaison or keeping communication between its parts when all other means have failed."

43 "Proceedings of a Board," August 8, 1919, p. 9, File 321.9, box 487, Separate Air Force, RG 18, Air Corps Central File 1917–1938, NARA.

44 Ibid.

45 Ibid., 11.

46 Ibid., 11 and 13. Navy Capt. Henry C. Mustin, who later in 1919 commanded the US Fleet Air Detachment, Pacific Fleet, and, in 1921, would become Assistant Chief of the Bureau of Aeronautics, testified concerning attitudes of French and Italian military and British Royal Navy professionals. Mustin confirmed that officers in those services believed they should train their own aviation personnel and conduct experimental work that required "the cooperation or assistance of other branches of the service."

47 Ibid., 10.

48 Synopsis of Testimony Delivered by Gen. Mitchell before the House Military Affairs Committee, January 8, 1925, File 321.9, box 487, Separate Air Force, RG 18, Air Corps Central File 1917–1938, NARA; "Memorandum for Gen. Menoher: Comments on H.R. 16151, Introduced by Mr. Curry of California, March 1, 1921," File 321.9, box 487, Separate Air Force, RG 18, Air Corps Central File 1917–1938, NARA. Mitchell restricted his concession to battlefield coordination, however, writing that "training, sector, depth of reconnaissance methods and supply" should remain under Air Force command.

49 Giulio Douhet, *The Command of the Air* (1942, repr.: Washington: Office of Air Force History, 1983), xi.

50 Ibid., 216–17.

51 In constructing this argument, Douhet neglected to consider the potential value of aerial reconnaissance to an army in the opening days of war, such as had been demonstrated at the 1914 battles of the Marne and Tannenberg.

52 Douhet, *Command of the Air*, 277.

53 Ibid., viii.

54 Ibid., viii–ix.

55 Ibid., passim; William Mitchell, *Winged Defense: The Development and Possibilities of Modern Air Power—Economic and Military.* 1925. Reprint, Mineola: Dover Publications, 1998, passim.

56 William Mitchell, "Aeronautical Era," *Saturday Evening Post* (December 20, 1924), 101; William Mitchell, "America in the Air: The Future of Airplane and Airship, Economically and as Factors in National Defense," *National Geographic* (March 1921), 330–52; William Mitchell, *Our Air Force: The Keystone of*

National Defense (New York: E. P. Dutton, 1921); William Mitchell, *Winged Defense: The Development and Possibilities of Modern Air Power—Economic and Military* (1925. Reprint, Mineola: Dover Publications, 1998).

57 William Mitchell, "Aeronautical Era," *Saturday Evening Post* (December 20, 1924), 101. Mitchell wrote: "In the development of air power one has to look ahead and not backward, and figure out what is going to happen, not too much what has happened. That is why the older services have been psychologically unfit to develop this new arm to the fullest extent practicable with the methods and means at hand."

58 Mitchell, "Aeronautical Era," 3–4, 99–100, 103.

59 Mitchell, *Winged Defense*, 341–45.

60 Ibid., 345.

61 Waller, *A Question of Loyalty*, 11–16.

62 Ibid., 20.

63 Cooke, *Billy Mitchell*, 196–97.

Conclusion

1 National Security Act of 1947, Public Law 235, 80th Cong., 1st sess. [July 26, 1947], http://intelligence.senate.gov/nsaact1947.pdf (accessed June 8, 2011).

2 James Noffsinger, *World War I Aviation Books in English: an Annotated Bibliography* (Metuchen: Scarecrow Press, 1987) documents a marked decline in interest in Great War military aviation while the Second World War was in progress. Of the 1,663 titles Noffsinger catalogued fewer than one hundred were published in the 1940s, the only decade after the Great War's end in which the number of published works dropped below triple digits.

3 Adrian R. Lewis, *The American Culture of War: The History of US Military Force from World War II to Operation Iraqi Freedom* (New York: Routledge, 2007), 42–44.

4 R. G. Price, "Casualties of War—Putting American Casualties in Perspective," http://rationalrevolution.net/articles/casualties_of_war.htm (accessed June 25, 2011) puts US and USSR military casualties in the Second World War at 295,000 and 13,600,000 respectively; See also http://www.abmc.gov/search/wwii.php (accessed June 25, 2011); www.secondworldwar.co.uk/index.php/fatalities (accessed June 25, 2011).

5 Lewis, *American Culture of War*, 37.

6 Basil Liddell Hart, *The Real War, 1914–1918* (Boston: Little, Brown, 1930).

7 Basil Liddell Hart, *Liddell Hart's History of the First World War* (London: Cassell, 1970), 355.

8 Ibid., 358.

9 Henry Arnold, *This Flying Game* (New York: Funk and Wagnalls, 1936); Lionel Charlton, *War Over England* (London: Longmans, Green, 1936);

Frank Morison, *War on Great Cities* (London: Faber and Faber, 1937); J. M. Spaight, *Air Power in the Next War* (London: Geoffrey Bles, 1938).

10   Edward Jablonski, *The Knighted Skies: A Pictorial History of World War I in the Air* (New York: Putnam, 1964), 73.

11   Conversation with the author, League of World War I Aviation Historians biennial seminar, Ottawa, Canada, 1994.

12   Jablonski, *The Knighted Skies*, 25.

13   Ibid., 29.

14   Ibid., 73.

15   Ibid.

16   Ibid., 203–04.

17   Ibid., 217.

18   Irwin B. Holley, Jr., *Ideas and Weapons: Exploitation of the Aerial Weapon by the United States during World War I; a Study in the Relationship of Technological Advance, Military Doctrine, and the Development of Weapons* (Hamden: Archon Books, 1971), 31.

19   "Legend, Memory and the Great War in the Air," www.nasm.si.edu/exhibitions/gal206/index.cfm (accessed June 27, 2011) catalogues five single-seat fighters and one multi-seat bomber present in the gallery.

20   Courtland Bryan, *The National Air and Space Museum* (New York: Abrams, 1979), 2, 171.

21   Ibid., 2; "The 20 most visited museums in America," http://experience.usatoday.com/weekend/story/my-weekend-experience/2015/06/10/20-most-visited-museums-usa/71028302/ (accessed January 22, 2016) puts 2014 attendance figures at 6,700,000.

22   John Toland, *No Man's Land: 1918–the Last Year of the Great War* (New York: Smithmark, 1980).

23   Ibid., 10.

24   Ibid., 318–19.

25   Ibid., 431.

26   Ibid., 10, 64, 183–86, 314, 317–18, 424, 431–32, 436, 470.

27   Lyn MacDonald, *1915: the Death of Innocence* (London: Headline Book Publishing, 1993), 70.

28   Merrion Harries and Susie Harries, *The Last Days of Innocence: America at War, 1917–1918* (New York: Random House, 1997), 149.

29   Ibid.

30   Ibid., 416–17.

31   John Keegan, *The First World War* (New York: Knopf, 1998), 359.

32   Richard Holmes, *The Little Field Marshal: A Life of Sir John French* (London: Cassell, 2004), 352.

33   John Moore-Brabazon to Charles Fairbairn, October 26, 1918, Moore-Brabazon Papers, RAF Museum, London.

34   H. A. Jones, *The War in the Air: Being the Story of the Part Played in the Great War by the Royal Air Force* (London: Oxford, 1935), 5:240–41. During the final Turkish retreat, the official air historian credits No. 67 (Australian) Squadron's photographic section, with the help of a special staff at Weli Sheikh Nuran, with providing army staffs with prints made from plates exposed over the Turkish lines less than four to five hours earlier.

35   Nicholas Watkis, *The Western Front from the Air* (Phoenix Mill, UK: Sutton, 1999); Terrence J. Finnegan, *Shooting the Front: Allied Aerial Reconnaissance and Photographic Interpretation on the Western Front—World War I* (Washington, DC: National Defense Intelligence College, 2006); Birger Stichelbaut, Jean Bourgeois, Nicholas Saunders and Piet Chielens, eds., *Images of Conflict: Military Aerial Photography and Archaeology* (Newcaste upon Tyne: Cambridge Scholars Press, 2009); Gail Ramsey, *The Great War from the Air Then and Now* (Harlow: Battle of Britain International, 2013); Birger Stichelbaut and Piet Chielens, *The Great War Seen from the Air In Flanders Fields 1914–1918* (Brussels: Mercatorfonds, 2013); Von Hardesty, *The Camera Aloft: Edward Steichen in the Great War* (New York: Cambridge University Press, 2015). Hopefully, these works, all but one of which have appeared in the last decade, reflect the beginning of a trend in which historians will at last acknowledge the true value of aviation in the Great War.

Index